Assessing Deaf Adults

Critical Issues in Testing and Evaluation

Judith L. Mounty and David S. Martin, Editors

Gallaudet University Press   Washington, D.C.

© Gallaudet University Press
Washington, D.C. 20002

http://gupress.gallaudet.edu

© 2005 by Gallaudet University.
All rights reserved
Published in 2005
Printed in the United States of America

The tests and examinations discussed throughout this book have been copyrighted and/or trademarked by their respective owners. In the chapter titled "Certification Testing for Therapeutic Recreation: Equity, Access, and Preparation," (pp. 125–137), the name of the National Council for Therapeutic Recreation Certification (NCTRC) is a registered trademark, as is the phrase "Certified Therapeutic Recreation Specialist."

Library of Congress Cataloging-in-Publication Data

Assessing deaf adults : critical issues in testing and evaluation / Judith L. Mounty and David S. Martin, editors.
    p. cm.
  Includes bibliographical references and index.
  ISBN 1-56368-323-7 (alk. paper)
    1. Deaf—Ability testing. 2. Deaf—Psychological testing. 3. Educational tests and measurements. I. Mounty, Judith L. II. Martin, David S.

HV2395.A77 2005
153.9'3'0872—dc22
                                      2005041443

∞ The paper used in this publication meets the minimum requirements of American National Standard for Information Sciences—Permanence of Paper for Printed Library Materials, ANSI Z39.48-1984.

This book is dedicated to Ludmila Rose Mounty-Weinstock. Now a young woman on the brink of postsecondary education, she has faced many challenges in learning because of the early circumstances of her life. In sharp contradiction to what standardized test scores would suggest, she has succeeded academically and in all other areas because of her unflinching motivation and innate intelligence. It is my hope that this book will enlighten the minds of the many who unwittingly place roadblocks in the paths of deaf and hard of hearing people so that Ludmila may follow her dreams and excel in her chosen career.

Judith L. Mounty (a.k.a. Mom)

Contents

Foreword   xi
Oscar P. Cohen

Acknowledgments   xiv

Section I. The Context

Overview of the Challenge   3
David S. Martin and Judith L. Mounty

Historical Reflections
on Testing Individuals Who
Are Deaf and Hard of Hearing   11
Marjorie Ragosta

Section II. Test Development Issues

Test-Taking for Deaf
and Hard of Hearing Individuals:
Meeting the Challenges   27
Robert B. Weinstock and Judith L. Mounty

Access Considerations and
the Provision of Appropriate
Accommodations: A Research
Perspective From a Testing Organization   37
Ruth Loew, Cara Cahalan-Laitusis, Linda Cook, and Raylene Harris

Use of Technology
and Principles
of Universal Design
to Improve
the Validity
and Fairness of
Licensure Tests   54
Neal Kingston and Michael Ehringhaus

Contents

Considerations in Developing
Licensing Tests That Are
Accessible for All Candidates   65
Carolyn Emrick Massad

The Psychometric Properties
of Intellectual Tests
When Used With Deaf
and Hard of Hearing Individuals:
Practices and Recommendations   75
Susan J. Maller and Jason C. Immekus

Section III. Administrative Issues

Equity in Testing Deaf
and Hard of Hearing
Individuals—Legal Considerations   93
Rosaline Hayes Crawford

Sign Language Interpretation
in Testing Environments   109
Phyllis Rogers

Section IV. Cases From Specific Professions

Certification Testing
for Therapeutic Recreation:
Equity, Access, and Preparation   125
Anne Simonsen

GRE Performance
and the Deaf Community   138
Charlene Sorensen

Maximizing Access to Licensure
for Deaf and Hard of Hearing
Social Workers   149
Teresa V. Mason and Judith L. Mounty

New Hurdles: The Impact
of Recent Federal Mandates
on the Assessment of Deaf
and Hard of Hearing Teachers
and Teacher Candidates   156
Paul S. Singletary

Section V. Summing Up

Summary and Recommendations   171
Judith L. Mounty and David S. Martin

Epilogue: Fort Monroe Revisited   174
Robert Clover Johnson

Contributors   181

Index   187

Foreword

I'm a cautious guy. I want to know that my doctor, barber, and auto mechanic have passed tests before they work on me, my hair, or my car. The same applies to the neighborhood firefighters, police, and my grandchildren's teachers. At the same time, I am a believer in equal opportunity and social justice. Historically, deaf and hard of hearing people have demonstrated various levels of competence in a multitude of jobs, in a range of professions. They have also historically experienced discrimination and oppression.

Assessing Deaf Adults is an important response to the tidal wave of high-stakes testing that has come to dominate educational policy. This courageous work is aimed at preventing a terrible mistake from continuing to occur. A disturbing phenomenon has emerged: The testers' attempt to address a social inequality—the achievement gap between the poor and affluent, as well as between persons with and without disabilities—is yielding the unintended consequence of *increasing* the gap between deaf and hard of hearing persons and their hearing peers.

Many tests that purport to measure intelligence really measure how much and what kind of academic instruction people have had, not their inherent abilities. The conditions that help or hinder an individual's effort to succeed, and equity variables affecting the system within which the individual competes, are heavily governed by specific social policies. For example, Hernstein and Murray's misguided thesis that certain ethnic groups are socially unequal because they are intellectually unequal has been used to justify continuing inequalities (Hernstein and Murray, 1994). However, evidence shows the opposite to be true, that groups score unequally on tests predominantly as a *result* of their being treated unequally by society (Fischer et al., 1996, p.172).

Historically, deaf and hard of hearing persons constitute such a group—commonly demonstrating low performance on tests developed for persons with full access to the spoken form of the language used on the test. However, their low performance also is related to a variety of other factors, including, crucially, those that stem from the social-political context. Similar to other oppressed minorities, deaf and hard of hearing people historically have carried a stigma of inferiority based on the wider society's perception of them. In some cases, this situation has led to anxiety, fatalism, and resignation. In others, it may lead to rejecting the wider culture's expectations and standards, thus adopting an oppositional stance. Either reaction is likely to bring down the average school and test performance. At the same time, youth from advantaged groups demonstrate the reverse: They experience, to their profit, society's positive perception of them (Fischer et al., 1996, p. 174).

When there is a disconnect between what a test is intended to measure and whether it does, or when a test is negatively discriminatory for a particular group, such as deaf and hard of hearing persons, an injustice occurs.

In the Epilogue to this volume, "Fort Monroe Revisited," Robert Clover Johnson recalls Alan Crammatte's 1980 account of the "humanitarian revolution" that occurred between 1960 and 1980, where "deaf and hard of hearing persons were brought out of the closet of meek isolation into the active arena of competition for training, jobs, and recognition." Johnson talks about that period as fostering the emergence of deaf and hard of hearing teachers, professors, social workers, lawyers, linguists, historians, chemists, writers, and doctors—feats that would have astonished deaf and hard of hearing people as recently as the 1950s.

David Martin, Judith Mounty, Robert Clover Johnson, and their colleagues are concerned that the gains of the humanitarian revolution for deaf and hard of hearing persons will be reversed if the high-stakes testing movement is allowed to proceed unchecked. And they are right to be.

Who would argue that the successes of Crammatte's deaf and hard of hearing individuals were a fluke? These men and women have "aced" the most rigorous tests of all. They have become leaders in their communities, formed bonds with both deaf and hearing colleagues, made significant contributions to their companies and organizations, served as role models for deaf and hard of hearing youth, and extended the baton of their successes to others with similar aspirations and abilities. What were the assessment systems in place to allow for these deaf and hard of hearing teachers, chemists, lawyers, doctors, and programmers to become successful? Given the intrinsic disadvantages and inequalities facing deaf and hard of hearing persons in current high-stakes testing, it is not absurd to wonder whether many of them, if subjected to today's tests (which are often tantamount to being tests of English rather than of the actual substance of the test, because full access to spoken English is not available), might never have had the opportunity to realize their professional dreams.

This is not an argument against rigorous testing for deaf and hard of hearing individuals. They are as obligated to demonstrate competence as their hearing peers. On the contrary, what is presented is a systematic logical perspective, in a social context, by which to understand the complexities of testing deaf and hard of hearing individuals. The advocates of high-stakes testing probably have commendable aims. But as H. L. Mencken said, "For every human problem, there is a neat, simple solution; and it is always wrong." It would be appalling if the current generation of deaf and hard of hearing youth were held back by well-intentioned but misguided testing practices.

I myself am not a good test-taker as a hearing person. I didn't do well on the SAT or the Miller Analogies Test. I'm not sure how I would do on today's tests. I'm not sure how the members of Congress who voted to pass the No Child Left Behind legislation (one of the driving forces for high-stakes testing today) would do on them, either. It's all very well to propose testing as a way of closing an inequality gap, but actually devising a test that would help to do that is a far trickier job. Test-makers need to be intelligent problem-solvers. We need to work not simply harder, but *smarter*, in order to design tests that are both fair and relevant for everyone, including deaf and hard of hearing individuals. *Assessing Deaf Adults: Critical Issues in Testing and Evaluation* is a contribution toward that goal.

Joe Scott, reflecting on his arrival as basketball coach at the Air Force Academy, commented, "I didn't realize how deep 25 years of losing goes. It affects everyone from the top on down. A college basketball program isn't just the coaches and players. It's the support, the administration, and the community. The losing culture was so embedded there." For too long, deaf and hard of hearing children grew up with the inevitable sense of belonging to a "losing culture," characterized by a dearth of role models, opportunities, hopes, and aspirations. The past quarter-century has seen the emergence of a class of deaf and hard of hearing leaders previously unknown in the United States. Largely due to them, more and more deaf and hard of hearing youth are dreaming previously unimaginable dreams about opportunities and possibilities. The era of the "losing culture" has passed. We cannot let it return.

Oscar P. Cohen

REFERENCES

Fischer, C. S., Hour, M., Jankowski, M. S., Lucas, S. R., Swidler, A., and Voss, K. (1996). *Inequality by design: Cracking the Bell Curve Myth.* Princeton, NJ: Princeton University Press.

Hernstein, R. L., and Murray, C. (1994). *The Bell Curve: Intelligence and class structure in American life.* New York: Free Press.

Acknowledgments

In any undertaking of the considerable breadth and depth as is this volume, a number of individuals are indispensable to its completion. We would like to gratefully acknowledge the assistance of these persons. First, we express gratitude to Ivey Pittle-Wallace of Gallaudet University Press, for her patience, guidance, and unstinting support throughout the entire process of assembling this book. Second, we would like to thank current and former colleagues and co-workers at Gallaudet University and Educational Testing Service for sharing their knowledge throughout the years and for offering support in many ways as we prepared this book. Third, we are humbly grateful to the countless deaf and hard of hearing individuals, their families, and their advocates who have shared their experiences and struggles with testing. Fourth, we are deeply thankful for the understanding and support of our families, as this book often demanded our time over and above our many other commitments.

Last, we acknowledge the significant contributions of the numerous chapter authors, whose impressive biographies are listed in the contributors section; without them, we would simply have no book to contribute to this field.

Section I *The Context*

Overview of the Challenge

David S. Martin and Judith L. Mounty

A significant part of the story of American education since the 1970s has been the steady growth in the access certain groups have to services and opportunities that were heretofore closed to them because of the lack of legal protections. For persons who are deaf or hard of hearing, that increase in legal access has resulted from three specific pieces of legislation: Section 504 of the Rehabilitation Act, the Education for All Handicapped Children Act (now known as the Individuals With Disabilities Education Act), and the Americans With Disabilities Act. In different ways, these laws expanded the opportunities for all persons with disabilities, but they also gave rise to complex new issues that have been the subject of subsequent litigation and negotiation. In at least an indirect sense, the area of testing deaf and hard of hearing persons of all ages is one example of such an issue: Without the legislation, testing may not have been implemented, or individuals with disabilities may have been excluded. However, because testing is now required as part of equal access to education, new challenges have emerged related to equity and fairness in testing individuals with disabilities.

GROWING USE OF HIGH-STAKES TESTING

Since the mid-1990s, more and more states in the United States have implemented high-stakes testing for two purposes: as a condition of promotion, continuation, or graduation for elementary and secondary school students, and for licensure and certification of a wide range of professionals. As a result, deaf and hard of hearing adults, who previously had been denied access to certain professions, began to have such access, but increasingly they are being required to take and pass licensure examinations administered by a state agency. Colleges and universities that had excluded deaf and hard of hearing persons from their student bodies due to a lack of required accommodations opened their doors but required deaf and hard of hearing persons to take and pass certain entrance examinations in the traditional format. The inclusion movement in elementary and secondary education, as it has involved more and more deaf and hard of hearing students, has added fuel to this fire of educational testing and potential inequities for deaf and hard of hearing persons.

Thus, across all levels of education and in a number of professions, whereas testing of deaf and hard of hearing candidates or students had been a non-issue, it was now a clear issue—an ironic result of laws that were designed to be highly beneficial to all persons with disabilities. In fact, it has been reliably reported that students with disabilities consistently fail state tests at rates that are 35–45% higher than those for non-disabled students (Ysseldyke, et al., 1998). If we extend this computation, this statistic would mean that students with disabilities are failing such tests at the rate of 75–80% on their initial testing—far greater than would be expected when examining other criteria such as grade-point average.

EQUAL STANDARDS AND FAIR ASSESSMENT

Deaf and hard of hearing persons can and should be held to the same high standards as hearing persons—whether for school or college examinations or professional licensure and certification. However, an equally essential consideration is that while the standards should be equivalent, the means of assessment must be equitable. Therefore, in an effort to enhance equity and access, formal measurements of professional expertise must address specific variables that affect the development and experiences of deaf and hard of hearing people. Local, state, and federal agencies that use such assessment results to make important judgments about deaf individuals must be well trained in the appropriate administration and interpretation of assessments.

In this sense, the stakes are high for everyone—for deaf and hard of hearing persons in terms of the decisions that will be made about their lives as a result of any assessments and for decision-makers in terms of being able to make fair and defensible decisions in a highly complex domain.

TASK FORCE ON EQUITY IN TESTING

In 1987, the National Task Force on Equity in Testing Deaf Teachers was initiated and headquartered at Gallaudet University. The focus at the time was on advocating for fair testing of deaf candidates for teacher certification in an era when the field of deaf education had a re-awakening of interest and awareness of the need for more deaf and hard of hearing teachers. Some serious barriers were beginning to be experienced nationally, which persist to the time of writing this book. Several cases were addressed by the task force, and individuals were advised as to appropriate actions to take; in addition, some state agencies were advised on appropriate accommodations to make. By the mid-1990s, the task force realized that problems of licensure for deaf persons were not limited to the teaching profession, as more and more deaf adults began to seek careers in a broader range of professions. Thus, the task force broadened its title to the National Task Force on Equity in Testing Deaf Professionals. Several national position statements were developed by the task force, and it continued to advise both states and individuals on proper ways to proceed in the case of apparent inequities.

By the year 2000, the significant increase in the implementation of high-stakes testing in schools indicated that still another broadening of mission would be appropriate. As a result, the task force changed its name again to its present title of the National Task Force on Equity in Testing Deaf and Hard of Hearing Individuals. Membership is open to all who are interested and includes a broad array of representatives from various fields, including education, occupational therapy, psychology, the law, and others. Entities represented include schools, programs, and postsecondary institutions that teach deaf and hard of hearing individuals, the Educational Testing Service, the Council for Exceptional Children, the National Board for Certification in Occupational

Therapy, the National Therapeutic Recreation Association, the Laurent Clerc National Deaf Education Center at Gallaudet University, and the Governor's Office of Disabilities for the State of Maryland. In recent years, guests and attendees at thrice-yearly meetings have included attorneys from the U.S. Office of Civil Rights, the U.S. Department of Justice, the Association of Social Work Boards, and testing companies such as Harcourt and Measured Progress.

THE BASIC PROBLEM: THE TYPE OF ENGLISH USED IN STANDARDIZED TESTS

For many deaf and hard of hearing persons, English is not fully accessible and may not function as a true first or primary language. Yet tests for school graduation, university admissions, and licensure are embedded in the English language with all of its nuances, some of which will be explained below. Such tests thus evaluate the individual's knowledge of English as much if not more than the content or skills that the tests purport to measure. However, the problem is not simply one of English-as-a-second-language (ESL); if it were, then the same accommodations afforded to a hearing non-native speaker of English would suffice for deaf and hard of hearing individuals. The following anecdote told by Gallaudet University professor of deaf studies, Ben Bahan, during a 1990 presentation at the Educational Testing Service and elsewhere illustrates how environmental access to English is markedly different for deaf and hard of hearing learners of English compared with hearing ESL learners. This is true regardless of whether the individual is a native American Sign Language (ASL) signer, a later learner of ASL, or someone who does not use sign language at all.

Two strangers, one deaf and the other a recent hearing immigrant, have just left an adult education center where they each attended English classes at different levels taught by different teachers. As it happens, the unit they both had just learned in their classes focused on the structure of "have been." At the bus stop, the two strangers encounter two hearing, native speakers of English engaged in conversation while waiting for a bus. The immigrant is able to eavesdrop and is surprised to hear them using the very sentence structure he has just learned about in class.

(Speaker #1) "I saw John today, and he wanted to know what have you been doing since you two last went out."

(Speaker #2) "Oh, I hope you didn't tell him I have been going bowling with Charlie."

The hearing ESL learner is able to experience the newly learned language structure being used in a naturalistic context. In contrast, the deaf individual sees two people talking, and, by observing their proximity to one another, can surmise a shared level of intimacy, but has no idea what they are saying and certainly does not have the same opportunity to apply what he has been learning in class. Instead of benefiting from conversational application, the deaf individual's environmental exposure to English is restricted to recognition of environmental printed words and phrases such as: bus stop, "Stop" (sign), Wal-Mart (across the street), and "Sale 30–50% off on red tag items." (Benjamin J. Bahan, Personal Communication, August, 24, 2004.)

RESEARCH

This book provides a digest of research relevant to this challenge, including work done by educational researchers, legal experts, test developers, and others. Considerable knowledge has been added to the field as a result of the research, which will be reported in a subsequent chapter. Yet, as so frequently happens with research other than medical research, a significant gap in time and awareness exists between the research results and any application to the changing of practices and related policies. Specifically, we can now identify some critical points about language-learning and access by deaf and hard of hearing persons. Yet this knowledge generally remains unknown to or unaccepted by test developers, policy makers, and those who use test results to make decisions about this population. The challenge now is how to narrow that information gap such that relevant knowledge and research results can be applied to the benefit of equity in testing deaf and hard of hearing persons.

FUNDAMENTAL PROBLEMS IN TEST CONSTRUCTION

Since the great majority of school-based tests, college-entrance tests, and licensure tests are of the multiple-choice variety, it is now appropriate to list some of the fundamental problems they pose for this population:

1. Some items in such tests contain *item bias* in the sense that they presume experience or present some content that would not be equally accessible to a deaf person, such as items related to music or rhyme, or (especially in the days prior to closed captioning), television, movies, and other staples of "hearing" culture.
2. Many such tests include some items that are embedded in *figurative or colloquial* English. A deaf person who has attained some level of mastery of the English language through reading and writing, using strategies less tied to phonological processing due to restricted or no auditory input, would not be able to access the intent of the item simply because it was worded by a hearing test developer who assumed a knowledge of colloquial English. Often there is not sufficient redundancy within the item to allow the test-taker to discern the meaning from context. This problem is particularly relevant when such language is not one of the constructs that is being tested, yet it prevents the test-taker from accessing the meaning of the item.
3. Many such tests provide *inadequate context* in the "stem" of the item (that portion of the item which describes the situation on which several subsequent multiple-choice items are based); research indicates that deaf readers require a fuller context before being able to make a selection (citation?).
4. Some items use words that have *multiple* meanings in cases where the deaf or hard of hearing test-taker might only have had access to a single meaning for the same word. If an alternate meaning, other than the one that the deaf or hard of hearing person knows, was intended by the test developer, then the deaf or hard of hearing person will get that item wrong. Related to this

problem are words on the test that are used in ways that are not frequently used in other non-testing contexts.

5. Some items use *multiple embedded dependent clauses* in item wording. Deaf and hard of hearing candidates can easily become lost in that complexity and miss the intent of the question itself. Test-makers sometimes do such embedding in order to increase item difficulty or get more information into less space or time, even though such structures are not the specific structures that are being measured by the test.

Other problems could be identified, but even one error resulting from any of the above five flaws could result in a candidate not meeting the cut-score (sometimes referred to as "cut-off" score) and mean the difference between graduation or non-graduation, or licensure or non-licensure, for a deaf or hard of hearing person. When one aggregates these flaws, the likelihood of the deaf or hard of person having a problem with a test because of its embeddedness in English increases severalfold.

APPROPRIATE REMEDIATION

Addressing such serious flaws is, however, another matter entirely, because deaf or hard of hearing test-takers constitute such a small minority of any constituency taking such examinations, whether it is a high school student body, a college-entrance cohort, or individuals seeking professional certification or licensure in a given state. Thus, while the technology of test development would, in theory, allow each of these flaws to be addressed and remedied by the production of an alternative form, such an action is not realistic. Alternative versions of the same test are costly to produce and would represent a discernable loss in revenue for the test developer in view of the small number of deaf and hard of hearing candidates paying fees for such alternative-version examinations. However, making test developers aware of these flaws may allow for modifications in the test development guidelines, since in some cases, the changes needed to increase equity for deaf and hard of hearing candidates may improve item clarity for all test-takers.

How else have test administrators chosen to recognize this inequity, after it has been brought to their attention through complaints, hearings, or litigation? One response has been to allow certain accommodations during examinations. These have in general fallen into several categories:

1. Allowing sign language interpreters for the giving of instructions by the test administrator; this accommodation is now required in law by the Americans With Disabilities Act, if it is requested.
2. Allowing the candidate additional time, most commonly 50% more. This accommodation allows some deaf and hard of hearing candidates time needed to process English and may create a more level playing field.
3. A private room or work station so that the deaf or hard of hearing examinee can work at his or her own pace without the pressure of a group-administered test.

4. A paper-and-pencil version of a test that is usually computer administered, especially when it is not possible to grant extended time for the computer-delivered version.
5. Sign language interpretation of the entire examination by a certified sign language interpreter.

Let us now examine each of these accommodations and their consequences. Allowing a sign language interpreter for the instructions, which is now required for all who request it, can avoid any ambiguities in what is expected of the test-taker. It also ensures that the candidate has equal access to information that may impact safety and comfort. Allowing additional time to take the test has enabled some deaf and hard of hearing test-takers, whose score was close to passing, to pass because of the removal of a very limited time constraint. In the case of an individually administered examination, again the pressure of time and peer group is removed and can make a difference for deaf and hard of hearing test-takers whose scores are bordering on passing in any case. But none of these accommodations may sufficiently compensate for the fundamental flaw of unequal access to English.

In the case of the fifth accommodation—allowing a sign language interpreter to sign the entire examination—there is the risk of altering what is being measured or creating an unduly challenging or much easier examination because both the language and the modality have been changed. Off-the-cuff interpretation without advance preparation is virtually impossible. Considerable expertise and collaboration are needed to create a test translation, whether for presentation via video technology or live with an interpreter. And there are other factors to consider as well, such as the interpreter's skill level and whether he or she is knowledgeable about the test material.

If these accommodations are not capable of fully addressing the problem, then what other options for action are available? One option has been for the decision-making body to award a waiver and simply excuse the deaf or hard of hearing individual from the examination. However, this action is definitely less desirable in the eyes of both hearing officials and the Deaf community because it then could permit deaf or hard of hearing persons who are genuinely not qualified to pass and either graduate or become licensed. Is any other option available?

ALTERNATIVE ASSESSMENTS

One of the critical problems with licensure testing and high-stakes testing for students has been the basing of important educational decisions on a single criterion—namely, a written examination. This limitation applies to hearing, non-disabled individuals as well as those with disabilities, but may have graver implications when the single measure directly or indirectly focuses on a given disability. A clear option is a multiple-measures approach to evaluation, not restricted to multiple-choice examinations.

The state of the art in educational measurement has grown significantly since the early 1990's when the American Educational Research Association (AERA) officially endorsed the validity of certain non-quantitative, or qualitative, methods in research and evaluation. While certain qualitative techniques had been utilized for many years, they were accorded an important legitimacy by the action of the AERA. Some of these techniques, which can be adapted to the measurement of deaf and hard of hearing individuals, include:

1. The analysis of candidate *portfolios,* which are an accumulation of data showing the level of mastery of a subject. Oftentimes, well-constructed and validated sets of rubrics are useful in the hands of a panel of reviewers when applied to student or candidate products. This alternative is available to deaf students with multiple disabilities now, but is viewed as highly exceptional and is not available to the deaf and hard of hearing population as a whole.
2. Live or videotaped *observations* of students or candidates involved in a particular task, which is being evaluated for competency. This process requires trained observers using a systematic observation protocol.
3. *Interactive interviews* of students or candidates in reference to a specific skill or understanding, using a systematic interview protocol that has been pilot-tested and validated by a trained interviewer.
4. *Open-ended essay* tasks that require the student or candidate to express in their own words, with elaboration, their response to a situation or problem (as opposed to responding to a multiple-choice item).

It is easily seen how such methods present a double-edged sword. Individually or in combination, each approach could contribute to a comprehensive and balanced assessment of any individual's understanding, and some professional groups and examination authorities are looking at these alternatives as possibly promising. However, at this time, they are expensive to administer on any large scale, and it is probably unrealistic to expect the wide-scale implementation of such alternatives in the foreseeable future. Nevertheless, they might be able to be used to *supplement* rather than *supplant* regularly administered measures; if deaf and hard of hearing persons had access to such alternative means, a more complete picture of competency would emerge. Deaf and hard of hearing candidates actually might meet criteria with more rigorous assessment than that required of the hearing person because they would take both the regular examination as well as an alternative assessment of some kind.

DILEMMAS

This book, then, is to some degree about difficult choices—dilemmas—which face persons who are deaf or hard of hearing, and decision-makers (who more often than not tend to be hearing persons) who must make decisions about their qualifications and futures. The dilemmas include how to accommodate with existing examinations, how to equate results for deaf and hearing persons, how to create more accessible items and formats, how to decide among alternative assessments in terms of value and application, and how to ensure that all of these actions are financially feasible in view of budget restrictions in both the public and private sectors. None of these dilemmas is easily resolved, and each will require much experimentation and debate. It is hoped that readers will achieve a deep understanding of all of the issues attendant on this sensitive area, such that the goal of both equity and maintenance of high standards can be achieved by deaf and hard of hearing persons of all ages.

REFERENCE

Ysseldyke, J. E., Thurlow, M. L., Langenfeld, K. L., Nelson, J., R., Teelucksingh, E., & Seyfarth, A. (1998). *Educational results for students with disabilities.* Minneapolis: National Center on Educational Outcomes. (ERIC Document Reproduction Service No. ED425590)

Historical Reflections on Testing Individuals Who Are Deaf and Hard of Hearing

Marjorie Ragosta

For many years, I was a staff member at Educational Testing Service (ETS) in New Jersey, where (among other pursuits) I was intimately involved with test development issues related to accommodations and fairness for test-takers who have disabilities. My prior experience with deaf or hard of hearing individuals was only in relation to adults who had acquired difficulty with their hearing but had grown up as native speakers of English and could read English with reasonable competence.

Since 1939, the College Board has sought to provide special test administrations of the Scholastic Aptitude Test (SAT) to students with disabilities in order to minimize the effects of the disabilities on their test performance. The first adaptations of the SAT were responses to efforts by blind people and their advocates for an accessible version of the test. The College Board developed a Braille version, and gave extra time to test-takers since it takes longer to read Braille. A large-type version of the SAT was not difficult to produce and could be used by many visually impaired test-takers. When blind veterans of World War II began returning to college, cassette versions of the SAT were developed for those who had no experience with Braille. Adaptations were made for veterans with physical disabilities—individual administrations of the test with extra time and perhaps an amanuensis to mark the answer sheet. As wounded war veterans expanded on what blind advocates had begun, special test administrations, although still relatively few, became less unusual. From the beginning, however, test scores from all special administrations were flagged to indicate that the scores were obtained under nonstandard conditions rather than the normal standardized testing requirements.

Civil rights legislation made the next impact on the testing of individuals with disabilities. The 1977 regulations implementing Section 504 of the Rehabilitation Act of 1973 required that admissions tests for students with disabilities be validated to ensure that they measured the students' aptitude and achievement rather than any disabilities extraneous to what was being measured. It also required that the test scores from special test administrations NOT be flagged. Because the regulations were seen by testing professionals as impossible to implement, the Office of Civil Rights held them in abeyance and asked the National Academy of Sciences to appoint a Panel on Testing of Handicapped People to study the issues. Their report, submitted in 1982, began a lengthy program of research at the Educational Testing Service (ETS), funded jointly by the College Board, the ETS, and the Graduate Record Examinations Board.

But even before the panel's report was issued, the College Board and the ETS had begun preparing for the possibility of validity studies. The first step was a small pilot study to interview students with disabilities in selected colleges and universities about their experiences with college-entrance examinations. As a Research Scientist at ETS, I was asked to undertake this preliminary task before any further research was begun. I almost turned down the request. I had little experience nor expertise in the area of disabilities and frankly was afraid of being inadequate for the task. My prior experience with deaf and hard of hearing individuals was only in relation to adults who had acquired difficulty with hearing but who had grown up as native speakers of English. In retrospect, I now believe that this lack of knowledge and experience is fairly typical of many testing professionals and often creates, in and of itself, a handicapping condition for people with disabilities. Despite these misgivings, however, I agreed to do the interviews.

I consulted with the individuals responsible for setting up special test administrations, which revealed that accommodations for the SAT primarily consisted of the use of alternative formats—Braille, large-type, or cassette tests—as well as additional testing time. Deaf or hard of hearing students were given written rather than oral instructions, a tap on the shoulder when time was up, and perhaps extra time. At that time, I did not question the appropriateness of these accommodations because they appeared to be reasonable.

PILOT STUDY

Individual interviews lasted about a half-hour and utilized a specially developed questionnaire. The 30-minute interviews occurred at sites with populations large enough to ensure that they could be conducted efficiently with a wide variety of students with disabilities. Although this study and subsequent research was conducted across many disability groups, for purposes of this chapter, I will focus exclusively on issues and research involving deaf and hard of hearing individuals.

My first lesson about this population was very enlightening and, at the same time, frustrating. At a large state university where I had interviewed students with many different disabilities, my schedule called for interviewing deaf students during my last day on campus. Instead of a series of interviews, I received a daylong, comprehensive overview about the population from the hearing director of the program for deaf students and his deaf assistant. Finally, for the last half-hour of the day, I was allowed to interview a large group of deaf students in a conference room with a sign language interpreter. The scope of the problem of testing deaf students then became overwhelmingly apparent.

How could the SAT scores of these students who were using a signed language distinct from English mean the same thing as those of hearing students raised in an English-speaking environment? Although most of these deaf young people had also been raised in an English-speaking environment, they had not had access to English, let alone to incidental learning and information-gathering in that language.

I tried to imagine being deaf. What if I were placed in a soundproof booth in a classroom of people learning Chinese? It was beyond my imagination to conceive of learning under those conditions. From my first encounter with deaf students, I was concerned that there was no suitable accommodations for standardized testing that would make their test scores comparable to the test scores of the general population for whom the tests were originally designed and intended.

TEST VALIDITY STUDIES OF THE SAT

After the pilot study was completed, the work of establishing a database for future validity studies of the SAT and Graduate Record Examination (GRE) began, and a research and development plan was initiated. By the time the Panel on Testing of Handicapped People released its report, the comprehensive research study was set to begin. Between 1982 and 1986, ETS researchers published twenty-seven technical reports, journal articles, and other reports, culminating in the publication by Allyn and Bacon of the book, *Testing Handicapped People* (Willingham, Ragosta, Bennett, Braun, Rock, & Powers, 1988).

Although no GRE test-takers had identified themselves as having a hearing loss, enough deaf and hard of hearing SAT test-takers were available for research on test performance, student descriptive information, test completion and reliability, construct validity, and predictive validity. Since the application for a special test administration only inquired if the student had a visual, hearing, learning, or physical disability, further breakdown within categories was impossible.

SAT Test Performance

The mean SAT-Verbal and SAT-Mathematical scores of the 752 deaf or hard of hearing students from special test administrations were 291 and 375, respectively. The Verbal mean was 1.22 standard deviations below the mean of 425 for all college-bound seniors taking standard administrations over the same period of time, and the Mathematical mean was .79 of a standard deviation below the analogous mean of 467 (Willingham et al., 1988, p. 53).

The mean scores of deaf and hard of hearing students were the lowest of all disability groups taking special administrations of the SAT and reflected the English language deficiencies of deaf and hard of hearing individuals as documented in the literature review conducted for the study.

Student Descriptive Information

The Student Descriptive Questionnaire accompanying the SAT was completed by 537 deaf and hard of hearing test-takers, a return of 71%. Many of their responses paralleled those of the general population. In a few cases, the responses of deaf and hard of hearing individuals differed:

- The mean self-reported, high school grade-point average (HSGPA) of deaf and hard of hearing students from special test administrations was .38 of a standard deviation below that of all college-bound seniors: 2.83 compared with 3.06.

- Although ethnic minorities comprised 18% of all college-bound seniors, they represented only 10% of the deaf and hard of hearing respondents.

- Compared with all college-bound seniors, fewer deaf and hard of hearing students from special test administrations attended public high schools: 70% vs. 81%.

- Fewer deaf and hard of hearing respondents rated themselves as being in the top 10% of their classes in spoken expression, written expression, creative writing, or music.

A special questionnaire was then developed in order to obtain information from test-takers with disabilities about their reactions to special testing accommodations and to the test itself. Overall, 97% of respondents to the SAT survey reported that their special accommodations were satisfactory, but only 88% of deaf and hard of hearing respondents did. Their sources of difficulty and dissatisfaction included the following:

- Asked about aspects of the test that were difficult because of their disability, 59% of deaf and hard of hearing respondents reported a problem with vocabulary, 51% with reading comprehension, and 40% with the amount of reading, while 24% reported no difficulty because of their disability.

- In open-ended responses, the test itself was criticized as being hard to comprehend, too advanced, having vocabulary that was too difficult, and being unfair to deaf and hard of hearing test-takers. Dissatisfaction with the conditions of testing was reflected in several comments about not having a sign language interpreter.

Psychometric Characteristics

The comparability of SAT scores for disabled and non-disabled groups of students depends on several psychometric characteristics, including the level of performance, test completion rates, the reliability of the test, and unexpected differential performance.

Test completion rates. Two measures of test completion rates were obtained for those completing the entire test and those completing 75% of the test. Both measures were needed in order to examine the possible effects of the extra time given to disabled individuals in special test administrations. The ratio of these two measures for students with disabilities compared with non-disabled students gave quite different results. For all disability groupings, the ratios of those completing 75% of the test clustered around the score of 1.00 for individuals from standard test administrations. The deaf and hard of hearing students' ratio was 1.01. These results indicated that virtually equal percentages of disabled and non-disabled test-takers were completing 75% of the test questions in each section of the test.

When the ratios were obtained for those *finishing* each section of the test, however, the data presented a different picture. Compared with the ratio of 1.00 for individuals from standard test administrations, the ratios of students with disabilities finishing each section ranged from 1.11 to 1.25, with a ratio of 1.22 for deaf and hard of hearing students. These results indicate that more of the students with disabilities from special test administrations were able to complete the final question in each section of the test.

Reliability. Reliability was evaluated using internal-consistency standard errors of measurement. For the non-disabled group, the raw-score standard errors were 3.74 for the 85-item Verbal section and 3.12 for the 60-item Mathematical section. Without exception, the standard errors for all disability groups were virtually identical to these values, differing by only a few hundredths of an item.

Unexpected differential item performance. The analysis of differential item performance was intended to detect broad, general classes of items that function differently across groups. In the 162 pairs of cluster performances studied (9 groups by 18 clusters on each of 2 test forms), only 5 instances of deviant cluster functioning were consistent across both forms of the test, and only 2 of those were instances of differential difficulty. Neither of those instances involved deaf and hard of hearing students.

Three instances of differential *easiness* were found, two of which involved deaf and hard of hearing test-takers. These differentially easy clusters were both in the Mathematical section. One cluster was composed of quantitative-comparison items with algebra content. The other was a cluster that was considered low in reading load, with items composed only of mathematical symbols. One possible explanation for the differential easiness might have been that item clusters were disproportionately loaded with items near the end of the test sections, thus giving an advantage to students who had the extra time. However, when the individual items were examined, some but not all of the items supported this hypothesis, suggesting that extra time alone is not a sufficient explanation. Another perhaps more powerful explanation for the differential easiness of both clusters for deaf and hard of hearing test-takers is that the items are relatively free of English-language difficulties.

Construct validity. Factor-analysis as a standard methodology for assessing construct validity was used in this study in conjunction with the data from the differential item performance just discussed. A two-factor model was hypothesized—the Verbal and Mathematical factors of the SAT—and item clusters were used.

For the test-takers from standard test administrations, the percentage of performance variation on item-parcels, which was accounted for by the hypothesized factor structure, was 96% for the Verbal factor and 100% for the Mathematical factor. For deaf or hard of hearing test-takers, those figures were 97% for the Verbal factor and 99% for the Mathematical factor. Overall, the hypothesized two-factor model was found to fit the data quite well for all groups.

Predictive validity. Several months were spent attempting to acquire the necessary FYAs of students from special test administrations. After several rounds of data collection involving 500 institutions, we obtained validity study data from 145 schools. The final database was composed of 1,200 students with disabilities from regular and special test administrations (Regulars and Specials) and 6,255 control students composed of a random sample of, at most, 50 students from each of the institutions that provided data.

Only 84 deaf and hard of hearing students from special test administrations were found, although 130 were identified who had taken regular test administrations. The deaf and hard of hearing Specials located for this study had somewhat higher mean SAT scores than the population from which the subset was obtained, as might be expected since these students had been accepted for college and attended long enough to get first-year grade-point averages. Deaf and hard of hearing Specials consistently earned lower scores than their Regular counterparts. Mean scores for SAT-Vs were 356 for the Regulars and 315 for the Specials. SAT-M means were 438 and 429, respectively.

One other note about the composition of the deaf and hard of hearing students in this validity study should be mentioned. More than in other disability groups, deaf and hard of hearing students tended to cluster at specific institutions which had strong support services for deaf students. Three such institutions supplied most of the data obtained, but one of those had no control group data and could not be used for the validity study. The other two institutions provided 63 of the 84 individuals from special test administrations. The final 21 Specials were located in institutions distributed across the United States and had mean SAT scores of 369 Verbal and 484 Mathematical—higher than their clustered counterparts.

Methodology. Traditional validity studies use HSGPA together with SAT-Verbal and -Mathematical scores (SAT-V and SAT-M) to predict first-year averages (FYAs). For the 145 institutions in the study, the FYAs in each school were converted to standard scores, and separate regression equations were obtained using only data from the control students in each school. Then, for each disabled student, a predicted FYA was obtained by substituting a person's HSGPA and SAT scores into the prediction equation for the institution the person attended. The differences between the actual and the predicted FYAs, called *residuals,* would be expected to cluster around zero (the mean of the control group) if the groups were roughly comparable.

Results. When college performance was predicted from high school grades and SAT scores, the mean residuals of deaf and hard of hearing students were 0.25 for Regulars and 0.27 for Specials. These were the most discrepant scores of any group. The positive residuals indicate that the equation based on control students underpredicted the college performance of deaf and hard of hearing students and that they actually performed *better* than predicted. A negative mean residual would indicate overprediction and poorer-than-expected performance.

An additional set of regression analyses were developed for deaf and hard of hearing students because of the restricted sources of data. The underprediction of college performance for deaf and hard of hearing students can perhaps best be understood by dividing them into the three groups of such students referred to earlier when the database for this study was being built: students from a separate unit within a large technical university, students from an institution in which they were mainstreamed and offered excellent support services, and students scattered among other mainstream colleges and universities. The results differ for students from Special and Regular SAT administrations.

Specials. An examination of the mean residuals for these three groups from regressions based on high school grades and SAT scores from Special test administrations showed severe underprediction (.73) at the separate unit in the technical university, which was only partly offset by moderate overprediction at the mainstream school, which had strong support services. The 21 students in the third group, from other mainstream institutions across the country, had a mean residual close to zero.

Regulars. For individuals with SAT scores from standard test administrations, the results are rather different. While the performance of students at the mainstream institution was fairly predicted on average, the performances of students from the separate institution and from the third heterogeneous group were quite strongly underpredicted.

THE STUDY OF ADMISSIONS DECISIONS

Before discussing the conclusions and recommendations resulting from the research already reported, we need to look at a related study on admissions decisions for college applicants with disabilities. Because the "flagging" of test scores from special test administrations appeared to be discriminatory, the regulations implementing Section 504 of the Rehabilitation Act of 1973 mandated that test scores from special test administrations not be flagged. Although the mandate was held in abeyance, there was a need for a study of the extent to which admissions standards are applied equally to applicants with and without disabilities.

Residual analyses of the differences between actual and predicted admission rates for subgroups of applicants with disabilities showed significant differences for two groups: students with learning disabilities versus deaf and hard of hearing students. The small group (N + 75) of deaf and hard of hearing applicants had a large positive residual, indicating that they were far more likely to be admitted than was predicted. Further analysis revealed that this result was largely based on the scores from a single institution with a special unit for deaf students.

CONCLUSIONS AND RECOMMENDATIONS

The series of studies described thus far considered the extent to which nonstandard test administrations for examinees with disabilities were comparable with tests regularly administered to college applicants. The major differences in comparability were: (1) the greater likelihood that students from special test administrations could complete the test, and (2) the consistent overprediction of college performance evident in SAT scores from special test administrations across all disability groups. Timing studies to determine an equitable amount of extra time were recommended and subsequently reported (Packer, 1987; Ragosta & Wendler, 1992), but those results made no practical difference in timing for deaf or hard of hearing examinees.

How can the SAT be said to be comparable for deaf students and non-disabled students? Perhaps there are two answers (Willingham et al., 1988, p. 166). The research suggests that the test results are comparable because the test measures the same cognitive abilities in the same way, the items within the sections of the test are similarly interrelated, and there is little evidence of differential item difficulty within the Verbal and Mathematical sections of the test. A different answer is that the test cannot be comparable because there is no hope of disentangling the effects of the disability on the skills, especially the verbal skills, in English, which the test intends to measure. One possibility for improving the comparability of test performance for deaf students might be to translate an admissions test into the signed language used by the candidates. Another possibility is a recommendation that the national admissions tests should not be used at all for individuals who primarily use a signed language. One of the 14 final conclusions and implications of the research related solely to deaf and hard of hearing students was:

A test translated into a manual language, (if feasible), might better assess the academic potential of deaf students, particularly those entering special programs where sign language is used for instruction. If admissions tests are used in such programs, special norms for deaf students could be helpful (Willingham et al., 1988, p. 184).

* * * * *

By the time the ETS series of validity studies was completed, I had become very concerned with the educational and testing issues of individuals with disabilities, especially those involving deaf and hard of hearing persons. I was a member of the ETS Committee on Handicapped People, formed in 1981. I had also become an active member of the Association on Handicapped Student Service Programs in Postsecondary Education (AHSSPPE). I began attending meetings of the National Task Force on Equity in Testing Deaf Persons in the late 1980s and early 1990s at Gallaudet University, described elsewhere in this volume. I was at Gallaudet, eating lunch in the university cafeteria, where I first fully realized the enormous similarities and differences between the students that I had known all my life and these deaf and hard of hearing students: Of course these students were quieter and their hands flashed their communications, but there was no mistaking the vigor and vitality of the communication within the many groups of students. In this scenario, they were not disabled at all.

A Request for a Proposal (RFP) was issued in 1987 by the U.S. Department of Education for research that was relevant to progress in education and rehabilitation of the deaf. Years earlier, in 1965, the U.S. Department of Health, Education and Welfare (HEW) had published a report, *Education of the Deaf*, prepared by the HEW Secretary's Advisory Committee on the Education of the Deaf, chaired by Homer Babbidge, Jr. The Babbidge report began:

The American people have no reason to be satisfied with their limited success in educating deaf children and preparing them for full participation in our society.

The report went on to outline the elements of the educational system, to describe its effectiveness, to set forth factors in the selection of programs, to identify needs for improvement, and to make recommendations. The new research was to chart the progress made since the Babbidge report and to make recommendations for the future. Presented with the possibility of an opportunity to learn more about deaf and hard of hearing individuals, the author responded to the RFP and was subsequently awarded the grant to conduct the study.

PROGRESS IN EDUCATION AND REHABILITATION OF DEAF AND HARD OF HEARING INDIVIDUALS

During the early months of the grant, an advisory panel was set up to guide the progress of the study, and site visits were made to six states to interview people in education and rehabilitation.

The advisory panel. The members of the advisory panel were Thomas Allen, Gallaudet University; Glenn Anderson, Arkansas Rehabilitation Research and Training Center; Claudia Barguest, Columbus State Community College; Edward Franklin, Johnson County Community College; Gerilee Gustafson, Signing Exact English Center for the Advancement of Deaf Children; T. Alan Hurwitz, National Technical Institute for the Deaf; Judith Mounty, South Shore (MA) Educational Collaborative; Stephen Quigley, Consultant; and Gloria Wright, Arkansas Rehabilitation Services. The panel was a cooperative and well-informed group, dedicated to improving conditions for deaf and hard of hearing individuals at all stages in their lives.

Site visits. Site visits were a reality-based introduction to the progress and problems set forth by the advisory panel and encountered in the literature. In two locations, the exclusively oral approach to education was still strongly defended, and sign language was discouraged. In other locations, innovative programs used both sign and oral approaches and had deaf or hard of hearing people involved as administrators, teachers, and/or paraprofessionals. Many people in the field of deaf education were concerned about the definition of "least-restrictive environment" as it affected deaf students. In the field of rehabilitation, concern was expressed about the confusion resulting from the payment of Supplementary Security Income (SSI) to young people with disabilities, who must prove themselves incapable of work in order to receive the benefits and who then are ironically encouraged to go to work and give up their benefits.

In one location, people in rehabilitation were proud of placing deaf students in the workforce and directed me to visit a job site where a minimum wage was offered for a dead-end position. I was not given an opportunity to see the deaf individuals at work, but it was hard to envision much of a future for them. In another location, deaf and hard of hearing students had opportunities for after-school employment even before they graduated from secondary education. What emerged from the site visits was a realization of the scope of the problems involved with the education and rehabilitation of deaf and hard of hearing individuals.

Progress. There had been much progress since the time of the Babbidge report. By 1988, sign language had become much more accepted and was in general use in the education of most deaf and many hard of hearing individuals. In some locations, it had officially been recognized as a "foreign" language, making it possible for hearing students to study it for high school or college credit. Total Communication (TC) became the dominant approach used to educate deaf children, although the meaning of TC differed from location to location. Stanford Achievement Test scores had improved somewhat for deaf and hard of hearing examinees. Postsecondary programs had proliferated since 1965 when only the Gallaudet College and Riverside Community College programs had been reported. Since then, Gallaudet had become a university, the National Technical Institute for the Deaf had been established at the Rochester Institute of Technology, and support services had been developed in many mainstream colleges and universities.

Over a period when vocational rehabilitation found itself constrained to serve fewer clients, the numbers of deaf and hard of hearing clients had grown, and the success rate remained higher than that of most other disability groups. Rehabilitation funds had helped to create additional personnel in service to deaf and hard of hearing people: Rehabilitation counselors for the deaf, state coordinators for the deaf, interpreters, and other specialists.

The consciousness of the general public had been raised with respect to deaf and hard of hearing individuals. Deaf actors and playwrights had succeeded on Broadway, in television and movie productions, and with the National Theatre of the Deaf. Deaf students had demanded and gotten a deaf president for Gallaudet University. Deaf people in the hundreds had earned master's degrees and close to 100 had earned doctorates. And with the passage of Public Law 99-457 in 1986, efforts at early identification of and intervention with deaf infants were finally under way. Progress had been made in the quarter of a century since the Babbidge report, but there was still a long way to go.

We had not yet fully identified the broad components of education that would ensure the best possible outcomes for deaf individuals from birth to adulthood. The final report of the study (Ragosta, 1990, March) called for a long-term program of research, based on rigorous data collection on individual students at all levels from early identification and subsequent participation in early intervention programs to adulthood. Data included objective evaluation and assessment of the individual as well as the characteristics of the programs to which the individual has been exposed. Part of the data could be obtained from documents already required by law, if the documents could be standardized: the Individualized Written Family Plan (IWFP) at the time of early identification, the Individualized Education Plan (IEP) during elementary and secondary school, and the Individualized Written Rehabilitation Plan (IWRP) leading to employment. Presenting pertinent information in a standardized format would facilitate a smooth transition from early childhood to adulthood as well as advance the potential for research.

Such a broad program of research depends for its success on the development of standardized instruments to measure the individual's progress as well as the characteristics of the programs and people to whom the individual has been exposed. It also calls for work on the establishment and maintenance of standards of quality and minimum competency for teachers of deaf students, which may be quite different from that of teachers in general, and the development of reasonable accommodations for testing and/or alternative assessments.

Given the goals of early identification of deaf infants—early provision of the rich social interaction important to all children's development, optimal educational experiences and employment opportunities, and supportive services to facilitate progress from infancy to successful adulthood—the opportunity to identify and build on the components of success has never been greater. Assessment, evaluation, and testing should not inhibit that progress but be the very foundation upon which progress depends.

Other activities in which I engaged that have bearing on this volume included directing and collaborating on studies that led to the publication by Willingham et al. (1988), enabling the establishment of the ETS Committee on Testing People with Disabilities, and directing a federal grant that studied progress in the education and rehabilitation of individuals who are deaf and hard of hearing. In a variety of ways, these activities played a role in developing the points described in this chapter.

* * * * *

The findings of the research presented here clearly indicated the need for continuing research on testing deaf individuals, but I was soon to retire. At the same time, postdoctoral fellowships were being announced to qualified candidates competing for the opportunity to do research at ETS. I had identified a person with all the credentials, who had directed a school program for deaf and hard of hearing children and was interested in ways of making standardized tests and testing more accessible to deaf and hard of hearing persons. She was also hard of hearing herself and could begin to sensitize testing professionals about accommodations just by her physical presence. In August 1989, Judith Mounty became a postdoctoral fellow at ETS and stayed on as a research scientist until July 1996.

During her time at ETS, Dr. Mounty worked with several testing programs to identify and examine the problems that deaf and hard of hearing people often experience with standardized tests, and begin to explore possible solutions. The projects included:

- Thorough review of many tests and identification of the kinds of grammatical constructions and types of vocabulary selections that are likely to cause problems for deaf and hard of hearing candidates. This information was later applied to the revision of test development manuals and to the analysis of tests for potential bias, as will be seen in several chapters in this book.

- Examination of the quantity and quality of information that deaf candidates provided when asked to respond to an essay prompt by signing versus writing (Mounty, 1990a; 1990b).

- Development, through several separate efforts, of a process for identifying the challenges of translating tests developed in English to ASL.

  - Translation of the NTE Listening Comprehension Test to ASL

  - Translation and then administration via live interpreter (versus videotaped deaf actors) the English Language Proficiency Test (ELPT) (Mounty, Epstein, & Weinstock, 1997).

- Translation of reading passages from the National Assessment of Educational Progress (NAEP) and development of an early interactive video technology program to use for instruction and assessment. This project explored the use of ASL versus a more English-oriented sign version of the passages (Hansen, Mounty, & Baird, 1994; Hansen & Mounty, 1997; 1998).

- Exploration of the use of tools developed for assessing the English of hearing non-native speakers with the deaf and hard of hearing population (Mounty, Epstein, & Weinstock, 1997).

- Development of a checklist to assess ASL/signed language acquisition by children and adults (Mounty, 1993; 1994).

SUMMARY

The corpus of work encompassed within my career and then extended by Judith Mounty provided important insights into various aspects of testing deaf and hard of hearing individuals. These points related to the limitations of existing accommodations, questions about test equity, perceptions of test difficulty by deaf test-takers, English decoding issues, the possible inappropriateness of test scores being used as primary indicators of skills and knowledge for deaf test-takers, underprediction of school or job performance by standardized tests, identification of grammatical constructions that constitute inequity in testing for deaf persons, and issues pertinent to translation of tests developed in English into ASL. These and related issues growing from them are topics now dealt with in the chapters which follow.

REFERENCES

Hansen, E. G., Mounty, J. L., & Baird, A. (1994). Interactive video and sign language for improving literacy skills of deaf students. In T. Ottman & I. Tomek (Eds.), *Proceedings of ED-MEDIA 94-World Conference on Educational Multimedia and Hypermedia.*, Vancouver, British Columbia, Canada: Association for the Advancement of Computing in Education (pp. 241–245).

Hansen, E. G., & Mounty, J. L. (1997). *Final report: Videodisc technology and sign language for improving reading skills of deaf middle school students* (U.S. Department of Education grant number H180G20021). Princeton, NJ: Educational Testing Service.

Hansen, E. G., & Mounty, J. L. (1998). Interactive video technology and sign language for learning and performance support for deaf students. In A. Weisel (Ed.), *Proceedings of the 18th International Congress on Education of the Deaf* (ICED), (I, 100–103), Tel Aviv, Israel: Ramot Publications, Tel Aviv University.

Mounty, J. L. (1990a). *A study of signed and written essays produced by prospective deaf teachers.* (Postdoctoral research report.) Princeton, NJ: Educational Testing Service.

Mounty, J. L. (1990b). Testing deaf individuals: Equity in test conditions and test format. In D. Ellis (Ed.), *Selected Proceedings of the 1990 AHSSPPE Conference* (pp. 13–17). Columbus, OH: Association on Handicapped Student Service Programs in Post-Secondary Education.

Mounty, J. L. (1993). *Signed language development checklist: Training manual.* Princeton, NJ: Educational Testing Service.

Mounty, J. L. (1994). *Signed language development checklist.* Princeton, NJ: Educational Testing Service.

Mounty, J. L., Epstein, K. I., & Weinstock, R. B. (1997). *Using the English Language Proficiency Test with deaf and hard of hearing students: An overview and update.* Report submitted for publication.

Packer, J. K. (1987). *SAT testing time for students with disabilities.* (ETS Research Report No. 87-37). Princeton, NJ: Educational Testing Service.

Ragosta, M. (1990, March). Progress in education and rehabilitation of deaf and hard of hearing individuals. Report in acknowledgement of support from U.S. Department of Education: OSERS (Contract No. 300 87-0056).

Ragosta, M., & Wendler, C. (1992). *Eligibility issues and comparable time limits for disabled and nondisabled SAT examinees.* (ETS Research Report No. 92-5). Princeton, NJ: Educational Testing Service.

Willingham, W., Ragosta, M., Bennett, R. E., Braun, H., Rock, D. A., & Powers, D. (1988). *Testing handicapped people.* Boston: Allyn and Bacon.

Section II *Test Development Issues*

Test-Taking for Deaf and Hard of Hearing Individuals: Meeting the Challenges

Robert B. Weinstock and Judith L. Mounty

Even the most able and accomplished deaf and hard of hearing people often do not do well on standardized tests. The principal author remembers consoling a deaf college classmate whose Graduate Record Examination (GRE) scores were very low. She was a straight-A student, well respected by peers and professors alike for her intellect and work ethic—but as she read her score report, she was devastated. She thought her dreams of graduate school were fading away. Of course, the situation turned out not to be so dire; she was accepted into a master's degree program on the strength of her academic record, excelled in the program, earned the appropriate licenses and certifications, and became a successful teacher and administrator.

Our acquaintance is not alone in her experience. We know of many students who aspire to professional careers, but who are stymied by the corresponding standardized test. Those who do surmount this obstacle face one later—the examination for certificate or licensure. We know of outstanding classroom teachers who are unable to pass teacher licensure examinations; people with master's degrees in social work who cannot obtain their critical license; law school graduates who are unable to pass the bar examination; and architecture school graduates who struggle to pass the nine-part examination to become licensed architects.

Why do so many seemingly capable deaf and hard of hearing people have difficulty with standardized tests, especially licensing examinations that are arguably the most "high-stakes" of all? The reasons are many and varied, and they are addressed by most of the other authors in this volume as well. Briefly, they have to do with the language, content, and format of tests, deaf and hard of hearing people having less than full access to English; and their corresponding unfamiliarity with the culture of testing (Ragosta, 1989).

To a far greater extent than most people realize, full access to the spoken form of a target language provides the foundation for facility with that language in a variety of print contexts. Native fluency involves understanding not just the mechanics of a language, but also its registers, its formal and informal uses, its nuances, and its subtleties. One of the authors (Weinstock) teaches college-level English and communication studies classes, and often has to explain to students why a sentence in an essay, while grammatically and syntactically correct, does not "sound" right in print.

Similarly, in our experience with deaf and hard of hearing students of all ages, we have seen misunderstanding of textbook exercises and test questions because the language in these items is excessively complex, ambiguous, or convoluted (or the opposite: insufficiently detailed). Students need to spend a great deal of time decoding questions, and even then may not fully understand them. Hearing people typically decode such items on the basis of linguistic familiarity or an innate knowledge of "what sounds right." Their deaf and hard of hearing counterparts usually cannot apply this strategy.

WHY DO DEAF AND HARD OF HEARING CANDIDATES CHALLENGE TEST ITEMS?

Deaf and hard of hearing test-takers typically challenge individual test items or groups of items. Some have challenged entire tests. Some have become advocates for systemic change.

Some deaf and hard of hearing candidates challenge test items because the language of the question impedes their understanding of that question. To a far greater extent than most people realize, full access to the spoken form of a target language provides the foundation for facility with that language in a variety of print contexts. When the language used in test items is excessively complex, ambiguous, or convoluted, the candidate may need to spend a great deal of time decoding the question, and even then may not fully understand it.

Candidates also challenge questions that ask for information that may not be within their experience or to which they may not have full access. Questions about music or that require familiarity with intonation or voice inflection patterns may be problematic. Finally, candidates have challenged questions because the answer choices do not allow for the possibility that deaf and hard of hearing people may learn things differently and do things differently. A social work licensing candidate who is deaf or hard of hearing may have learned how to conduct intake interviews with clients who are deaf or hard of hearing. Very likely, the techniques and the protocol differ somewhat from that used by hearing candidates, owing to the unique communication situation. Cultural and experiential differences often mean that a more direct and less formal interaction style may be used. Deaf and hard of hearing social workers often—albeit with caution—share a bit more of themselves in establishing rapport with clients. If a question asks how intake interviews are conducted, and the answer choice closest to the deaf or hard of hearing person's experience is not presented, the candidate may feel that the question is inappropriate or perhaps culturally insensitive and should not be counted.

CANDIDATE CHALLENGES TO INDIVIDUAL TEST ITEMS

Nearly every standardized test has provisions for candidates to report what they believe are irregularities in test items. Typically, after taking the test, the candidate informs the test center supervisor or proctor that he or she wishes to question an item or items. Most candidates will remember the specific item, or will have made a mental note of it (e.g., "Verbal Subsection 1, Question 21"). It is amazing how well some candidates remember items that they subsequently challenge, right down to the answer choices. Candidates may also write to the testing company after leaving the testing room. This step usually must be done within a fixed time period.

The testing company will review the complaint. If it is about ambiguous wording, test development specialists are consulted. It is exceedingly rare that an item is discarded, however. Items in the final forms of tests have already been vetted; in effect, they have stood the test of time, they have been psychometrically validated, and they have been answered by hundreds or even thousands of test-takers. In all likelihood, the challenge will be denied.

On some tests, including the Scholastic Assessment Test (SAT), individual questions or entire sections of questions are experimental. Candidates do not know which question(s) or which section does not count toward their score. If they challenge one of these questions, there is a greater likelihood that their comments be considered; however, there may not be a concomitant adjustment to the candidate's score because the item was not counted in his or her score in the first place.

CANDIDATES' ACROSS-THE-BOARD CHALLENGES

The authors of this chapter know of several instances where deaf or hard of hearing candidates challenged multiple items on tests, or even entire tests. One case involved a Praxis II subject assessment; the others were state-level licensing examinations. This section describes two of these challenges and their outcomes.

A deaf candidate applying for a teaching license in a southeastern state took an Educational Testing Service (ETS) Praxis II subject assessment several years ago. While taking the test, he identified approximately 20 items that he felt he could not answer. According to the candidate, these items concerned pronunciation, poetry, and phonetics. He stated that some questions were "sound-based"—that is, they were answerable by candidates with normal hearing because those candidates had the ability to select the answer on the basis of which one "sounded right," whereas deaf candidates did not have this facility. ETS staff participated in a review of the test and suggested that approximately 15 items should be discarded for this particular candidate. The test was re-scored without these questions, and the candidate's revised score met the state standard for licensure. Note, however, that this case did not succeed in moving either the licensing body or ETS to further investigate how the issues might more broadly impact deaf and hard of hearing candidates for teacher licensure.

A candidate for a counseling license in a southwestern state failed the state-developed and administered examination and filed a formal complaint. The case ultimately came to the attention of the state attorney general's office, which entered into a consent agreement with the candidate and the state agency that administered the examination. The agreement called for a review of the test by an independent and impartial panel of professionals with expertise in the following: test development, the language challenges faced by deaf and hard of hearing candidates, and the content covered by the test. The attorney general's office contacted the authors, who recruited a professor from the department of counseling at Gallaudet University as the content-area expert.

The panel members began their work by reading the test individually and proposing the classification of each item into one of nine content domains. These domains included normal human growth and development; abnormal human development; appraisal or assessment techniques; counseling theories; counseling methods or techniques; research, lifestyle, and career development; social, cultural, and family issues; and professional orientation. During their first face-to-face meeting, the panelists reviewed each other's proposals and reached consensus on which questions fit into which content domain. They created a matrix using Microsoft Excel, then painstakingly reviewed each test item for context, phrasing, grammar and syntax, vocabulary, and other issues. They concluded that some 30 items out of 200 would be problematic for deaf or hard of hearing candidates and noted items that would be problematic for non-native users of English generally. The licensing agency accepted the reviewers' recommendations in their entirety and removed these questions from scoring for this particular candidate. As a result, the candidate was able to obtain a license.

As with the Praxis II case, the dispensation was for the individual candidate, with no assurance that other "similarly situated" candidates would receive the same consideration. While it is commendable that the dispensation was made at all, the very fact that so many items on both tests were problematic points to a greater, systemic problem. The best item-writing guides, the best fairness reviews, and the best pre-testing regimens did not prevent these flawed items from being included on the tests. They also did not result in changes to the tests themselves.

Granted, it is difficult to retrofit an existing test. It is time-consuming and expensive to create new test forms. The reality is nonetheless that just as important knowledge, skills, and abilities of deaf and hard of hearing candidates are not being assessed by existing problematic items, neither will they be assessed by eliminating those items. Absent a supplemental evaluation of the candidate that addresses targeted knowledge, skills, and abilities in some other way, unqualified candidates may still be entering the profession.

This situation makes it imperative that we "get in on the ground floor" to attack the problem before it even occurs. This process is the focus of the following section.

GETTING IN ON THE GROUND FLOOR

The test development process is fairly straightforward and relatively standard. Figure 1 shows the test development process and timelines for the North Carolina Essential Knowledge and Skills battery, which is used to assess K-12 students' performance.

Typically, the test development process begins long before the test is ever given and long before a single test item is even written. It is necessary to conduct a job analysis or a practice analysis first. In the early 1990s, one of the co-authors of this chapter and several colleagues at ETS conducted a job analysis of teachers of deaf and hard of hearing students. This study "involved a multi-method approach that included subject-matter experts and a national survey" (p. 4). ETS staff developed an outline of the "knowledge and skill domains thought to be important for newly licensed teachers of deaf and hard of hearing students, reviewed the specifications for an existing test and the test itself, and finally circulated this material to an advisory committee" (p. 5). The committee

Test-Taking for Deaf and Hard of Hearing Individuals

**North Carolina Testing Program
Multiple Choice Test Development Process Flow Chart**

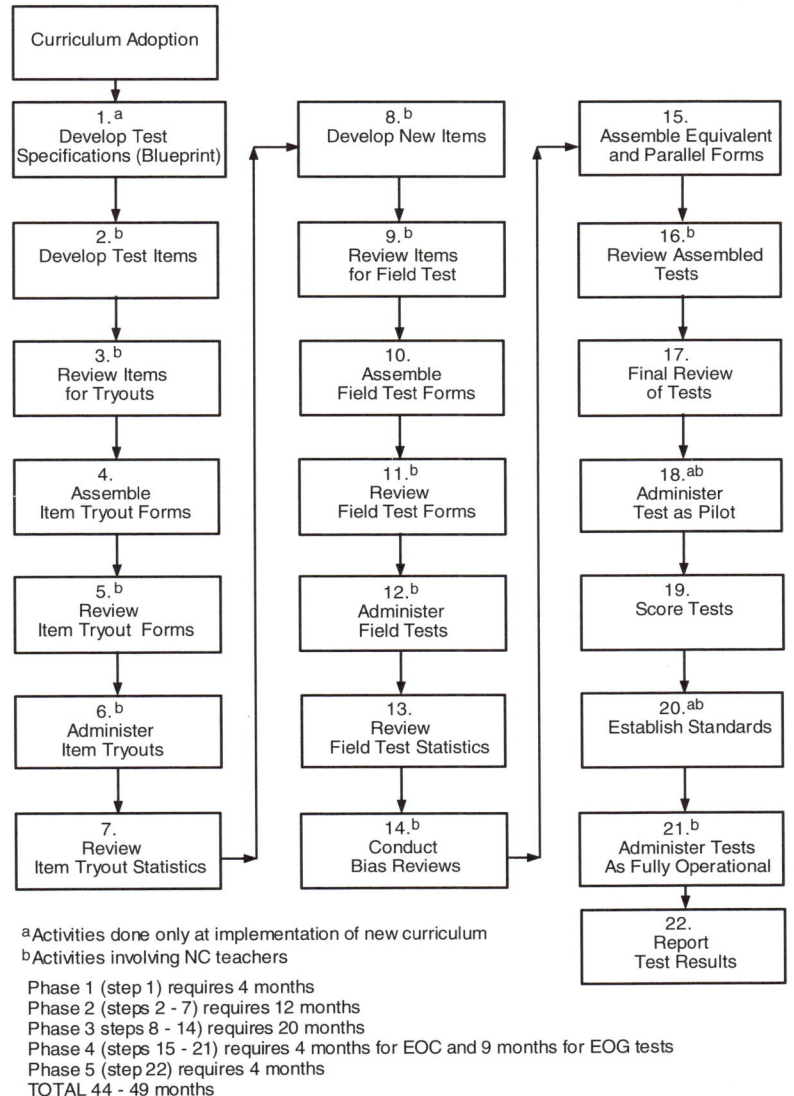

```
                    ┌─────────────────┐
                    │   Curriculum    │
                    │    Adoption     │
                    └────────┬────────┘
                             ▼
    ┌──────────────┐   ┌──────────────┐   ┌──────────────────┐
    │     1.[a]    │   │     8.[b]    │   │       15.        │
    │ Develop Test │──▶│ Develop New  │──▶│ Assemble Equiv.  │
    │Specifications│   │    Items     │   │and Parallel Forms│
    │ (Blueprint)  │   │              │   │                  │
    └──────┬───────┘   └──────┬───────┘   └────────┬─────────┘
           ▼                  ▼                    ▼
    ┌──────────────┐   ┌──────────────┐   ┌──────────────────┐
    │    2.[b]     │   │    9.[b]     │   │      16.[b]      │
    │ Develop Test │   │ Review Items │   │ Review Assembled │
    │    Items     │   │for Field Test│   │      Tests       │
    └──────┬───────┘   └──────┬───────┘   └────────┬─────────┘
           ▼                  ▼                    ▼
    ┌──────────────┐   ┌──────────────┐   ┌──────────────────┐
    │    3.[b]     │   │     10.      │   │       17.        │
    │ Review Items │   │   Assemble   │   │   Final Review   │
    │  for Tryouts │   │Field Test Fm.│   │     of Tests     │
    └──────┬───────┘   └──────┬───────┘   └────────┬─────────┘
           ▼                  ▼                    ▼
    ┌──────────────┐   ┌──────────────┐   ┌──────────────────┐
    │      4.      │   │    11.[b]    │   │     18.[ab]      │
    │   Assemble   │   │    Review    │   │    Administer    │
    │Item Tryout Fm│   │Field Test Fm.│   │  Test as Pilot   │
    └──────┬───────┘   └──────┬───────┘   └────────┬─────────┘
           ▼                  ▼                    ▼
    ┌──────────────┐   ┌──────────────┐   ┌──────────────────┐
    │    5.[b]     │   │    12.[b]    │   │       19.        │
    │    Review    │   │  Administer  │   │   Score Tests    │
    │Item Tryout Fm│   │ Field Tests  │   │                  │
    └──────┬───────┘   └──────┬───────┘   └────────┬─────────┘
           ▼                  ▼                    ▼
    ┌──────────────┐   ┌──────────────┐   ┌──────────────────┐
    │    6.[b]     │   │     13.      │   │     20.[ab]      │
    │  Administer  │   │    Review    │   │    Establish     │
    │ Item Tryouts │   │Field Test St.│   │    Standards     │
    └──────┬───────┘   └──────┬───────┘   └────────┬─────────┘
           ▼                  ▼                    ▼
    ┌──────────────┐   ┌──────────────┐   ┌──────────────────┐
    │      7.      │   │    14.[b]    │   │     21.[b]       │
    │    Review    │──▶│   Conduct    │──▶│ Administer Tests │
    │Item Tryout St│   │ Bias Reviews │   │As Fully Operatnl │
    └──────────────┘   └──────────────┘   └────────┬─────────┘
                                                   ▼
                                          ┌──────────────────┐
                                          │       22.        │
                                          │      Report      │
                                          │   Test Results   │
                                          └──────────────────┘
```

[a] Activities done only at implementation of new curriculum
[b] Activities involving NC teachers

Phase 1 (step 1) requires 4 months
Phase 2 (steps 2 - 7) requires 12 months
Phase 3 steps 8 - 14) requires 20 months
Phase 4 (steps 15 - 21) requires 4 months for EOC and 9 months for EOG tests
Phase 5 (step 22) requires 4 months
TOTAL 44 - 49 months
NOTES: 1. Whenever possible, item tryouts should precede field-testing items.
2. Professional development opportunities are integral and ongoing to the curriculum and test development process.

was deliberately diverse with respect to educational philosophy regarding language and communication, positions (teachers, administrators, and teacher educators), settings (mainstream and residential schools), hearing status, as well as race/ethnicity, gender, and geographic region of the United States. The committee met at ETS in March 1992 and reviewed a revised content outline.

After this meeting, ETS staff developed a survey instrument. This instrument had five domains: basic skills, educational foundations, specialty area knowledge, language and communication skills for teachers of deaf and hard of hearing students, and biographical information. Questions for the first four domains had an importance rating scale.

The results of the survey were used to develop an examination "blueprint," which was shared with a test development committee in the fall of 1995. This committee, along with ETS test development specialists and research staff, laid the final groundwork for what is now known as the Praxis II Education of Deaf and Hard of Hearing Students subject assessment.

The process described above is typical of Praxis Series test development: "committees of educators (practicing teachers and faculty who prepare teachers) are convened, and work with ETS subject experts, using the results of the job analysis to create test specifications. Test specifications define the content areas to be measured by the test. They are sometimes referred to as the 'blueprint' of the test, as they describe and define the content architecture of the test. The process of deriving test specifications from the job analysis creates the connection between the test content and the job-related knowledge and/or skills being measured" (ETS, 2004). What was unique in this case, however, is that deaf and hard of hearing individuals were involved in each step of the process.

Job or practice analyses should be done periodically so as to capture the inevitable changes in pedagogy and practice. The Association of Social Work Boards (ASWB) conducts practice analyses for each of its examination levels approximately every seven years.

Pools of examination items are drafted and extensively vetted and pre-tested. Psychometricians, working in concert with subject-matter experts, develop baseline data for what percentage of test-takers should answer each item correctly. The goal of ASWB and indeed all organizations that use tests is to find items that "1. fit, 2. are pertinent to the profession, 3. are just hard enough but not impossibly difficult, and 4. do not present unfair obstacles to candidates of different genders, ethnic groups or geographic locations, or for whom English is a second language" (http://www.aswb.org/exam_info_examdev.shtml).

As structured as the test development process may be, there is a point where the test specifications—what is to be measured—meet the reality of *how* it is measured through test items. A professional test developer or an external content area expert who is writing items, often being paid by the item, has to ask an appropriate stem (question) and create a key (correct response) and detractor items (incorrect responses). While doing so, the item writer usually has access to an item-writing guide, a document that includes information on the proper format and structure of test questions. Most item-writing guides also include language and style rules, typically those incident to the discipline or specific to the testing organization. With few exceptions, item-writing guides are proprietary and confidential. An Internet search elicited several guides in the public domain, including:

- http://www.nbme.org/PDF/ItemWriting_2003/2003IWGwhole.pdf); the item-writing guide of the American Board of Veterinary Practitioners

- (http://www.abvp.com/pdfs/form_pdf/item_writing_guide.pdf), the item-writing guide of the National Commission on Certification of Physician Assistants, Inc.
- (http://www.nccpa.net/pdfs/Test%20Committee%20Handbook.pdf), and an abbreviated version of the item-writing guide of the Society for Human Resource Management Certification Institute (http://www.hrci.org/faq/faq_6.html).

The co-authors have been permitted to review several item-writing guides during their work with testing entities, most recently the one used by the Association of Social Work Board for its series of tests licensing social workers at different levels. We have noticed a few common themes.

First, while nearly every item-writing guide calls for clarity in writing, none sets a target reading level. None seems to identify or recognize the potential problem of the esoteric "language of testing" or suggest that it be abandoned due to potential discrimination against professionals who are non-native speakers of English. And while pre-testing is conducted routinely, sampling strategies may not result in inclusion of members of the populations who are most likely to be affected by language issues—including people who are deaf and hard of hearing.

Second, question types that are most often problematic for deaf and hard of hearing test-takers, such as negative stems ("which of the following is not," "all of the following are true except," "all but one of the following," etc.), are frequently adopted.

Third, for many items, the answers depend on candidates' ability to analyze the underlying spoken language, parsing not only written English syntax but also "auditory" memory.

The authors believe that the issues confronting deaf and hard of hearing candidates are similar to those encountered by other linguistic minorities. This point suggests that collaboration would be helpful—on the premise that what benefits one group will benefit all. As our society becomes increasingly diverse, we can all benefit from increased attention to what works best for the largest number of people.

RECOMMENDATIONS

The recommendations that follow are for both test-takers and test-makers.

1. Preparation

Before taking any standardized test, candidates should know exactly what it is they are studying for, what kind of question types to expect, and how well they have to do to pass the test. While of course everyone wants to do as well as possible, it is wise to keep in mind that for most licenses and certifications, one only needs to *pass*. The candidate who answers all questions correctly and the candidate who obtains the minimum passing score will both become licensed or certified. The opposite is true for admissions tests such as the GRE, civil service examinations, promotional examinations, and the like.

Candidates must be able to read and understand test questions and possible responses. They must understand, insofar as possible, the "language of testing." They should understand how to read and answer questions with negatives ("Which of these is not . . .") and qualifiers ("all of the following except"). They must watch carefully for all-inclusive or all-exclusive answer choices ("all of the above," "none of the above") or partially-inclusive answer choices (a. and b. only). They should recognize key words and phrases that are often used in test questions and responses. These usages can provide clues to the correct response.

Generally, hearing test-takers are more likely to be familiar with the "language of testing" than their deaf and hard of hearing peers because tests are more a part of their school experience. Elementary, middle, and high school curricula may place greater emphasis on standardized testing, either as a measure of the student's achievement or the school or school district's performance. Students are told from an early age that they will encounter the PSAT/NMSQT, the SAT, the ACT, and other tests for college admissions. Increasingly, hearing students are taking Advanced Placement courses or examinations in high school. These tests are far less frequently encountered in students and programs for students who are deaf or hard of hearing. Many deaf and hard of hearing students do not have the facility with English to participate in this kind of testing in the early years. Since English is not fully accessible as a native language, there is not the same foundation with which to make sense of the more esoteric and truncated "language of testing." Later, although commercial test preparation classes and materials are widely available, the majority of these are auditorially-based. A deaf student typically needs to arrange for support services, such as note-takers, computer-assisted real-time captioning, or interpreters to obtain the full benefit of in-person classes, and has to rely on the visual channel with material on compact disk or online.

2. Accommodations

Candidates who are deaf or hard of hearing should be clear about which accommodations are available for the test they plan to take and should assess their need for test accommodations. They should follow to the letter the test provider's instructions for requesting accommodations. Typically, one has to complete and submit with the test registration form a supplemental application for test accommodations. In most cases, one has to provide medical certification of hearing loss. Some testing companies want to know if similar accommodations were provided to the test-taker for tests in the past.

The most frequently requested accommodation is extended time. While very little research has been conducted and there is no conclusive link shown between extended time and test performance for deaf or hard of hearing candidates, many candidates request extended time anyway. The perception is that additional time allows deaf candidates to process the English language constructions to which they have had less access and with which they are less familiar than hearing candidates. This accommodation makes good sense. The limited research conducted (Willingham et al., 1988; Ragosta & Wendler, 1992) suggests that for most deaf and hard of hearing candidates, "time and one-half," or 50% more time, is about what is needed and ultimately used.

Some candidates request written instructions, or ask that a sign language interpreter sign the test instructions. In rare cases, entire tests have been interpreted. This accommodation presents a whole set of issues which are beyond the scope of this chapter, but which are treated in the following chapter on pages 40–41.

3. Study Materials

Testing companies typically provide candidates with study guides that include sample questions. We have seen some especially comprehensive study guides, and we have seen others that provide only one or two sample questions. All candidates would benefit from the opportunity to see more sample questions, but this benefit is especially true for deaf and hard of hearing candidates, given their hampered access to what we have been referring to as "the language and culture of testing."

The larger testing companies provide print-based, computer-based, or Internet-based study materials, sometimes as extra-cost items. Commercial publishers produce aftermarket study materials, which are sometimes helpful. Unfortunately, some aftermarket study guides are based on discontinued or outdated material or do not represent accurately the type of questions found on the actual test. This situation is truly a case of *caveat emptor*—let the buyer beware.

4. Study in Advance

Candidates should study diligently, either alone or in formal or informal groups. Commercial test preparation courses may be helpful if they are accessible—typically through the provision of interpreters or through online content. Practice tests should be taken under true test conditions—in a quiet environment without distractions, with actual time limits.

SUMMARY

In this chapter, we have examined standardized tests from the perspective of the deaf or hard of hearing test-taker, presented examples of candidate challenges to tests, reviewed the test development process, and made suggestions for more effective test-taking.

We close this chapter with the thought that licensing and certification authorities and testing companies should adopt a more inclusive approach to test development—one that uses the concepts of universal design. Changes that benefit one population will benefit others. Douglas Forer at ETS said it best several years ago (D. Forer, personal communication, November 28, 2004). He likened the test development landscape to that of *Field of Dreams*, the 1989 baseball fantasy movie in which a farmer in Iowa, hearing voices, constructs a baseball diamond on his cornfield. The voices tell him, "If you build it, they will come"—and indeed they did.

Build a good test, and they will come.

REFERENCES

American Board of Veterinary Practitioners. (2001). *Item writing guide.* Retrieved November 25, 2004, from http://www.abvp.com/pdfs/form_pdf/item_writing_guide.pdf.

Americans with Disabilities Act of 1990, 42 U.S.C. §12101 *et seq.*
Association of Social Work Boards. (2004). *ASWB exam information: Examination development.* Retrieved from http://www.aswb.org/exam_info_examdev.shtml.
Educational Testing Service. (2004). *Validity for licensing tests: A brief orientation.* Princeton, NJ: Educational Testing Service.
National Board of Medical Examiners. (2002). *Constructing written test questions for the basic and clinical sciences* (3rd ed.). Retrieved November 25, 2004, from http://www.nbme.org/PDF/ItemWriting_2003/2003IWGwhole.pdf.
National Commission on Certification of Physicians' Assistants, Inc. (2002). *Item-writing guide.* Retrieved November 25, 2004, from http://www.nccpa.net/pdfs/Test%20Committee%20Handbook.pdf.
Ragosta, M. (1989). *Considerations on testing individuals who are deaf or hard of hearing.* Unpublished manuscript.
Ragosta, M., & Wendler, C. (1992). *Eligibility issues and comparable time limits for disabled and nondisabled SAT examinees.* (ETS Research Report No. 92-5). Princeton, NJ: Educational Testing Service.
Rosenfeld, M., Mounty, J. L., & Ehringhaus, M. E. (1994). *A transportability study of the reading, writing, and mathematics skills important for teachers of deaf and hard of hearing students.* (ETS Research Report 94-53). Princeton, NJ: Educational Testing Service.
Rosenfeld, M., Mounty, J. L., & Ehringhaus, M. E. (1995). *A job analysis of the knowledge and skills important for newly licensed (certified) teachers of deaf and hard of hearing students* (ETS Research Report 95-9). Princeton, NJ: Educational Testing Service.
Society for Human Resources Management Certification Institute. (2004). *An insider's look at item writing.* Retrieved November 25, 2004, from http://www.hrci.org/Certification/EXAMDEV/INSIDER/.
Willingham, W., Ragosta, M., Bennett, R., Braun, H., Rock, D., & Powers, D. (1988). *Testing handicapped people.* Boston: Allyn and Bacon.

Access Considerations and the Provision of Appropriate Accommodations: A Research Perspective From a Testing Organization

Ruth Loew, Cara Cahalan-Laitusis, Linda Cook, and Raylene Harris

Fair assessment of examinees with disabilities has been a growing national concern since the early 1990s. The 1990 Americans With Disabilities Act (ADA) made the regulations of Section 504 of the Rehabilitation Act (1973) mandatory for private agencies. The major focus of the new regulations was the removal of physical barriers. However, the regulations apply to, and have had great impact on, less overt barriers in educational settings. Since the passage of this legislation, testing agencies have seen a major increase in accommodations requests. At the same time, attention has been focused on issues of fairness and on the validity of inferences made from test scores obtained by examinees with disabilities, regardless of whether or not the individual received accommodations.

Testing organizations such as Educational Testing Service (ETS) offer a unique vantage point for the consideration of issues in testing examinees with disabilities, including deaf and hard of hearing adults. ETS has years of experience testing a wide variety of examinees and consequently is in an ideal position to conduct research on test development and accommodations for deaf and hard of hearing test-takers.

In this chapter, we provide an overview of accommodations for deaf and hard of hearing individuals taking high-stakes graduate and professional tests; discuss research concerning this population of test-takers, including a recent study of a licensure test for teachers of deaf and hard of hearing students; and summarize some of the challenges facing those who undertake research in this field.

STANDARDIZED TESTING AND DEAF AND HARD OF HEARING TEST-TAKERS

Deaf and hard of hearing individuals typically do not perform as well on standardized tests as do their comparably qualified hearing peers (Martin & McCrone, 1990). In some cases, tests contain content not fully accessible to deaf and hard of hearing individuals (music, phonetics, etc.). A more pervasive issue that probably contributes to the pattern of low performance, however, is reduced language access. An individual with congenital or early-onset deafness has a very different English-language acquisition process than does a hearing child. As a result, a deaf individual's English mastery is

---

Any opinions expressed herein are those of the authors and not necessarily of Educational Testing Service.

often not as advanced as that of hearing peers; for example, deaf and hard of hearing 17- and 18-year-old students' median Reading Comprehension subtest score on the Stanford Achievement Test corresponds to about a 4.0 grade level for hearing students (Holt, Traxler, & Allen, 1997). In standardized tests, familiar vocabulary may be used in unfamiliar ways. Sentences may be long and/or complex, the result of collapsing two or more sentences into one to economize on space and/or the test-taker's time, and vocabulary words or test questions typically appear with little or no context (Mounty, 2001). For someone without full native mastery of English, such uses of language in standardized testing may constitute a barrier. Because of the challenges that standardized tests present for deaf and hard of hearing test-takers, accommodations are often required to make tests more accessible to this population.

ETS HISTORY AND POLICY: TESTING INDIVIDUALS WHO ARE DEAF OR HARD OF HEARING

History

ETS has a long history of providing accommodations for test-takers with a variety of disabilities. In 1937, well before there was any legal mandate to serve individuals with disabilities, the College Board, one of the founding organizations of ETS and now a major client, made the Scholastic Assessment Test (SAT) available in Braille for students who were blind (Ekstrom, 1998; P. Taylor, personal communication, February 2004). ETS, from its inception in 1947, has provided support, research, and accommodations for individuals with disabilities.

An informal group was established at ETS in the late 1960s to advise testing programs about disability issues. This group was succeeded in the early 1970s by a more formal body, the Committee for Handicapped People, which was responsible for drafting policy statements, addressing problems of identifying test-takers who required accommodations, and recommending ways to comply with Section 504 of the Rehabilitation Act (the first civil rights legislation specifically addressing Americans with disabilities) (P. Taylor, personal communication, October 2003).

With the inception in 1990 of the ADA, which applied, as Section 504 had not, to private testing organizations, the number of test-takers requesting accommodations for disabilities began to increase sharply (P. Taylor, personal communication, October 2003). As a consequence, ETS's disability work intensified, and, in 1997, the organization created their Disability Policy Team, composed of representatives from the various ETS testing programs (Graduate Record Examination, Graduate Management Admission Test, Praxis, etc.), Disability Services (the area that processes registrations and requests for accommodations), and Test Development. In 1997, the Office of Disability Policy succeeded the earlier Committee for Handicapped People, and this group continues to be the key advisory group for disabilities issues at ETS today. Among other responsibilities, this office coordinates the work of the Disability Policy Team and establishes accommodations policies.

Accommodations for Deaf and Hard of Hearing Test-Takers

Although the earliest accommodations ETS offered were for test-takers with orthopedic disabilities and for blind individuals, ETS has for some time offered accommodations for test-takers who are deaf or hard of hearing as well. Appropriate accommodations vary, depending on the characteristics and objectives of the test and the characteristics of the test-taker (degree of hearing loss, communication skills and preferences, educational background).

Access to Communication in the Test Environment

Accommodations to facilitate access to communication in the test environment include assistive listening devices; oral or sign language interpreters for spoken directions and other communications with test center personnel; preferential seating; and print copies of spoken directions. Such accommodations are rarely problematic, since, for the most part, they do not affect test content, but serve merely to equalize access by helping to ensure that candidates understand what is happening in the testing environment.

Access to Content

A few ETS tests of general knowledge include content that is inaccessible or at least problematic for deaf and hard of hearing test-takers. In most cases, these items represent only a small portion of the test and are not central to the constructs being assessed. Therefore, for a deaf or hard of hearing test-taker, it is usually possible to either omit such items or to select a test form that does not include them, while still obtaining a meaningful score.

Access to the Language of the Test

As indicated above, hearing loss can profoundly impact the learning and mastery of spoken and written language, which in turn impacts most educational testing. In the following sections, we describe several ways to increase the accessibility of test material for deaf and hard of hearing test-takers.

Writing Test Material Accessibly

One way to address this language issue is not through accommodations, but through the language of the original test: writing test material—if language is not part of the test construct—in ways that facilitate access by those who do not have full native command of English (if English is the language of the test). An example of this approach will be discussed later in this chapter.

Extended Time

Typically, however, whether or not language accessibility is considered in test design, extended time is requested by deaf test-takers. The usual rationale is that extended time addresses the slower English-language processing that results from hearing loss. Test-takers who are deaf or hard of hearing typically find it difficult to judge, for example, which answer choice "sounds right" when they have never experienced spoken language as have their hearing peers. They may need to laboriously try out all the options, whereas a hearing peer might be able to quickly use his or her auditory linguistic experience to rule out some of the choices. Furthermore, a hearing test-taker may automatically process some of the specialized uses of English prevalent in standardized tests (such as "which of the following"), whereas a deaf or hard of hearing counterpart may need to carefully consider the meanings of these phrases.

This accommodation relates to access to test language only indirectly, to be sure, but it is usually the only accommodation available to address this difference between deaf and hard of hearing test-takers and their hearing counterparts.[1]

There are no hard data, to the authors' knowledge, on the effects of extended time on deaf and hard of hearing individuals' test performance, nor are there data to help decide, if extended time is granted, how much time is appropriate (time and a half, double time, or some other figure). ETS graduate and professional tests commonly grant up to double time for those deaf and hard of hearing test-takers who ordinarily use this accommodation.[2]

The consequences of hearing loss on English-language mastery, and therefore on the need for extended testing time, are often attributed to the use of a sign language as a native or primary language. However, early-life hearing loss impacts the acquisition of a spoken language (and therefore of its written/read form) whether or not the child is exposed to a sign language. Furthermore, even a partial hearing loss can affect language acquisition, so to the extent that additional test time addresses the language consequences of hearing loss, it is relevant for both deaf and hard of hearing test-takers, signers and non-signers alike (Jarrow, 2001).

Sign Language Translation

Another accommodation sometimes requested is sign language interpretation of the test itself. This accommodation is *not* currently offered for ETS graduate and professional tests, nor for those sponsored by the College Board (for example, SAT or Advanced Placement tests [AP]). There are several reasons for this policy:

1. Any translation can alter the construct being assessed, including translations from one spoken language to another (Gierl, 1999; Hambleton, 2001). Examples particularly relevant to sign languages include geometric figures or graphs, for which the iconicity of the signed descriptions could either point to or obscure the correct answer, and physical education tests, for which the signed descriptions of bodily motions (such as hitting a ball) typically provide more information about those motions than do the English-language descriptions. This additional information, again, could either help the test-taker identify, or divert the test-taker away from, the correct response.
2. Often the language of the test is an essential part of the construct being assessed. An extreme, but clear, example is a foreign-language test. Offering an American Sign Language (ASL) interpretation of a French test would not assess the test-taker's knowledge of French. Subtler examples include technical vocabulary, which in some fields may be important to assess in English.

3. Real-time "on-the-fly" translation can vary significantly from one interpreter to another (Mounty, 2001). Thus, the standardization of a standardized test can be lost.

One possible solution to some of the problems of offering an ASL interpretation is to develop standardized videotaped or computer-delivered signed translations of tests for which language is not a key part of the construct. Prerecording makes it possible to control both construct change and standardization of translation. At ETS, this approach was used for the Listening Skills section of the Praxis Core Battery, for which a prerecorded ASL version was offered (Ragosta, 1989) until the Listening Skills test was discontinued in the 1999–2000 testing year. This approach has not been widely adopted, however, largely because the limited research on videotaped signed translations of standardized tests indicates that test-takers with hearing losses do not necessarily benefit from ASL translations, even if these translations are carefully crafted for accuracy and prerecorded (Hollenbeck, Tindal, Brown, & Almond, 2003).

In at least some states, for K–12 testing, signing deaf and hard of hearing test-takers are permitted to sign their responses to essay questions. These responses are then translated and transcribed by an interpreter/scribe and are scored along with responses that were originally composed in English (Johnson, 2003; Massachusetts Department of Education, 2004). Because this approach makes it difficult if not impossible to completely differentiate the test-taker's contribution from that of the interpreter/scribe, it has not been used for ETS tests.

Special Issues Presented by Listening and Speaking Tests or Sections

Typically, language tests assess receptive language through both listening and reading. Some also assess expressive language through speaking, writing, or both. Listening and reading sections are generally designed to test different skills. Reading sections assess navigation skills and assume that the test-taker will reread the passage in whole or in part as needed to find key words or phrases. Listening sections, on the other hand, are inherently linear and typically assess the ability to answer questions based on a single hearing, as in ordinary conversation.

The feasibility of offering accommodations for these tests depends on the objectives of the particular test and the details of the test-taker's disability. For an ETS listening section or test, if the essential construct is the ability to comprehend spoken language (i.e., speech per se is essential to the construct), then the options include:

- an oral interpreter (typically for a hard of hearing test-taker). Even this accommodation may change the construct somewhat, since recorded listening sections sometimes are intended to assess comprehension of naturalistic conversations, in which there is background noise or two speakers overlapping one another. These aspects of a listening section are difficult or impossible for an oral interpreter to replicate. Nevertheless, this is a reasonable accommodation for some tests and some test-takers.

- omission of the listening section

- denial of accommodations (e.g., if the assessment is a listening *test*, not a listening *section*)

For some tests, however, although the construct is the ability to comprehend communication in the target language that is typically spoken, speech per se is not part of the construct. For example, the goal might be to determine how the student can communicate in a classroom in the target language, and classroom communications that would be spoken for most students would typically be written for a deaf student. In this case, another option may be to permit the test-taker to read a print script of the listening section. This process does not replicate the original precisely, since the listening section may include false starts, overlapping voices, and so on; but it may provide a functional equivalent for a deaf or hard of hearing test-taker. However, if the listening section does NOT assess fundamentally different uses of language from the reading section—and this would be unusual—then this accommodation may simply provide a redundant additional reading section. Again, the decision must be based on the test constructs and structure and the test-taker's characteristics.

For a speaking section of an ETS test, if speech per se is central to the construct, then the options may include the following:

- If the test-taker is comfortable speaking in a test situation, an assistive listening device, if this helps the test-taker hear his or her own speech, is generally not a problematic accommodation.

- If the test-taker is not comfortable speaking in a test situation, the options are to omit the section or to deny accommodations.

If speech per se is not central to the construct, then it may be possible to substitute writing for speaking as a functional equivalent for a deaf or hard of hearing test-taker. If the test already includes a writing section, this accommodation could amount to giving the deaf or hard of hearing test-taker a redundant second writing section, depending on the types of language and content assessed in the two sections. This again must be decided test by test and test-taker by test-taker.

Recognizing that there are many unanswered questions about the validity of scores for this population of test-takers, ETS has an ongoing program of research concerning assessing test-takers with disabilities, including those who are deaf or hard of hearing.

ETS RESEARCH PERTAINING TO DEAF AND HARD OF HEARING TEST-TAKERS

Review of Previous Research

A number of ETS research studies have addressed the test performance of deaf and hard of hearing individuals. Ragosta and Nelson (1986) found that the performance of deaf and hard of hearing students on the Test of English as a Foreign Language (TOEFL) was closer to the performance of foreign students than to that of native speakers of English. Research on the SAT conducted in the early 1980s indicated that deaf or hard of hearing and learning-disabled students had lower mean scores on both

Verbal and Mathematical sections than test-takers without disabilities (Willingham et al., 1988). Researchers also examined how well test scores predicted first-year grade-point average (FYGPA) in college and found that SAT scores underpredicted FYGPAs for students with hearing losses (Willingham et al., 1988), which suggests that standardized test scores may not accurately represent the abilities of deaf and hard of hearing test-takers (Mounty, 1990). Mounty, Epstein, and Weinstock (1997) adapted the English Language Proficiency Test (ELPT) for use with deaf and hard of hearing students by translating listening sections into ASL, thereby transforming that portion of the test into an assessment of functional through-the-air communication rather than of English mastery. Their preliminary findings were that the test was effective in differentiating levels of ASL and English proficiency among deaf and hard of hearing test-takers. Another study considered the effects of test modifications on deaf test-takers' performance. Mounty compared deaf test-takers' responses to written essay prompts with their responses to prompts that were presented in both written and signed form; in addition, comparisons were made between essays that were written and essays that were signed (Mounty, 1989). Findings included that (a) a high proportion of individuals with proven academic success failed to produce passing scores on written essays, (b) signed essays earned scores as good as or better than those assigned to written essays, and (c) different presentation modes for essay topics appeared to result in differential effects for deaf test-takers.

Rosenfeld, Mounty, and Ehringhaus (1994) conducted a study to determine if the reading, writing, and mathematics skills that were included in the test specifications for the Praxis I Basic Skills Assessment and the Pre-Professional Skills Tests (PPSTs) were important for newly licensed teachers of deaf and hard of hearing students. They concluded that the content of the Praxis I and PPSTs were appropriate for entry-level teachers, but they emphasized that this finding does not imply that the test items and mode of assessment were appropriate for deaf and hard of hearing candidates. Rosenfeld, Mounty, and Ehringhaus (1995) also conducted a job analysis to determine the specialty-area knowledge that should be included on a licensure test for teachers of deaf and hard of hearing students. The job analysis provided test developers with recommendations for including specific knowledge statements in the test. Knowledge statements regarding language and communication skills were not recommended because there was not sufficient consensus in the field regarding the language and communication skills important for newly licensed teachers to permit development of a single proficiency measure. This job analysis led to the development of the current Praxis II Education of Deaf and Hard of Hearing Students (EDHH) teacher licensure test. Research on the EDHH test now in progress at ETS is described later in this chapter.

In addition, ETS has conducted several studies that examined the impact of interactive video and sign language on the test performance of deaf or hard of hearing students. The first study (Hansen, Mounty, & Baird, 1994) explored the potential of interactive video technology and sign language for improving the reading comprehension and test-taking skills of deaf junior high and high school students. This preliminary research indicated that the use of multimedia technology and sign language was highly motivational to students. A second study (Hansen & Mounty, 1998) examined the impact of sign language versions of science and history tests on the test performance of 11 deaf or hard of hearing children ages 7–17. This study indicated that students who had access to a sign language version of the science test, in addition to a written English version of the test, performed significantly better than students with access only to the written English version. No significant difference was found on the history test between the test-takers who received the sign language version in addition to the written English test and those who received only the written English version of the test.

Most recently, ETS researchers have examined how deaf and hard of hearing test-takers perform, relative to hearing test-takers, on the Praxis II, EDHH teacher licensure test (Harris, Loew, Cahalan-Laitusis, & Cook, 2004). The following section summarizes this study.

Current Research: Differential Item Functioning Analysis of the Praxis Education of Deaf and Hard of Hearing Students (EDHH) teacher licensure test

The Deaf community has long viewed the participation of deaf individuals in the education of deaf students as beneficial because deaf teachers can serve as role models who understand the students' academic and social concerns from personal experience.[3] With the increasing emphasis on oral-only educational methods in the late nineteenth century, however, the percentage of teachers in schools for the deaf who were themselves deaf declined from 42.5% in 1870 to 14.5% in 1917 (Jones, 1918; cited by Moores, 1996, p. 25).

In the mid- and late-twentieth century, the reintroduction of sign language into programs for deaf students, the increasing diversity of approaches to deaf education, and the disability rights movement all led to renewed interest in bringing deaf teachers into programs for deaf students. However, by this time, standardized tests had become gatekeepers to the profession, creating yet another hurdle for deaf would-be teachers.

Until the mid-1990s, the National Teacher Examinations, the predecessor of the ETS Praxis teacher licensure testing program, offered a licensure test for teachers of the deaf that was grounded in the oral approach. It became outdated as approaches to the education of deaf and hard of hearing students diversified and as its emphasis on oral methodology limited the test's accessibility to these test-takers.

A new test was therefore developed, on the basis of the job analysis cited above (Rosenfeld, Mounty, & Ehringhaus, 1995), by a committee of hearing, deaf, and hard of hearing individuals representing a broad spectrum of approaches to deaf education. This range of perspectives was maintained throughout the test development process and the pre-testing of test questions. A full history of the test can be found in Harris et al. (in progress).

The test was developed with deaf and hard of hearing test-takers in mind. Since EDHH is a test of content, not of English-language skills, test language was controlled for accessibility to deaf and hard of hearing candidates. For example, item writers avoided the use of the passive voice, endeavored to make pronoun references clear, introduced topics early in sentences, provided more context in both stimuli and stems than is typical for multiple-choice (MC) items, used declarative sentences where possible, and tried to minimize the use of negation. Deaf culture was included in the content specifications because the development committee deemed this information important.

Description of the Test

Designed for individuals who have recently completed a teacher preparation program in the education of deaf and hard of hearing students, EDHH consists of forty-four-option MC questions and two constructed-response (CR) questions covering two general content categories, "Human Development and the Learning Process" and "Educational Policies and Practices." The CR questions require examinees to apply their knowledge of the field to situations they may face in teaching deaf and hard of hearing students and can be answered from different philosophical perspectives (Educational Testing Service, 2004). Three different forms of the test have been used since the test was introduced.

Description of the Study

Since accessibility to deaf and hard of hearing test-takers was included in the design of EDHH, the purpose of the study was to compare the test performance of these test-takers to that of hearing test-takers by examining differential item functioning (DIF) for deaf and hard of hearing, as well as hearing, test-takers who took EDHH over a period of several years. DIF procedures were used to examine differences among item types while controlling for differences in overall ability, as measured by test score. DIF exists when two groups of people (in this case, hearing vs. deaf and hard of hearing), matched in terms of their relevant knowledge and skills, perform differently on a test item. While a variety of statistical procedures exist for examining DIF, this study employed the Mantel-Haenszel statistic (MH D-DIF[4]), which is used operationally on most tests administered by ETS. (See Holland and Thayer, 1988, for a full explanation of DIF analyses.) The CR items were not included in this analysis because they differ from form to form, and the sample size on each individual form was too small to permit within-form comparisons. Only items that were worded identically across all three forms of the test (a total of 29 MC items) were included in the analyses. Data were collapsed across the three forms to increase the number of candidates available for the analysis.

A total of 880 tests were administered over the seven-year period from 1997 to 2003. Of this number, 617 were included in the study. The study was limited to first-time test-takers. The final sample of test-takers included 67 who reported being deaf or hard of hearing (37 deaf and 30 hard of hearing) and 550 who reported being hearing.

Two researchers (one hearing and one deaf) categorized by content area each of the 29 items that appeared across all three test forms. These researchers also identified the items that exhibited DIF for deaf and hard of hearing test-takers compared to hearing test-takers. (From the total of 29 items, 7 items exhibited DIF.) Four coding categories emerged. Three of these categories pertain to test content: Deaf culture, aural/oral approaches, and linguistics. The fourth category, negative stem, relates to the language of the items.

Items classified as "Deaf culture" relate to the customs and social norms of the Deaf community of the United States. Those classified as "aural/oral approaches" are about educational methods that emphasize the use of residual hearing and the development of speaking skills. "Linguistics" items focus on analysis of the phonological, morphological, syntactic, or semantic structure of language, whether spoken, written, or signed. The stems of "negative stem" items contain words such as *not, never,* or *no* (e.g., "the aided audiogram shown above suggests that John can probably NOT comprehend . . .").

Results

Because the sample of deaf and hard of hearing test-takers is quite small (N + 67) for the type of analysis carried out, the results of the DIF analysis should be interpreted with caution. For the purpose of these analyses, hearing test-takers were considered the reference group, and deaf and hard of hearing test-takers were combined into a single

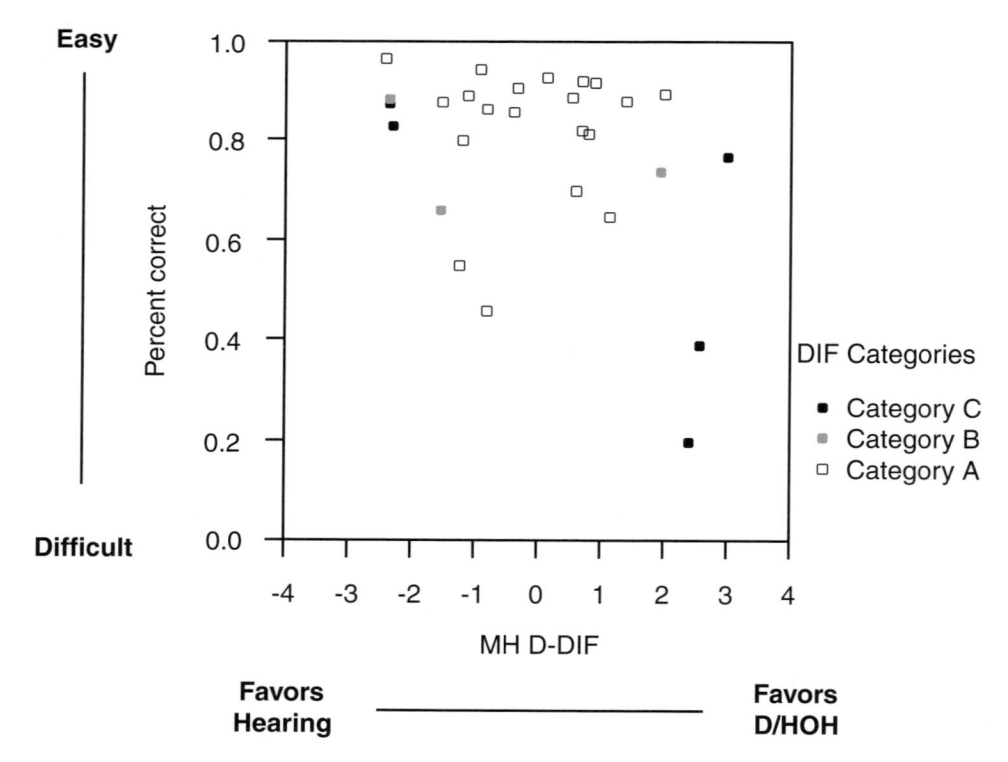

Figure 1. Test items by percentage correct, DIF values, and DIF categories.
Note. Category A contains items with negligible DIF. Category B contains items with slight to moderate values of DIF, and Category C contains items with moderate to large values of DIF. "D/HOH" = Deaf/Hard of Hearing

Appropriate Accommodations and Access

focal group. Figures 1–3 display the cross-classification of items by percent correct (i.e., difficulty of the item) and by MH D-DIF values (Holland et al.) for the 29 items classified in several different ways.

Figure 1 displays the three DIF categories (A, B, and C) that are used as standard practice at ETS to identify items that display various levels of DIF. Of the 29 items analyzed, 5 were identified as having category C DIF, and 3 had category B DIF. Three items favored deaf and hard of hearing examinees, and four items favored hearing examinees. One item had a high DIF value favoring hearing test-takers, but this finding was not considered to be significant because only one test-taker who was deaf or hard of hearing got the item wrong, so the variance was too small to consider this a category B or C DIF item.

Figure 2 displays items broken out by the two general test content categories: Human Development and the Learning Process (HDL) versus Educational Policies and Practices (EPP). No clear differences were found between these two categories. The items are again cross-classified by percent correct and MH D-DIF value.

Finally, Figure 3 displays cross-classification by the coding that researchers used to characterize the subset of items that performed differently for hearing and deaf/hard of hearing test-takers (oral/aural approach, Deaf culture, linguistics, and negative

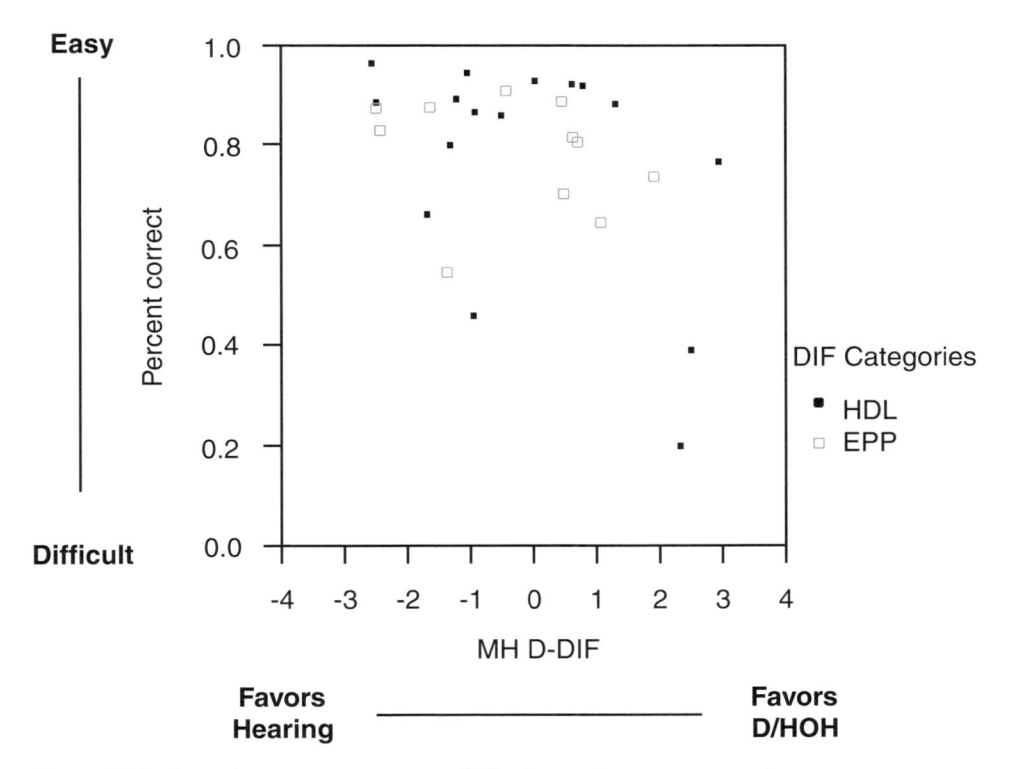

Figure 2. Test items by percentage correct, DIF value, and content categories.
Note. HDL indicates Human Development and the Learning Process, and EPP indicates Educational Policies and Practices.

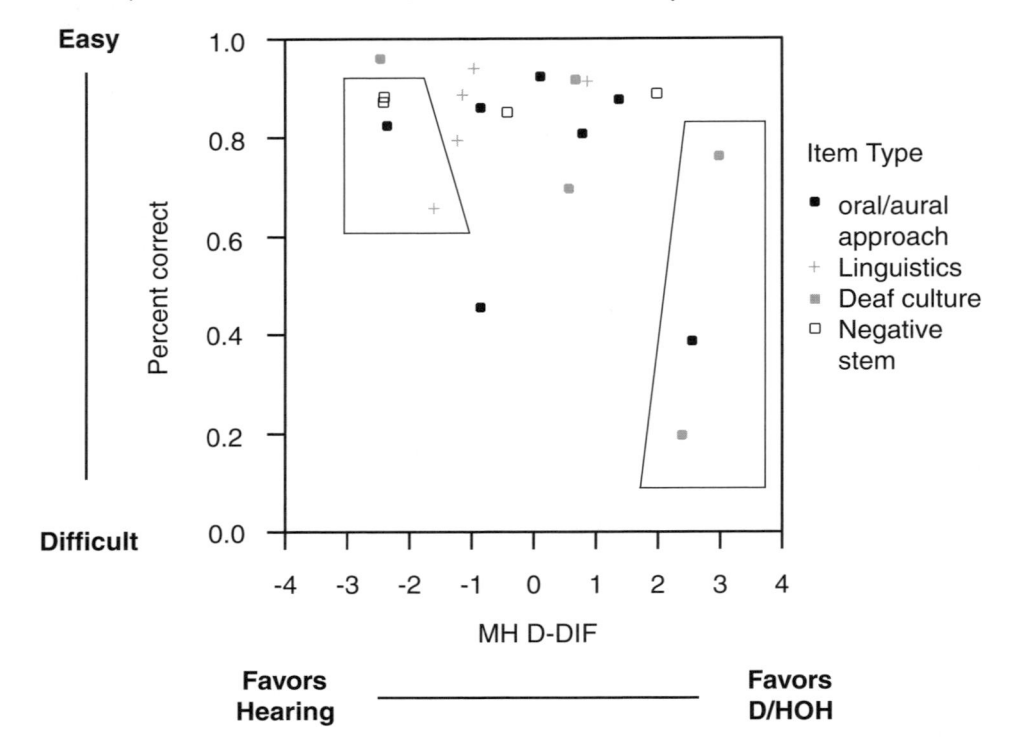

Figure 3. Test items by percentage correct, DIF values, and item characteristics

stem). The items with significant DIF are outlined. Three items, one aural/oral and two Deaf culture, favored deaf and hard of hearing examinees, and four items, one aural/oral, one linguistics, and two negative stem, favored hearing examinees. A quick review of the information in Figure 3 shows that half (two of the four) of the negative-stem items had DIF favoring hearing test-takers: one category C and one category B. Also, 40% (two of five) of the Deaf culture items had DIF. (Both items were category C items, and both favored deaf and hard of hearing test-takers.) One-third (one of three) of the linguistics items showed B DIF favoring hearing test-takers, and two of the seven oral/aural approach items had C DIF: one item favoring deaf and hard of hearing test-takers and one favoring hearing test-takers.

Although the generalizations that can be made on the basis of this study are limited due to the small sample size, the results do indicate some general trends that might be useful to investigate further. In particular, the results suggest that test questions categorized as "Deaf culture" have a slight tendency to favor deaf and hard of hearing test-takers, whereas items classified as "negative stem" have a slight tendency to favor hearing examinees. The elimination of negative-stem items from future test forms may be advisable. In addition, identifying material on Deaf culture in the EDHH preparation materials and elsewhere may be helpful to hearing candidates.

Future research on EDHH could include examining scores from the CR items when a sufficient sample size is obtained, as well as continuing to collect survey data and replicating the MC study when more data are available.

Discussion of Past and Current Research

The research reviewed in this chapter has focused on a variety of issues related to the assessment of deaf and hard of hearing test-takers. In particular, most studies were concerned with obtaining fair and valid scores for this population of test-takers. As Willingham et al. (1988) point out, "In evaluating the validity of a test for a subgroup such as handicapped people, the primary concern is fairness, and the measure of fairness is comparability" (p. 13). Willingham et al. continue by saying that score comparability implies comparable meaning and interpretation of test scores, not necessarily the same distribution of scores for different groups of examinees. They point out five important aspects in which scores should be generally comparable. Four of these aspects are relevant for this discussion: reliability, factor structure, item functioning, and predicted performance.

Several issues face researchers evaluating test characteristics, such as those mentioned by Willingham et al. for populations with disabilities. These issues impact the interpretation of the results of the studies reviewed in this chapter as well as the evaluation of EDHH carried out by Harris et al. The most salient issues are summarized below.

Challenges of Conducting Research on Candidates With Disabilities

Pitoniak and Royer (2001) classify three categories of challenges that face researchers studying testing accommodations for populations with disabilities: small sample size, variability in examinees, and variability in accommodations. The first two of these categories have significant implications for the interpretation of the results of the Praxis EDHH study, and all three challenges have implications for the interpretation of the results of the studies reviewed in this chapter.

Sample Size

Sample size is one of the most seriously limiting aspects of empirical research conducted with populations with disabilities. This point is particularly true of populations with sensory disabilities such as hearing losses and visual impairments. Many of the psychometric analyses required to evaluate the four aspects of comparability of scores described above require sample sizes in excess of 100. This situation often requires accumulating responses of examinees across possibly diverse settings, or, as in the case of the EDHH study, accumulating scores across a period of time—in some cases, a fairly extended time period. Not only do small sample sizes pose a problem for evaluating the validity of tests, but they are also a complicating factor whenever a new assessment is introduced; it is desirable to pilot-test the changes on examinees with disabilities prior to implementing the changes. The results of the EDHH study have been interpreted with a high degree of caution, simply because the sample—which was accumulated over a four-year period and across three different test forms—is quite small for the types of analyses carried out.

Classifying Examinees According to Their Disabilities

A major complication in most studies conducted with populations of examinees with disabilities is that it is difficult to classify examinees according to disability because of variation within the population and because some examinees have multiple disabilities. This issue is certainly pertinent for any research with a deaf and hard of hearing population. The range of disability varies greatly in this group, and consequently the results of any study carried out with this group of test-takers will be contingent upon how the examinees are classified.

Variation in Accommodations

As mentioned previously, variation in accommodations is also a factor in the interpretation of the results of any study of the fairness or validity of scores that are obtained by test-takers with disabilities. As reported by Geisinger (1994), the number of different accommodations (or combinations of accommodations) available to examinees is almost limitless. Because accommodations are often administered in concert, it is very difficult to determine the effect of a particular accommodation on the fairness and validity of a test score for a particular group of examinees.

A key issue related to the interpretation of the results of studies, such as those reported in this chapter, which is not mentioned by Pitoniak et al., is that the majority of these studies are nonexperimental in nature (i.e., students are not randomly assigned to conditions). In this situation, it could be quite misleading to generalize the results of the study to a larger population beyond the immediate study group. Without random assignment of students to treatments, it is impossible to control for the effects of competing hypotheses on the results of the study.

SUMMARY

In this chapter, we have provided an overview of accommodations for deaf and hard of hearing individuals taking high-stakes graduate and professional tests. We have also discussed research concerning this population of test-takers, including a recent study of a licensure test for teachers of deaf and hard of hearing students (the Praxis EDHH teacher licensure test). Finally, we have summarized some of the challenges that face those interested in doing research in this field, including sample size, the difficulty of classifying examinees according to their disability because of population variation and multiple disabilities, and the nonexperimental nature of most studies.

In this chapter, we have tried to demonstrate both the importance and the complexity of preparing fair and valid assessments for test-takers who are deaf and hard of hearing. The work recently conducted on the Praxis EDHH test is a good example of the type of research that can inform the design and development of assessments for examinees with hearing impairments. Research on this test was as timely as possible, given that several years were required to accumulate sufficient data to support the EDHH analyses. Empirical findings such as the results of this study provide very important information for test designers and test developers as they consider future types of assessments for deaf and hard of hearing examinees. Consequently, it is important for researchers to look for ways to overcome some of the obstacles to doing this type of research, such as small sample sizes, which have been outlined in this chapter.

The development and delivery of accessible tests for deaf and hard of hearing test-takers is challenging for most testing organizations. Although a great deal has been accomplished over the past decade, continued work in this area is important to ensure the fairness and validity of test scores obtained by deaf and hard of hearing test-takers.

NOTES

1. The situation of a deaf or hard of hearing test-taker is comparable in some respects to that of an English Language Learner (ELL), the key difference being that a deaf or hard of hearing individual's limited exposure to English results from a disability. Extended test time is a common accommodation for ELLs on K–12 assessments. Most ETS graduate and professional assessments do not offer accommodations to ELLs. The Praxis program is the exception and offers extended time to ELLs as well as to some individuals with disabilities.

2. The College Board sets its own accommodations policies for its tests (PSAT/National Merit Scholarship Qualifying Test [NMSQT], SAT, Advanced Placement [AP]).

3. We follow the convention of using *Deaf*, capitalized, to refer to cultural identity, and *deaf*, lower case, to refer to audiological status.

4. MHD-DIF is a transformation of the Mantel-Haenszel statistic that centers the index about the value of 0 and puts the index on a scale roughly comparable to the ETS delta scale of item difficulty.

REFERENCES

Educational Testing Service. (2004). *Test at a Glance: Education of Deaf and Hard of Hearing Students*. Retrieved March 5, 2004, from http://www.ets.org/praxis/taags/prx0271.html.

Ekstrom, R. B. (1998, January). *Equity issues in the assessment of individuals with visual or hearing impairments*. Paper presented at the Test Interpretation and Diversity: Achieving Equity in Assessment Symposium, St. Petersburg, FL.

Geisinger, K. F. (1994). Psychometric issues in testing students with disabilities. *Applied Measurement in Education, 7*, 121–140.

Gierl, M. J. (1999). *Construct equivalence on translated achievement tests*. Unpublished manuscript.

Hambleton, R. K. (2001). The next generation of the ITC test translation and adaptation guidelines. *European Journal of Psychological Assessment, 17*, 164–172.

Hansen, E. G., & Mounty, J. L. (1998). Interactive video technology and sign language for learning and performance support for deaf students. In A. Weisel (Ed.), *Proceedings of the 18th International Congress on Education of the Deaf (ICED), Vol. 1* (pp. 100–103), Tel Aviv, Israel: Ramot Publications, Tel Aviv University.

Hansen, E. G., Mounty, J. L., & Baird, A. (1994). Interactive video and sign language for improving literacy skills of deaf students. In T. Ottman & I. Tomek (Eds.), *Proceedings of*

ED-MEDIA 94: World Conference on Educational Multimedia and Hypermedia (pp. 241–245). Charlottesville, VA: Association for the Advancement of Computing in Education.

Harris, R., Loew, R., Cahalan-Laitusis, C., & Cook, L. (2004, April). *Evaluation of deaf and hard of hearing examinees' performance on the Praxis Education of Deaf and Hard of Hearing Students Test.* Paper presented at the annual meeting of the National Council on Measurement in Education, San Diego, CA.

Holland, P. H., & Thayer, D. (1988). Differential item performance and the Mantel-Haenszel procedure. In H. Wainer and H. Braun (Eds.), *Test validity* (pp. 129–145). Hillsdale, NJ: Erlbaum.

Hollenbeck, K., Tindal, G., Brown, C., & Almond, P. (2003). *Computerized test accommodations for students who are deaf or hard-of-hearing.* Unpublished manuscript.

Holt, J., Traxler, C., & Allen, T. (1997). *Interpreting the scores: A user's guide to the 9th Edition Stanford Achievement Test for Educators of Deaf and Hard-of-Hearing Students* (Gallaudet Research Institute Technical Report 97-1). Washington, DC: Gallaudet University.

Jarrow, J. (2001, Winter). Extended time as an accommodation for deaf and hard-of-hearing students. *NETAC (Northeast Technical Assistance Center) Networks*, p. 5.

Johnson, R. C. (2003). High stakes testing conference held at Gallaudet. *Research at Gallaudet*, p. 9.

Jones, J. (1918). One hundred years of history in the education of the deaf in America and its present status. *American Annals of the Deaf, 63*(1), 1–43.

Martin, D., & McCrone, W. (1990). Testing the hearing-impaired teacher: Is fairness possible? *Journal of Personnel Evaluation in Education, 3,* 169–178.

Massachusetts Department of Education. (2004). *Requirements for the Participation of Students with Disabilities in MCAS.* Retrieved March 5, 2004, from http://www.doe.mass.edu/mcas/alt/spedreq_letter.html.

Moores, D. F. (1996). *Educating the deaf: Psychology, principles, and practices* (4th ed.). Boston: Houghton Mifflin Company.

Mounty, J. L. (1989). *A study of signed and written essays produced by prospective deaf teachers.* Princeton, NJ: Educational Testing Service.

Mounty, J. L. (1990). Testing deaf individuals: Equity in test conditions and test format. In D. Ellis (Ed.), *Selected Proceedings of the 1990 AHSSPPE Conference* (pp. 13–18). Madison, WI: Omnipress.

Mounty, J. L. (2001). *National Task Force on Equity in Testing Deaf and Hard of Hearing Individuals website.* Retrieved October 23, 2003, from http://gri.gallaudet.edu/TestEquity/stantest.html.

Mounty, J. L., Epstein, K. I., & Weinstock, R. B. (1997). *Using the English language proficiency test with deaf and hard of hearing students: An overview and update.* Washington, DC: Gallaudet University.

Pitoniak, M. J., & Royer, J. M. (2001). Testing accommodations for examinees with disabilities: A review of psychometric, legal, and social policy issues. *Review of Educational Research, 71,* 53–104.

Ragosta, M. (1989). *Considerations on testing individuals who are deaf or hard of hearing.* Unpublished manuscript.

Ragosta, M., & Nelson, C. (1986). *TOEFL and hearing impaired students: A feasibility study* (ETS RM-86-4). Princeton, NJ: Educational Testing Service.

Rosenfeld, M., Mounty, J. L., & Ehringhaus, M. E. (1994). *A transportability study of the reading, writing, and mathematics skills important for teachers of deaf and hard of hearing students.* (ETS RR-94-53). Princeton, NJ: Educational Testing Service.

Rosenfeld, M., Mounty, J. L., & Ehringhaus, M. E. (1995). *A job analysis of the knowledge and skills important for newly licensed (certified) teachers of deaf and hard of hearing students* (ETS RR-95-9). Princeton, NJ: Educational Testing Service.

Willingham, W., Ragosta, M., Bennett, R., Braun, H., Rock, D., & Powers, D. (1988). *Testing handicapped people*. Boston: Allyn and Bacon.

Use of Technology and Principles of Universal Design to Improve the Validity and Fairness of Licensure Tests

Neal Kingston and Michael Ehringhaus

Je ne parle pas français. J'ai étudié le français pendant trois années dans le lycée, mais en dépit de mes parents employant un précepteur privé pour travailler avec moi je l'ai trouvé une grande lutte et ai presque échoué. En fait, la seule raison que j'ai passée est parce que la section d'écoute de compréhension—en valeur 40 pour cent de l'essai—n'a pas été normalisée. Oui, chacun a pris les mêmes questions (c'était un examen de Regents d'état de New York, ainsi chaque étudiant III français dans l'état a pris le même essai), mais c'était à un moment où non toutes les écoles ont eu des joueurs de bande (et avant le joueur omniprésent de cassette) et ainsi mon professeur de salle de classe a lu un manuscrit.

Perhaps, like me, you do not speak French. Let me start again in English.

I do not speak French. I studied French for three years in high school, but despite my parents hiring a private tutor to work with me, I found it a great struggle and almost failed. In fact, the only reason I passed is because the oral comprehension section—worth 40% of the test—was not standardized. Yes, everyone took the same questions (this was a New York State Regents Examination, so every French III student in the state took the same test), but this was at a time when not all schools had tape players (and before the ubiquitous cassette player), so the classroom teacher read a script.

Being unable to comprehend spoken French, I paid no attention to the content of my teacher's words. Bored, and with little else to do during the test, I paid attention to the intonation and stress she placed on the words. I noticed in reading the questions, she stressed slightly one of the four answer choices; my French was sufficient to recognize the French version of the letters A, B, C, and D. Having no better chance to pass the test, and having been told that without three years of a foreign language I would not get into a college and would be drafted, go to Vietnam, and die (there have always been many forms of high-stakes testing), I chose whichever answer her voice stressed.

Everyone else in the class was busy listening to the content of the script and did not notice the slight stresses in her speech. When the tests were scored, I had answered 19 of the 20 questions in this section correctly—the highest score in the school—rather

---

The authors wish to thank Edmund Ashley, David Martin, and Judy Mounty for their thought-provoking comments on two earlier drafts of this chapter. The most rewarding writing is writing from which the author learns, and this has been such an experience.

than the 6 or 7 out of 20 that would have been my more typical score. So for the want of a standardized test, I passed French, graduated from high school, graduated from college, went to graduate school, earned a doctorate, and became a psychometrician.

Perhaps if I had learned French from birth, I would have done better; perhaps I have a learning disability that makes it harder for me to learn French than most people. On the other hand, I am a good psychometrician (though perhaps not an overly modest one), but if I had to take a psychometrician licensure examination in French, I would fail.

INTRODUCTION

Trybus and Karchmer (1977) reported the median reading comprehension score of deaf students age 20+ participating in the norming of the Special Edition of the Stanford Achievement Test for Hearing Impaired Students to be at grade level 4.5. Based on the same standardization sample, the median mathematics grade level was below 8.0.

Willingham, Ragosta, et al. (1988) reported the mean Scholastic Aptitude Test (SAT) Verbal score of deaf or hard of hearing students as 291—1.2 standard deviations below the mean score of the group of all college-bound students. This mean score is .5 standard deviations below the mean score of self-reported learning-disabled students and 1.0 standard deviation below the mean score of visually-impaired students. The mean SAT Mathematics score for deaf or hard of hearing students was 375—.8 standard deviations below the mean score of the group of all college-bound seniors, only .1 standard deviations below the mean of self-reported learning-disabled students, and .5 standard deviations below the mean score of visually-impaired students. Yet Braun, Ragosta, and Kaplan (1986) found that, on average, deaf college students earned first-year grade-point averages (FYGPAs) only slightly lower than that of the general college population.

From these three studies, as well as many other others with similar findings, we can see that there is a great discrepancy between the test scores of deaf or hard of hearing examinees and hearing examinees, that this discrepancy is larger in verbal assessments than mathematical assessments, and that these differences are not reflected in at least one other context (first-year college grades).

Holt (1993) found a similar lag for the sample used in the special norming of the 8th edition of the Stanford Achievement Test. In this study, the median reading comprehension score of 17-year-old students was at grade level 4.5. Furthermore, Holt reported the median scores for those 17-year-old students with profound hearing loss to be at a 3.8 grade equivalent, compared with a 5.8 for those with a less-than-severe loss.

Perfetti and Sandak (2000) reference a body of research which states that, "The evidence is that hearing readers automatically convert printed words into phonological forms." They also reference research that recoding mechanisms are different in people who have been deaf from birth: "The recoding systems include articulation, fingerspelling, sign-based recoding, or no recoding at all." Perfetti and Sandak go on to say, "Both deaf and less skilled hearing readers have learned to rely more on visual (orthographic) and contextual (semantic) information than phonological information."

A licensure test in written French may be more of an impediment for me as a hearing person than a licensure test in written English might be for deaf and hard of hearing individuals who have not had full access to oral English. Nonetheless, for many in this population, English does not function as a true first/primary language, so it is not an unreasonable leap to adopt the analogy of taking a test in one's second (less proficient) language to understand the negative impact on scores for this population.

RELIABILITY AND STANDARDIZATION — some history

In the middle of the 19th century, Horace Mann revolutionized the field of educational testing by introducing the concept of test standardization in Boston's schools. Prior to Mann, most American educators used the British tradition of oral exams with teachers asking probing questions that differed for each student. Mann implemented district-wide essay testing with all students answering the same questions. Standardization minimized intentional and unintentional biases of examiners and provided a demonstrably fairer and more equitable assessment of students than did oral examinations.

At the beginning of the 20th century, a number of measurement experts developed the concept of multiple-choice assessment to improve the efficiency of the assessment process. When World War I broke out, the armed services needed to assign specialties and train one million draftees. To do so, they developed the first large-scale standardized multiple-choice assessment program, the Army Alpha. Assessment efficiency was paramount in order to meet this national emergency.

It was clear that a test could not be useful for classifying people if individuals achieved dramatically different scores when tested with the same test on multiple occasions or with different forms of a test. This observation led to much research on test reliability—the consistency of test scores. With huge amounts of available data, psychometricians were able to develop new statistical techniques to estimate how reliable the scores from a given test were. Researchers and testing practitioners developed many ways of using statistical summaries of item quality to select and weight items to form the most reliable tests. Quickly, psychometricians discovered that the more one standardizes a test administration (i.e., makes the testing situation identical from one administration to another), the more reliable are the test scores. Furthermore, the logistically easiest way to standardize the testing environment across administrations was to standardize the testing environment within the administration. A single testing manual would be able to describe in detail the precise steps to be taken in administering a test to each examinee.

VALIDITY

Reliability considerations have gotten the lion's share of psychometric attention from test authors and publishers because, of all the important measures of test quality, it is the easiest one to assess and address with naturally occurring data. That is, many forms of reliability analysis can be applied using solely the data collected from operational test administrations. Thus, reliability information is easy and inexpensive to collect.

Moreover, there is a statistical relationship between reliability and another historically important quality of tests—validity. (In recent years, the concepts of reliability and validity have been merged into the overarching concept of generalizability. This concept refers to the extent one can generalize meaning from a test score.) I cannot do justice to defining validity in this chapter—many book-length treatises have been written on the subject (e.g., Messick, 1989), but suffice it to say that validity is the extent to which test scores measure what one intends them to measure. So if a test's scores are supposed to measure achievement in high school mathematics, but the test only asks questions about math learned in elementary school, scores will be of limited validity. Most inferences one might make regarding a student's knowledge of high school math are likely to be wrong.

In theory, a test cannot be more valid than it is reliable. In operational terms, this means that a test cannot correlate more highly with an external measure (a criterion used to assess validity) than it can with itself.

LICENSURE TESTING

The purpose of licensure testing is to protect the public from harm by setting qualifications for beginning practitioners. In some professions, these minimum qualifications include receptive or expressive English-language communication skills. In this situation, a component of the assessment process should test those skills. But in other professions, such skills are not considered of critical importance. In such cases, those skills should not be a requirement for licensure. While this may seem obvious on the face of it, and such licensure tests might not explicitly test English-language communication skills, it may well be that aspects of a test's design unintentionally raise barriers due to those extraneous skills.

Even if a test intentionally measures communication skills, much thought needs to be given to what kinds of communication skills are to be measured. If listening comprehension is important for a profession, but in that profession such communication typically occurs face-to-face, is it appropriate to test it in a disembodied way where body language is not part of what is being assessed? If a teacher is going to work primarily with deaf and hard of hearing students, might not expressive communication skills in sign language be as, or more important than, oral expression?

VALIDATION OF LICENSURE TESTS

Validation is the accrual of evidence to demonstrate what a test measures vis-à-vis the constructs which it was intended to measure. While validation should never be viewed as a single exercise at one point in time, specific approaches to validity studies are often used. While it is desirable to apply all of these techniques, licensure programs that test relatively small numbers of people each year usually use only one or two such approaches because the cost of a more comprehensive approach may be prohibitively expensive.

Content Validation

Many licensure tests depend primarily on an approach called content validation. Messick (1989, p. 17) describes content validity as being, ". . . based on professional judgment about the relevance of the test content to the content of a particular behavioral domain of interest and about the representativeness with which item or task content covers that domain." Content validity is, or at least should be, an integral part of the test development process because the same process of expert judgment is necessary to develop the blueprint that describes and guides the building of the test.

In the case of licensure testing, the process of building blueprints and building tests usually starts with a job analysis. In a job analysis, typical job incumbents or experts identify major and critical activities performed by people in a job class and determine the knowledge, skills, and abilities required to accomplish those tasks. Test blueprints are developed to ensure that all forms of the test reflect the findings of the job analysis.

Criterion-Related Validation

The scores from a licensure test can be statistically correlated with a measure of job success, (e.g., supervisor ratings or other empirical measures of the quality of work performance). A valid assessment should correlate positively with a reasonable measure of job success. This correlation should apply both to the population of test-takers as a whole and identifiable subgroups. Moreover, for a licensure test to be unbiased, the average criterion performance for people with a given test score should be the same regardless of the subgroup to which they belong. Note that there are many complex statistical issues associated with the assessment of potential bias in tests. These issues are beyond the exposition in this chapter.

LACK OF ACCESS AS A THREAT TO VALIDITY

If, for some examinees, the way language is used in the test poses difficulties that are unrelated or not closely related to the knowledge, skills, and abilities identified in the test blueprint, that language requirement will diminish the validity of test scores. That diminution is because a person relatively lacking in the knowledge, skills, and abilities of interest might, by virtue of his or her language facility, score higher than a person with more technical knowledge but less language proficiency, and vice versa.

Consider the two questions in the boxed text, each intended to determine whether a test-taker understands how to compute an arithmetic mean.

Version 1 is wordy. A test-taker who is not a native English speaker, is dyslexic, or has grown up with limited hearing, may be confused by the question or might require excessive time to answer the question due to its reading load—and thus, if there were many such questions, have insufficient time to finish the entire test. Many people who can compute a simple average will not realize that is what is required to answer the question because the more arcane term, *first moment,* is used.

Version 1

Fyodor Dostoevsky owns a manufacturing plant that produces volumetric analysis equipment made from thermoplastic resins. For the fiscal year beginning in July 2004, his company had quarterly sales of one million dollars, two million dollars, three million dollars, and four million dollars. Determine the first moment (measure of central tendency) of the sales data distribution.

(Correct answer is $2.5 million)

Compare this to version 2.

Version 2

A company has quarterly sales of one million dollars, two million dollars, three million dollars, and four million dollars. What was the arithmetic mean of the quarterly sales?

(Correct answer is $2.5 million)

Version 2 is significantly better and might be appropriate for a licensure exam where averages are typically applied to financial data. Still, the reading load and vocabulary of the item could be simplified further (as in version 3).

Version 3

What is the average of the following four numbers: 1, 2, 3, 4?

(Correct answer is 2.5)

A sometimes competing principle argues against taking linguistic simplification too far—the use of pertinent context and redundancy. Appropriate inclusion of redundant information provides people with less proficient or still-developing English reading skills with multiple opportunities to infer meaning. While version 4 is more complex than version 3, individuals with less proficient reading skills might perform better on such an item. More research on this issue is desirable.

Version 4

A teacher assigned homework with four parts and graded each part on a four-point scale. Keesha scored 1, 2, 3, and 4 on these parts. What is Keesha's average (arithmetic mean) score?

(Correct answer is 2.5)

If job success depends on an understanding of the arithmetic mean, examinees who can answer correctly any of the above questions will have the opportunity to be successful. The opposite, however, is not true. Examinees who answer the first question incorrectly might nonetheless understand the concept of arithmetic means and do well in their jobs.

A test that includes items like version 1 will be exclusionary. Some competent members of the profession will not be allowed to practice. Moreover, it is likely that entire classes of people, such as people who are deaf or hard of hearing, will be adversely impacted and potentially excluded from their chosen profession.

UNIVERSAL DESIGN

Once upon a time, and not a very long time ago, doorknobs in public buildings were round and needed to be grasped and rotated to allow someone to open the door. People who could not grasp and/or rotate, perhaps because of arthritis, neuromuscular condition, or possession of certain kinds of artificial limbs could not open these doors. Today, most doorknobs in public buildings are levers that can be operated by pushing them downwards with or without their being grasped. More people can open these doors by themselves. Today's doorknobs have been designed to be more universally accessible.

From this architectural tradition, the principle of extending access through universal design has been expanding to other parts of our lives, including testing.

General Principles of Universal Design for Tests

To maximize accessibility for deaf and hard of hearing individuals, several aspects of test questions should be considered.

Vocabulary

Often, tests contain non-discipline-specific vocabulary words that are familiar to hearing individuals but are rarely encountered by deaf and hard of hearing individuals. In general, one should minimize the use of words with multiple meanings and in particular the use of the low-frequency meaning of some words.

Idiomatic English

Some test questions and stimuli for questions include idiomatic English expressions. However, since idiomatic English is used most frequently in speech, hearing individuals are often more exposed to it than are deaf and hard of hearing individuals. This lack of or limited access to idiomatic English tends to be especially challenging for test-takers who have grown up profoundly deaf.

Language

The language used in tests is often refined specifically for testing purposes. Committees of educators and test developers carefully review the language of tests to ensure that each test question has one and only one correct response. However, for deaf and hard of hearing individuals, the resulting language used in tests is often atypical, idiosyncratic, confusing, or difficult to understand. While these individuals may very well not have difficulty comprehending other written material (e.g., magazines, textbooks, fiction), they are often thwarted in their efforts to successfully grasp what is being asked of them by decontextualized questions on a test.

Grammatical Construction of Test Items

Several grammatical constructions prove to be particularly difficult for deaf and hard of hearing individuals to decipher. While these constructions are often employed to save space and reduce the reading load of the test, they prove to be thorny, even unfair, for some test-takers. For example, long sentences with several embedded subordinate clauses can become difficult to process and confusing for individuals who are deaf or hard of hearing. Also, questions that contain a negative often introduce a further hardship for deaf and hard of hearing individuals (e.g., Which of the following is not an inference that can be drawn from . . .).

Use of Technology to Implement Principles of Universal Design for Licensure Testing

Many testing programs provide what are referred to as accommodations. An accommodation is a change in testing conditions that is intended to level the playing field for the person needing that accommodation, but would provide little or no advantage to other test-takers. The most common accommodation is extra time, though many (including the authors) believe that for many tests, extra time would help most test-takers.

Some accommodations, such as extra time, reflect the same approach that people might take outside of a testing situation. For example, people who read English slowly and require extra time to ensure that they understand the meaning of a written test might be mirroring the extra time they might take while performing the job for which they are licensed. (In most cases, the rationale for timing accommodations is more complicated. Unlike a test, on a job, a person will usually receive richly contextualized information from multiple and redundant sources.)

Other testing accommodations are made requiring examinees to depend on other people to help them take a test (e.g., having an aide write out an examinee's answers).

Still others are made in an all-or-nothing fashion that provides individuals with little choice or control (e.g., a single choice of font size for a large print test). Though relatively cost effective, some of these types of accommodations are not consistent with life outside of testing situations because they either restrict choices or foster undue dependency. We are all interdependent. The issue is whether some of us are required to be more dependent despite alternatives that could support greater independence.

Through principles of universal design, technology can be used to broadly make tests more accessible by providing multiple options for examinees to access the content of test items and then indicate their responses. The following are examples of such practices that could be made available to all examinees, but would be of particular interest in meeting the needs of examinees who are deaf or hard of hearing.

- Audio with controllable volume
- On-demand video presentation of instructions and/or items using sign language
- On-demand simplification and contextualization of English
- Instant messaging to communicate with proctors

Audio With Controllable Volume

Most test proctors cannot communicate by signing. Many may be unused to communicating with deaf or hard of hearing examinees who read lips or who need to be relatively near a speaker. Test directions can be provided aurally (as well as in print) by computer using sound files and headphones with volume controls so examinees with partial hearing can receive information in multiple ways to best meet their needs. With this option, examinees who need to can repeat aural information to ensure that they understand the instructions.

On-Demand Video Presentation of Instructions and/or Items Using Sign Language

Software exists to translate text into sign language. Unfortunately, the state of the art in commercially available translation software provides a word-by-word translation, and thus appropriate grammar and usage is ignored. Also, words not in the software dictionary are spelled. For some fluent American Sign Language (ASL) signers, the resulting translation might be more disconcerting than helpful—akin to taking a test in Pidgin English or non-native, grammatically incorrect English. Computer science advances in natural language processing make it likely that in a few years, translation software is likely to produce a more accurate ASL translation from written English.

In the meantime, although the approach is somewhat more expensive to implement, ASL (or other forms of signing) video translations of questions and stimulus materials can be produced and presented by computerized testing systems. That is, qualified translators could be recorded as they sign instructions or questions. The resulting digital video files could be played on demand by the test-taker and replayed if necessary.

Back-translation, a technique long used in the translation of tests from one written language to another, could be used to verify the fidelity of the translation. After the text is translated by one person into ASL, a second person views the translation and independently translates from ASL to written English. The resulting translation is compared with the original text. Any significant differences might point out problems with the choice of language in the original text.

Such an approach will ensure a quality translation and avoid aberrations that impact test validity, parallel to those described in the anecdote about the first author's experience with the French Regents Examination. That is, a testing agency can review and ensure the quality of one recorded video translation, even though they cannot control the quality of the translation of 10 or more individual translators at separate sites. Of course, this approach will not help all deaf or hard of hearing test-takers, since some do not have ASL proficiency. More research is needed in this area.

On-Demand Simplification and Contextualization of English

Test makers like questions to be sufficiently interesting to engage most examinees. Moreover, contextualization and redundancy can assist people with limited or developing reading skills. On the other hand, unless carefully applied, contextualization and even redundancy can increase the complexity of the language used to frame and ask the questions and might make questions more difficult. Thus language complexity might make questions more difficult for those examinees who have difficulty reading written English. One way to approach this issue is to allow examinees to switch back and forth between more and less contextualized versions of the same question.

Instant Messaging to Communicate With Proctors

During test administration, examinees sometimes need to ask questions of the test proctor. Examinees who are not native speakers of English, including some deaf examinees, may not readily be able to express their needs orally, but may be able to do so in writing. The use of instant messaging from within a test—sending a message from the examinee's computer to the proctor's computer—might be an effective communication mechanism, and at the same time will be less intrusive to other test-takers.

A CALL FOR RESEARCH questions

Providing examinees with a set of tools from which they can choose how best to respond to a test can be justified in one or both of two ways. Some will say this is an appropriate approach based on policy considerations. It is the fair thing to do. Others might believe that such an approach improves the validity or reliability of test scores. At this time, we have no evidence regarding the impact that providing such a system would have on either psychometric criterion; such research is needed.

This general question can be broken down into a number of separate, more focused questions. These questions can be asked regarding contextualization, including separate questions for different kinds or aspects of contextualization, and also for linguistic simplification, on-demand volume controlled audio, on-demand video of ASL translations, and use of instant messaging to the text proctor. Examples of such questions follow.

1. Does this practice increase the accessibility of the test for deaf and/or hard of hearing examinees (do test scores increase)?
2. How large is the effect (how much do scores increase)?
3. Does this practice increase scores differentially for deaf and/or hard of hearing examinees compared to examinees in general and compared to other identifiable subgroups of examinees?
4. What is the impact of this practice on test reliability?
5. What is the impact of this practice on test score validity?

CONCLUSION

Much should and can be done to improve the fairness and the psychometric characteristics of licensure tests taken by deaf and hard of hearing examinees. Much promise exists in applying the principles of universal design to the testing experience. Further research is now necessary to guide us in developing best practices in this area.

REFERENCES

Braun, H., Ragosta, M., & Kaplan, B. (1986). *The predictive validity of the Scholastic Aptitude Test for disabled students.* Princeton, NJ: Educational Testing Service.

Holt, J. A. (1993). Stanford Achievement Test—8th edition for deaf and hard of hearing students: Reading Comprehension subgroup results. *American Annals of the Deaf.* http://gri.gallaudet.edu/Assessment/sat-read.html.

Messick, S. (1989). Validity. In R. L. Linn (Ed.), *Educational measurement* (3rd ed., pp. 13–103). New York: Macmillan.

Perfetti, C. A., & Sandak, R. (2000). Reading optimally builds on spoken language: Implications for deaf readers. *Journal of Deaf Studies and Deaf Education, 5* (1), 32–50.

Trybus, R. J., & Karchmer, M. A. (1977). School achievement scores of hearing-impaired children: National data on achievement and growth patterns. *American Annals of the Deaf: Directory of Programs and Services, 122* (2), 62–69.

Willingham, W. W., Ragosta, M., Bennett, R. E., Braun, H., Rock, D. A., & Powers, D. E. (1988). *Testing handicapped people.* Boston: Allyn and Bacon.

Considerations in Developing Licensing Tests That Are Accessible for All Candidates

Carolyn Emrick Massad

Currently, state licensing laws directly affect about one-fifth, and perhaps as much as one-third, of the workforce (Young, 2004). The position in favor of licensing has consistently been that it protects the public from incompetents, charlatans, and quacks in important occupations or fields of practice. Generally, a state licensing board, receiving its charter from the state legislature, enforces and maintains control over a licensed occupation.

To become licensed usually requires candidates to meet some or all of four types of requirements. First, they must have successfully completed a formal educational program. Second, the candidates must have had some experience in the field in which they wish to be licensed. Third, they must have specified personal characteristics (e.g., residency within the state). Fourth, and most important, applicants for licensure must have successfully completed a written licensing examination.

The intent underlying licensing examinations is to provide information to state licensing boards that would help them determine the competence of candidates for licensure and protect the public from incompetent professionals and tradespeople (AERA, APA, & NCME, 1985; 1999). However, most written licensure examinations are developed to be valid for measuring solely the essential knowledge and skills necessary to enter a field. The measures are seldom sufficient to evaluate competent performance in the field. It is only after licensure and in the actual practice in the field that an individual's ability to perform a job safely and competently can be determined. Therefore, the written licensing examinations are generally the gatekeepers to licensing the rights of individuals to begin practicing in a field of licensure.

Because of the limitations of a single measure given at one point in time on the continuum of learning in any field, any examination should be of the highest quality and take into consideration the full range of the population to be tested. Naturally, the quality of measurement and recognition of the diversity of the population are critical in developing a written licensing examination that controls entry into practicing a profession or trade. Just as the concept of universal design—"the design of products and environments to be usable by all people, to the greatest extent possible, without need for adaptation or specialized design" (Mace, 1998)—has been applied in removing

---

A major portion of this chapter was first prepared for an invited presentation at the Gallaudet University National Conference on "High-Stakes Testing: Are Deaf and Hard of Hearing Children Being Left Behind?" held on November 15–16, 2002, in Washington, DC. It appears in "Maximizing Equity and Access in Test Construction," a technical report copyrighted © June 2003 and reproduced here by permission of the publisher, Harcourt Assessment, Inc. All rights reserved.

obstacles for people with disabilities in the physical world, this concept is now being applied in test development. A licensing examination needs to be the best it can be, and the diversity of the population must be recognized in developing that measure so that equity and access are maximized.

Specifically, the range of cognitive styles that impact how people have learned the knowledge and skills being tested must be recognized. Also, the language of the testing environment needs to be made as accessible as possible, particularly to the many individuals for whom English is not the first language, for whom English is not fully accessible, and for whom it may not have been the sole language for learning. Essentially, English or any auditorily-based language is never fully accessible to a person who is not fully hearing when growing up. For example, hearing people have the advantage of unhampered access to English and thus have easier access to incidental learning. They are also likely to be more familiar with the multiple meanings of words and idiomatic lexicon and expressions, as well as with complex English constructions (Karchmer & Mitchell, 2002; Marschark, 2001; Mounty, 2002; Randall, McAnally, Rittenhouse, Russell, & Sorensen, 2000). These features must be kept in mind by test developers, particularly if the results of the tests are to reflect what all prospective licensees need to know and are able to do.

Good licensing examinations must be both reliable and valid. An examination is reliable when results from administration to administration are consistent and when it is based on clear test specifications as well as established technical and professional standards. Validity of the examination is based on whether or not the examination tests job-related tasks or knowledge established by the results of a job analysis. Job analysis refers to procedures designed to obtain descriptive information about the tasks performed on a job and/or the knowledge and skills believed necessary for adequately performing those tasks (Gael, 1983). The information from the job analysis is essential to determine the content and skills to be measured.

There are many ways in which content and skills may be measured. However, there are excellent resources available to guide test developers and users. Some general guidelines for developing and using assessment measures are the focus of the *Code of Fair Testing Practices in Education* (1988), which was developed by the Joint Committee on Testing Practices of the American Psychological Association (APA), the American Educational Research Association (AERA), and the National Council on Measurement in Education (NCME). The code includes guidelines for developing and/or selecting tests, interpreting scores, and striving for fairness. The joint committee also produced the *Joint Standards for Educational and Psychological Testing* (1985; 1999), which provides the foundational guidance for all testing. Further, most test developers have their own guidelines for their test development work, including test-specific and testing program-specific guidelines.

Essentially, language is the primary medium of learning and testing. To develop tests that will provide good measures of what deaf and hard of hearing test-takers know requires an understanding of the test-takers' communication processes and skills and an awareness of how English generally functions for them. Especially for deaf and hard of hearing test-takers, the way in which written language is used in testing can create insurmountable hurdles and prevent an accurate assessment of what they know and can do (Mounty, 2002; Marschark, 2001; Martin, 2001; Randall, McAnally, Rittenhouse, Russell, & Sorensen, 2000). To meet the technical and professional standards embodied in the *Joint Standards for Educational and Psychological Testing* (1985; 1999), test developers must seek ways to maximize all test-takers' ability to demonstrate what they know on tests.

GENERAL GUIDELINES FOR TEST CONSTRUCTION

What follows are general guidelines that would be appropriate for constructing test questions for any population but that have particular relevance for testing deaf and hard of hearing candidates for licensure. The learning outcomes referred to in the excerpt below are the essential knowledge and skills in a field for which the test-taker has had entry-level preparation and seeks licensure.

Each type of test question is efficient for measuring some learning outcomes, but is inefficient or inappropriate for measuring others. The types of selected-response questions include the (1) true/false or alternative response, (2) matching, and (3) multiple-choice.

1. The true/false or alternative-response question is most useful where the desired outcomes are determining the truth or falsity of a statement, distinguishing between fact and opinion, or discriminating between appropriate and inappropriate responses, such as "yes/no," "right/wrong," "agree/disagree." The true/false or alternative-response question is generally inadequate for measuring the more complex learning outcomes.
2. The matching type of question is similarly restricted and is limited almost entirely to learning outcomes that call for the identification of simple relationships and the ability to classify things into given categories.
3. The multiple-choice question is the most generally adaptable and can be used effectively to measure a variety of learning outcomes, from the simple to the complex. However, even the multiple-choice question is inefficient or inappropriate for measuring some of the more complex learning outcomes.

Types of constructed response questions include (1) the short answer and (2) the essay or other types of open-ended questions.

1. The short-answer question, calling for a few words or sentences, effectively measures the recall of specific facts, but is generally inappropriate for measuring understanding, application, interpretation, and other complex learning outcomes.
2. The essay or other types of open-ended questions are the most effective for measuring the ability to organize data, for presenting original ideas, and for

problem-solving. Furthermore, if ability to write is being measured, the constructed response is the most direct measure.

Additionally, other measures of learning outcomes include: performance observations, interviews, in-depth observations, and long-term activities, such as projects, extended written assignments, and portfolios.

GUIDING PRINCIPLES

Regardless of the type of questions used in a measure, the fundamental principles in the construction of the questions are that they:

1. Measure only important content and skills and are based on a representative sample of the knowledge and skills identified as essential for the purposes of the measure,
2. Elicit only the outcomes that are to be measured, and
3. Do not prevent or inhibit the test-takers' demonstration of the desired outcomes.

Since most measures consist primarily of multiple-choice and constructed-response questions, the remainder of this chapter focuses on those two types of questions. Because the language of instruction in a field is typically English, the measures of knowledge and skills in a field are usually encoded in English. Therefore, attention also will be given to the importance of ensuring that the language of the measures does not prevent or inhibit test-takers' ability to demonstrate what they know and can do. To maximize equity and access requires careful examination of the questions and whether or not the English structure, usage, and vocabulary are appropriate for all test-takers.

Consequently, in measuring learning outcomes other than reading skills, it is important also to keep in mind that although the language of instruction in a field may be English, the measure should not be primarily a measure of reading ability in English; the focus must instead be on the content and skills being measured. Test developers want the test-taker to be able to obtain correct answers to questions that measure the attainment of the learning outcomes being tested. A measure would not be considered valid if the test-taker answered such questions incorrectly merely because of readability factors, such as inordinately complex sentence structures or exceptionally difficult vocabulary, or because the type of response called for was not clearly specified. These factors, which are extraneous to the purpose of the measure, limit and modify the test-taker's responses and prevent the test-taker from demonstrating the true level of achievement attained. Such factors are as unfair as determining a person's running ability when he or she has a sprained ankle; although a measure of running would be obtained, it would be restricted by a factor not intended to be included in the measure.

Good measurement requires that those who develop or review and select the questions that are to be used in tests, such as licensure tests, must establish criteria for determining whether questions are appropriate and valid for the purpose of the test. To discuss the criteria, it would be helpful to consider the vocabulary of measurement. To this end, consider the following diagram of a multiple-choice question:

Stem ⟶ **Who may write prescriptions for patients?**
Correct Answer ⟶ (A) Licensed psychiatrists *
(B) Registered physical therapists
(C) Registered nurses
(D) Licensed pharmacists

Note that A, B, C, and D are the options for the stem. Answers B, C, and D are distracters or incorrect options, while A is the key or correct answer. In addition, below is an example of a constructed-response question with its associated terminology.

Prompt ⟶ **Carefully read the passage above. Based on this information, describe in detail the three most common causes of indigestion. Use examples from the passage to support your answer. This is not a test of your writing ability, but your answer should be written as clearly as possible. You may use any one or combination of formats (e.g., lists, outlines, prose paragraphs, diagrams) that is appropriate for your response.**

CRITERIA FOR TEST-ITEM STRUCTURE

Now let us turn to the criteria for determining whether questions are appropriate and valid for the purpose of the test. The first, second, and third criteria below would apply to both multiple-choice and constructed-response questions.

1. The question should be about a concept, idea, or skill that is important for the test-taker to know or to understand as opposed to some obscure or trivial fact. In addition, for questions measuring skills, such as reading, the question should be as interesting as possible.
2. The question should be structured around *one* central idea or problem that is clearly and completely presented in the stem of the question. Those whose primary language is not English and those who have grown up without full accessibility to English understand a complete question better than an incomplete stem that is completed by the options.

- The stem should be meaningful by itself.

- The stem should include as much as is needed to answer the question and should be free of irrelevant material. When one is calling for a judgment or a conclusion, the criterion or authority that is the basis for the correct answer should be specified.

- The stem should not pose a form of the question "What do you think . . ." or "What would you do . . ." because the correctness of any of the options could then be defended.

- A negatively stated stem should be used only when significant learning outcomes require it. For example, knowing the "least important . . ." is seldom related to important learning outcomes.

3. The language of the question is most important. It should be clear and concise.

- The vocabulary should be as simple as possible unless vocabulary that is complex or difficult is being tested.

- The stem and options, if there are options, should be simple, short, and in straightforward context.

  – The information should be presented in the active voice and present tense whenever possible.

- The question should avoid complex structures that are unnecessary to measure what is intended.

  – Whenever possible, the subject and its verb should be together.

  – Sentences with multiple embedded clauses should be avoided, because they are particularly difficult for students who have not fully mastered English.

  – All parts of prepositional phrases should be kept together.

  – When using a pronoun, especially at the beginning of a sentence, its referent should be clear.

- The question should not contain double negatives. For example, it is inappropriate to ask the student to answer by identifying an option or writing about something that is not true or that is false or incorrect. As an extreme example, a student would be confused by having to recognize that it is *not* true that Louis Pasteur did *not* develop a process to make milk safe for consumption.

- When several questions are based on the same referent or on stimulus material such as a passage, graphs, or charts, each question should be independent of the other questions in the set. Moreover, it is imperative that the test-taker be able to arrive at the correct answer from the stimulus material. For example, arriving at the correct answer should not be based on having answered correctly a previous question in the set. In addition, for sets of multiple-choice questions, distracters in one question should not provide clues for answering another question in the set.

The fourth criterion below focuses only on multiple-choice questions.

4. The options of multiple-choice questions are as important as the stem. The difficulty of a question depends largely on the options. The finer the distinctions that must be made to select the correct answer from the distracters, the more difficult the question is.

- The correct answer to the question should be meaningful and related to important learning outcomes. Recognizing the fact that no option is a correct response is seldom related to important learning outcomes; therefore, "none of the above" should not be an option.

- If the question is asking for only one correct answer, there should be only one correct answer in the options available. "All of the above" should never be used as an option because it is inconsistent with there being only one correct answer.

- The distracters should be selected and formulated with care—incorrectness should not be the sole criterion. They should be plausible to test-takers. Nor should the distracters be deliberately tricky. Distracters should not be distinguished from the correct answer by factors related to language rather than content. For example, if the stem requires the correct answer to be a noun related to the target construct, all of the options should be nouns. Having a distracter be an adjective or other part of speech that is related to the target construct is inappropriate.

Sources of worthwhile distracters include the following:

  – Common misconceptions and common errors in technique

  – A statement which is itself true, but which does not satisfy the requirements of the problem

  – An incorrect statement that may sound plausible to those who have not attained the desired learning outcome

- The options should be phrased so that they all maintain a similar relationship to the thought in the stem. The options should be stated clearly and concisely.

- No clues should be given in the correct answer, such as similarity between the stem and the correct answer in wording, phraseology, or grammatical construction. If this similarity is not maintained between the stem and other options, the test-taker can respond based on the similarity alone. In addition, "textbookish" wording only in the correct answer is another clue.

The fifth criterion below focuses only on constructed-response questions.

5. Constructed-response questions provide a statement of the situation, setting, or problem along with response instructions.

   - The question or prompt specifies to what the test-taker is to respond. The greater the clarity and detail in the prompt of what is expected, the more likely the question is to measure what is intended to be measured.

     – The question should be as brief as clarity allows. Restatement may sometimes be necessary to prevent misunderstandings, but then perhaps the restatement alone may be all that is needed.

- Questions should not be able to be answered simply by "yes" or "no."

- There are basically two types of constructed-response questions:

  - Restricted-response questions, which provide highly structured directions and are typically scored by a point method, using a model answer as a guide

  - Extended-response questions, which do not describe a task too rigidly but indicate scoring criteria (This type of question is scored by the rating method, using defined criteria as a guide)

- Specific directions for responding may appear before or be included within the prompt. The greater the clarity and detail provided to the test-taker, the more likely the question is to measure what it is intended to measure. The response instructions include such things as:

  - Minimum or maximum length of response

  - Specific points to be covered and/or performance required, such as explaining a solution in addition to describing one, stating a position and providing a rationale for it, and so on

- Criteria for scoring, or rubrics, are an important part of the question. The criteria for scoring the question should accompany the question when constructed-response questions are reviewed, since they help to determine whether or not the question has been clearly and concisely stated. Generally three types of criteria apply:

  - Content criteria, which deal only with the presence of knowledge and its accuracy and not with the use of knowledge for application, analysis, synthesis, or evaluation. Responses are judged solely on whether the content of the response leads to the conclusion that the student is knowledgeable in the content area

  - Organization criteria, which deal with whether the response is logically presented

  - Process criteria, which deal with whether the process(es) required in the prompt and/or the response instructions were carried out in the response

- For example, criteria may focus on the problem-solving steps:

  - defining the problem

  - generating alternative solutions

  - weighing the alternative solutions and choosing among them

  - implementing the choice

- evaluating the outcome

or, they may be concerned with predicting what a character in a passage would do in a specified situation and supporting the prediction with details in the passage.

Not all types of criteria need to be included with each question. However, the criteria for a question should be clear to the test-taker, whether implied or explicit. The test-taker should not be asked to read the mind of the person who wrote the question.

- If the question is to measure content knowledge and skills other than writing, the response should not be evaluated on the basis of the responder's writing skills. But if the response is to be scored on writing skills as well as on content and/or other skills, this criterion should be made clear in the specific directions for responding, and the two scores should be kept separate so as to distinguish what is measured by each.

- If all test-takers are to be compared or evaluated based on the assessment of a learning outcome measured by constructed-response questions, optional questions or prompts should not be offered as alternatives from which test-takers may choose. Alternative prompts eliminate the ability to make comparisons and evaluate all test-takers on the same basis.

- When a test consists solely of constructed-response questions, a larger number of questions requiring relatively short answers, rather than a few questions requiring long answers, should be part of the test structure. Such an approach provides a broader sampling of the test-takers' knowledge and skills.

- The time limit, if any, and point value of each constructed-response question should be specified, whether they are in a test consisting of mixed types of questions or in one composed solely of constructed-response questions.

CONCLUSION

Ideally, tests for licensure will be developed that are equitable for and accessible to every test-taker seeking licensure, thereby being appropriate for the purpose for which they are intended: to help licensing boards determine whether candidates for licensure have the essential knowledge and skills necessary to begin practicing in the field.

REFERENCES

American Educational Research Association (AERA), American Psychological Association (APA), & National Council on Measurement in Education (NCME). (1985; 1999). *Standards for educational and psychological testing.* Washington, DC: American Psychological Association.

American Educational Research Association, American Psychological Association, & National Council on Measurement in Education. (1988). *Code of fair testing practices.* Washington, DC: American Psychological Association.

Gael, S. (1983). *Job Analysis: A guide to assessing work activities.* San Francisco: Jossey-Bass.

Karchmer, M. A., & Mitchell, R. E. (2002). Demographic and achievement characteristics of deaf and hard-of-hearing students. In M. Marschark & P. Spencer (Eds.), *Handbook of deaf studies, language, and education.* New York: Oxford University Press.

Mace, R. L. (1998). *A perspective on universal design.* An edited excerpt of a presentation at Designing for the 21st Century: An International Conference on Universal Design. Retrieved December 26, 2002, from www.adaptenv.org/examples/ronmaceplenary98.php.

Marschark, M. (2001, June). *Language development in children who are deaf: A research synthesis.* Alexandria, VA: National Association of State Directors of Special Education. (ERIC Document Reproduction Service No. ED455620)

Martin, D. S. (2001). *Multiple-choice tests: Issues for deaf test takers.* An issue brief of the National Task Force on Equity in Testing Deaf Individuals. Retrieved September 22, 2001, from http://gri.gallaudet.edu/TestEquity/mctests/html.

Massad. C. E. (2003). *Maximizing equity and access in test construction.* A technical report for Harcourt Assessment, Inc. Retrieved August 1, 2003, from http://www.HEMWEB/com/library.

Mounty, J. L. (2002). *High-stakes testing of deaf and hard of hearing children: Understanding the problem and finding equitable solutions.* Presentation at the Gallaudet University National Conference on High-Stakes Testing: Are Deaf and Hard of Hearing Children Being Left Behind? Washington, DC.

Randall, K., McAnally, P., Rittenhouse, B., Russell, D., & Sorensen, G. (2000). High stakes testing: What is at stake? Letter to the Editor, *American Annals of the Deaf, 145* (5).

Young, S. D. (2004). Occupational licensing. *The concise encyclopedia of economics.* Retrieved January 6, 2004, from www.econlib.org/library/Enc/OccupationalLicensing.html.

The Psychometric Properties of Intelligence Tests When Used With Deaf and Hard of Hearing Individuals: Practices and Recommendations

Susan J. Maller and Jason C. Immekus

Suppose a young, motivated deaf man, named Michael, seeks assistance from the state vocational rehabilitation agency. Michael hopes to attend Gallaudet University to study accounting. He sees a rehabilitation counselor for the deaf, Ruth, who is fluent in American Sign Language (ASL), but who has no advanced training in psychological assessment or measurement. The psychologist under contract tests Michael, as part of the eligibility determination for services. The psychologist is not trained to work with the deaf and hard of hearing population, yet has tested countless deaf people with the assistance of a certified interpreter with no training in psychology. Ruth receives the psychological report and is surprised to learn that Michael obtained a Verbal IQ of 79. She finds the results strange, as Michael appeared to be very bright when they had chatted in her office. Combined with his above-average Performance IQ, his Full Scale IQ suggests that Michael does not appear to be a good candidate for the state to fund his education. Ruth argues that the test of his Verbal IQ does not seem to be a valid indicator of his ability, and she works hard to get Michael to Gallaudet anyway. Michael succeeds in college, but the bruises to his self-esteem remain.

When Denise, who is profoundly deaf, was just 7 years old, her deaf parents decided that she would have a better social experience if she attended the state residential school. She was tested by Robert, the school psychologist, who was also deaf and who administered the Verbal Scale of a widely used intelligence test. Denise scored in the normal range, as compared with her hearing peers, which is about 15 points higher than most deaf examinees. Did her score mean that, as compared with her deaf peers, Denise (a) was gifted, (b) had better language skills, or (c) just got luckier by having a deaf psychologist? Did this score mean that Denise had average verbal intelligence, as compared with hearing peers? What did this score mean? Like many psychologists, Robert, in good faith, believed that the score told him *something*, even though he was not quite sure what.

These cases may seem recognizable, because they are all based on true stories. They highlight some familiar themes that raise critical ethical questions regarding intelligence tests and testing practices with deaf and hard of hearing examinees. Specifically, how does the diverse nature of the deaf and hard of hearing population (e.g., in terms of hearing loss, educational experiences, socialization, communication modality) affect the meaning of test scores? Further, how is the concept of intelligence defined? How are abstract definitions, also known as *constructs,* of intelligence operationalized? What evidence exists that the operational definitions (i.e., assessments, tests, instruments) measure what they claim to measure when used with deaf and hard of hearing examinees? What guidelines exist for test developers and practitioners? Even if it seems appropriate to violate the guidelines, what are the social consequences (Messick, 1989) that may result? This chapter will help to sort out some of these issues.

DEFINITIONS OF THE CONSTRUCT OF INTELLIGENCE

Despite the fact that there is no single, widely accepted definition of the construct of intelligence, it remains one of the most widely investigated domains regarding individual differences. The French psychologist Binet, for example, characterized intelligence as an internal process critical to an individual's ability to acquire and adapt information (Wolf, 1973). Wechsler (1944) defined intelligence as "the aggregate or global capacity of the individual to act purposefully, to think rationally and to deal effectively with his environment" (p. 3). Horn and Cattell (1966) proposed that global or general intelligence is composed of two interrelated abilities: fluid (novel problem-solving, including pattern recognition, flexibility, and adaptability) and crystallized (influenced by verbal ability and educational, cultural, and environmental factors) intelligence. Other noteworthy perspectives of intelligence include Gardner's (1993) position of multiple intelligences (e.g., mathematical, musical), as well as Feuerstein's (1980) stance that it is dynamic and modifiable. Intelligence historically has been considered to be a critical determinant of important outcomes such as academic achievement, environmental adaptation, and functioning (Ceci, 1996).

INTELLIGENCE OPERATIONALIZED

Intelligence is operationalized in terms of intelligence tests. The roots of modern intelligence tests can be traced to the Binet and Simon scale (Binet & Simon, 1905), developed by Alfred Binet to satisfy the French government's requests to identify students who might fail in the traditional educational system. It was claimed that intelligence tests were useful for identifying the "morons," "imbeciles," and "idiots" of society (Wechsler, 1944). Even within research and practice with deaf and hard of hearing individuals, Moores (1982) pointed out that intelligence tests were used to characterize deaf people's cognitive abilities as: "inferior," primarily based on the work of Pintner and his colleagues (Pintner, Eisenson, & Stanton, 1946; Pintner & Paterson, 1915), and "concrete," as per the work of Myklebust (1964), who posited that deaf and hearing people's cognitive functions were structured differently. Subsequent research finally led to the perception of "The Deaf as Intellectually Normal," (Moores, 1982) based on findings that deaf and hearing people score similarly on nonverbal intelligence tests (Rosenstein, 1961; Vernon, 1976), and this conclusion has been supported (Braden, 1984; 1985; Lavos, 1962; Maller & Braden, 1993) using scores from modern intelligence tests.

Intelligence tests now play a critical role in making high-stakes decisions related to classification, diagnosis, placement, and program planning (Sattler, 2001; Stinnett, Havey, & Oehler-Stinnett, 1994). To discourage potential adverse social consequences (Messick, 1989) of test use, practitioners are encouraged to: (a) interpret scores in the context of other clinically meaningful information (e.g., background information or other indicators of ability), and (b) consider the meaning of scores in relation to theory and supporting research (Kamphaus, Petoskey, & Walters Morgan, 1997). Despite these recommendations, some psychologists use tests with questionable validity for deaf and hard of hearing examinees "for purposes other than assessing cognitive ability" (Gibbins, 1989, p. 98). For example, without sufficient validity evidence, psychologists may believe that the Wechsler Verbal IQs provide insight into a deaf or hard of hearing person's English-language skills. Despite questionable validity (Maller, 2003), severely and profoundly deaf people are often administered verbal intelligence tests (Maller, 1991), usually resulting in scores about one standard deviation below hearing examinees (Braden, 1994).

Support for the routine use of performance scales with deaf and hard of hearing examinees stems from studies reporting that they obtain comparable scores to hearing examinees. Thus, nonverbal and performance measures more commonly used are, because they "reduce the verbal knowledge needed to understand directions" (Braden, 1994, p. 80). Performance tests require the use of fine motor skills, such as physical manipulation of objects (e.g., replicating block designs and arranging pictures into a sequential order). For example, deaf and hard of hearing and hearing examinees have been reported to obtain comparable scores on the Wechsler Performance Scales such as the Wechsler Intelligence Scale for Children—Third Edition (WISC-III; Wechsler, 1991; Maller & Braden, 1993; Sullivan & Montoya, 1997) and the Wechsler Intelligence Scale for Children—Revised (WISC-R; Wechsler, 1974; Phelps & Branyan, 1988). Severely and profoundly deaf people, however, have been reported to obtain lower nonverbal IQs than hearing examinees on the Leiter-Revised (Leiter-R; Roid & Miller, 1997), the Comprehensive Test of Nonverbal Intelligence (CTONI; Hammill, Pearson, & Widerholt, 1997), and the Universal Nonverbal Intelligence Test (UNIT; Bracken & McCallum, 1998). Deaf individuals tend to obtain lower scores on motor-free intelligence tests (Braden, 1994; Goetzinger & Rousey, 1957), which do not require motor skills for nonverbal problem-solving. Additional studies are needed to determine whether the scores from widely used tests are technically sound and fair measures for deaf and hard of hearing people.

PROFESSIONAL GUIDELINES

The widespread use of tests has prompted three key professional organizations to issue guidelines for test developers and users, the *Standards for Educational and Psychological Testing* (American Educational Research Association [AERA], American Psychological Association [APA], & National Council on Measurement in Education [NCME], 1999). These standards state that test scores of members from special populations should be investigated to determine whether they function appropriately for such groups. That is, a test must possess adequate *psychometric* (technical) properties (e.g., reliability, validity, norms) for the group for which the test is being administered. Few test developers provide evidence of the psychometric properties of their tests when administered to deaf and hard of hearing people, probably due to the: (a) expenses associated with work concerning low-incidence populations, (b) skills required in psychometrics and in working with deaf and hard of hearing individuals, and (c) diverse nature of the deaf and hard of hearing population (e.g., db loss, age of onset, etiology, languages used, parental hearing loss, ethnicity) (Maller, 2003). Regardless, it is ultimately the responsibility of practitioners to understand the way a test functions for a specific group and the implications for a given individual by reading test manuals and examining published research to avoid misuse of test scores (Standard 11.15).

ACCOMMODATIONS AND MODIFICATIONS

Several standards may apply to test adaptations frequently used with deaf and hard of hearing people. Specifically, Standard 10.7 recommends that the psychometric properties of test scores administered using accommodations be investigated. Standard 9.3 states that intelligence tests should be administered in an examinee's native language. Standard 9.11 emphasizes that interpreters be fluent in the language of the test and the examinee.

Test *accommodations* provide equal access for persons with disabilities and may include special seating arrangements or enlarged print. Such accommodations do not alter the measurement of the construct. *Modifications*, however, may change item content (Thurlow, Ysseldyke, & Silverstein, 1995), thus potentially altering test constructs. Therefore, practitioners must consider whether test adaptations (e.g., signed or gestured administrations) change the nature of the test construct. For example, if an examiner asks a child, "If I have two pens in each hand, how many do I have altogether?" In English, this item might be rather sequential in nature, but in ASL, the examiner may show PENS-TWO (right hand), PENS-TWO (left hand), bring both hands together. This process would make it very simple for an examinee to see that the answer is four. Conversely, it may be very difficult to judge why a deaf child is unfamiliar with a full credit answer (e.g., due to differential opportunities to learn or differences in language, culture, and socialization). Regardless, adaptations need to be investigated for validity across versions. There have been several attempts to adapt intelligence tests for deaf people (e.g., Kostrubala & Braden, 1998; Maller, 1994; Ray, 1979; Miller, 1984; Porter & Kirby, 1986; Ray & Ulissi, 1982; Sullivan & Montoya, 1997). Such adaptations either lacked sufficient psychometric evidence or have been shown to compromise validity (Maller, 1996; 1997; 2003).

Guidelines for test translation have been provided by Bracken and Barona (1991). They suggested several steps, which employ bilingual translators, blind-back translation (i.e., translating the translated version back to the language of the original language), and identification of discrepancies between versions. The process is then repeated until further improvements cannot be made and the translated version is approved by bilingual reviewers. Finally, technical evidence must be provided regarding the construct equivalence of both versions (Sireci, Bastari, & Allalouf, 1998). Some important technical (psychometric) properties will be discussed next.

NORMS

Intelligence tests are *norm-referenced* tests, in that an individual score represents the examinee's standing in relation to a representative peer group. According to Standard 10.9, the scores of members from low-incidence groups should be compared using norms based on individuals with similar characteristics. Special norms for deaf people were recommended (Anderson & Sisco, 1977; Hiskey, 1966; Sullivan & Vernon, 1979; Vernon & Brown, 1964; Vonderhaar & Chambers, 1975). Deaf norms were developed for the WISC-R Performance Scale (Anderson & Sisco, 1977). Braden (1985) reported that deaf norms did not improve the psychometric properties of the WISC-R for deaf examinees. Maller (1996) later argued that comparing deaf people to each other on tests that lack validity evidence is a larger problem not solved by deaf norms, because the scores may not measure the trait they claim to measure. In other words, special subgroup norms *do not* ensure that a test is valid for that group, because validity is based on empirical evidence. Conversely, unrepresentative norms do not, per se, guarantee that a test is biased, although they do raise concerns regarding potential bias. Instead, the degree to which deaf and hard of hearing examinees' scores are appropriate hinges on the test's psychometric properties for that population.

RELIABILITY

Reliability refers to consistency in measurement and must be reported for any testing purposes (Standard 2.1). Test-retest reliability indicates score stability over time. Internal consistency reliability coefficients report the interrelatedness of items, and can be estimated based on a single test administration. Information regarding the reliability of scores for deaf examinees, as well as other special populations, is rarely published by test developers. Current evidence regarding the stability of deaf or hard of hearing examinee's scores is based on outdated measures and research (e.g., Birch, Stuckless, & Birch, 1963; DuToit, 1954; Pinter, 1924), and is not applicable to current intelligence tests. Further, this evidence has been limited to nonverbal tests (Braden, 1994), with the result that the reliability of deaf and hard of hearing examinees' Verbal IQ is largely unknown. Because reliability is dependent on the sample in which the measures were obtained, research on the reliability of deaf and hard of hearing examinees' IQs is critically needed.

VALIDITY

Construct validity indicates that a test measures what it was designed to measure. According to Standard 1.2, test developers must provide evidence that test scores measure the intended construct. Messick (1989) stated that all validity (i.e., content, criterion, construct) evidence is ultimately subsumed under construct validity. A test that measures factors extraneous to the intended construct will yield test scores with *construct-irrelevant variance* (Messick, 1989). Instances in which construct-irrelevant variance exists in the test scores of deaf examinees is discussed by: **(a)** Braden (1994), who posited that verbal measures of intelligence may measure the effects of hearing loss in addition to verbal aptitude, and **(b)** Maller (2003), who explained how test items and scores may be biased against severely and profoundly deaf people who use sign language.

CONTENT VALIDITY

Content validity refers to the correspondence between test content and its associated domain, as judged by content experts (e.g., teachers). Professionals with expertise in testing deaf and hard of hearing individuals rarely, if ever, are consulted during intelligence test development to determine item content or format relevance for this population.

CRITERION VALIDITY

Criterion validity refers to the degree to which intelligence test scores relate to an external criterion, typically another test. The relationship, expressed as a correlation coefficient, between the test and criterion can be based on the administration of the tests at the same time (concurrent) or when the test is used to predict the criterion (predictive). The concurrent validity of deaf examinees' Wechsler Scale IQs has been reported (Phelps & Branyan, 1988; 1990), with moderate correlations with the Kaufman Assessment Battery for Children (Kaufman & Kaufman, 1983) and the Hiskey-Nebraska Test of Learning Aptitude (Hiskey, 1966). With the exception of *Coding* (.09), deaf examinees' WISC-III Performance Scale (Wechsler, 1991) scores were moderately correlated (.52–.67) with the Test of Nonverbal Intelligence (TONI-2; Brown, Sherbenou, & Johnson, 1990; Mackinson, Leigh, Blennerhassett, & Anthony, 1997).

In terms of predictive validity, TONI-2 scores were moderately correlated (.49–.71) with the Stanford Achievement Test (SAT; Holt, Traxler, & Allen, 1992; Mackinson, Leigh, Blennerhassett, & Anthony, 1997). Weak correlations were reported between WISC-R PIQs and SAT-Hearing Impaired scores (HIs; Braden, 1989), although WISC-R Performance IQ (PIQ) scores were moderately correlated with the Wide Range Achievement Test-Revised (Jastak & Wilkinson, 1984) by Phelps and Branyan (1990). WISC-III scores moderately predict academic achievement (Maller & Braden, 1993).

Some cautions regarding criterion-validity evidence should be noted. For example, it is largely unknown whether deaf and hard of hearing examinees' IQs predict academic or job performance, and/or other important outcomes. Furthermore, the degree to which deaf and hard of hearing examinees' test scores are related will depend, in part, on the types of tests. For example, Verbal IQ has been noted to be more strongly related to severely and profoundly deaf students' academic achievement than nonverbal IQ (Braden, 1994; Maller & Braden, 1993). Maller (2003) pointed out that criterion-related validity coefficients may be inflated due to *method bias*. Method bias results when correlations are stronger due to factors extraneous to test constructs and specific to the testing method. For deaf and hard of hearing examinees, correlations actually may be stronger because of language, educational, and socialization differences. Another caution is the possibility that the criterion measure may not be psychometrically sound (Messick, 1989). The research that does exist characterizing the relationship between deaf and hard of hearing examinees' test scores is largely based on outdated tests (e.g., WISC-R, WISC-III). As new intelligence tests emerge, research is needed regarding the criterion-related validity of instruments, such as the Wechsler Intelligence Scale—Fourth Edition (Wechsler, 2003), the UNIT (Bracken & McCallum, 1998), and the Wechsler Adult Intelligence Scale—Third Edition (WAIS-III; Wechsler, 1997).

CONSTRUCT VALIDITY

Standard 1.8 states that evidence should be provided to show that test scores represent their theoretical structure. Instruments that conform to their theoretical model have evidence of construct validity (Bollen, 1989). Factor analytic procedures are used to test the factor structure of intelligence tests across groups. There are two types of factor analysis procedures: exploratory factor analysis (EFA) and confirmatory factor analysis (CFA). EFA is data-driven; CFA theory-driven (Nunnally & Berstein, 1994). EFA should be used when there is limited *a priori* evidence to indicate the relationship between test scores and latent variables (e.g., intelligence). CFA directly tests the theoretical structure of an instrument. Each procedure has been employed to determine the construct representation of the test scores of deaf and hard of hearing and hearing examinees. Interested readers are referred to Gorsuch (1983) and Bollen (1989) for detailed discussions of the use of factor analytic techniques.

The factor structure of deaf examinee's WISC-III scores has been examined with EFA. Sullivan and Montoya (1997) factor-analyzed 106 deaf and hard of hearing children's (> 45-dB hearing loss in the better ear) WISC-III scores and found evidence of a two-factor solution, as opposed to the four-factor solution reported for the standardization sample (Wechsler, 1991). The two factors were labeled *Language Comprehension* and *Visual-Spatial Organization* and did not include a *Freedom from Distractibility* factor, consistent with previous research (Sullivan & Schulte, 1992). However, these results should be interpreted with caution, because: (a) the statistical procedure assumed uncorrelated factors, even though the factors are known to be correlated; (b) the sample sizes were small; and (c) the method did not account for the fact that the WISC-III was based on a theoretical model. Because intelligence tests are designed to represent a particular measurement model of intelligence, they should be examined based on a theoretically sound approach.

CFA is the theoretically preferred method for confirming whether a test represents its theoretical model. Multisample CFA has been recommended to test the theoretical model of an instrument simultaneously across groups (Byrne, 1998; Reynolds, 1982). Test-level bias occurs when test scores do not represent the same theoretical measurement model across groups, as determined by multisample CFA (Meredith, 1993). However, if the theoretical model "fits" across groups, as determined by a variety of fit statistics, the factor structure is said to be *invariant* (similar), and it is concluded that scores can be inferred to mean the same thing across groups. An advantage of CFA is that specific parts of the factor model (i.e., the relationship between the subtests and factors, known as factor loadings; error variances; and the relationships between factors) can be individually tested to determine what aspect(s) of the test differ across groups. Recent research has begun to investigate the measurement invariance of specific intelligence tests when used across deaf and hearing samples. Maller and French (2004) found that the two models of intelligence for the UNIT were essentially the same across deaf and hearing samples. However, they concluded that deaf examinees may obtain low scores on the *Analogical Reasoning* subtest and may not do well on measures of short-term memory. Maller and Ferron (1997) reported that the four-factor model of the WISC-III was acceptable across deaf and hearing samples, although many factor loadings, error variances, and covariances differed; thus, WISC-III scores may have different meanings for deaf and hearing people. Future research is encouraged for other intelligence tests.

PROFILE ANALYSIS

Profile analysis embodies the practice of interpreting subtest score patterns as an indication of an examinee's cognitive strengths and weaknesses (Kaufman, 1994; Sattler, 2001). Profile analysis is based on the potentially faulty assumption that subtest scores can be used as independent measures of the subordinate skills, despite reports that composite scores are: (a) more reliable, and (b) better predictors of academic success (McDermott, Fantuzzo, & Glutting, 1990). Typically, profile analysis is conducted through inferential judgment, but recent research (Glutting, McGrath, Kamphaus, & McDermott, 1992; Konold, Glutting, McDermott, Kush, & Watkins, 1999; Maller & McDermott, 1997) has used rigorous methods to report standardization sample profiles (known as *core profiles*) from various intelligence tests. Such information should be employed by practitioners to determine whether a deaf examinee's score pattern is clinically unique. Core profiles of the UNIT are provided by Wilhoit and McCallum (2002). In addition, Maller (1999) reported that while 5% of hearing children had unique WISC-III profiles, an alarming 35.5% of deaf children have unique profiles. However, in light of findings that WISC-III scores may not function the same for deaf examinees (Maller, 2000; Maller & Ferron, 1997), it would be expected that their profiles may, in fact, differ from the hearing population, as item and test scores are not invariant across groups, potentially affecting test scores. Thus, practitioners are discouraged from using profile analysis for deaf examinees. This recommendation is consistent with Standard 1.12 that states that evidence should be provided to support the practice of profile analysis.

DIFFERENTIAL ITEM FUNCTIONING

Differential item functioning, formerly known as *item bias,* indicates that the statistical properties of an item differs across individuals of equal ability (Holland & Thayer, 1988). Comparing item performance across groups of individuals with equal ability ensures that correct item responses are not due to ability differences. *Impact* occurs when an item is easier for one group than another due to ability differences. As such, differential item functioning (DIF) signals that an examinee's chance of obtaining a correct response is based, in part, on group membership (e.g., gender, ethnicity, socioeconomic status, language, culture, educational opportunities). Non-DIF items are identified as invariant. There are several available methods to examine DIF (Holland & Wainer, 1993). Due to the requirements to investigate DIF (e.g., large sample sizes, technical expertise, time, expenses), DIF studies involving deaf and other low-incidence populations are limited. DIF studies that have been conducted in the past, such as for the CTONI, were not based on state-of-the-art methods and results are questionable (Camilli & Shepard, 1994; Drossman & Maller, 2000). Today, the majority of intelligence tests lack sufficient evidence to conclude whether the properties of their items function similarly across deaf, hard of hearing, and hearing examinees. This point is especially true for tests that are recommended to be "especially suitable" for particular deaf and hard of hearing samples (e.g., children), such as the Leiter-R (Roid & Miller, 1997). DIF studies are also needed across the Wechsler Performance Scales, such as the WAIS-III and the Wechsler Intelligence Scale for Children—Fourth Edition (WISC-IV; Wechsler, 2003). Although DIF may not result in a decrease in an instrument's predictive validity (Rosnowski & Reith, 1999), it jeopardizes construct validity and yields questionable test scores (Maller, 2001).

Recent DIF detection research has found evidence of differential difficulty of various WISC-III Verbal Scale and Picture Completion items against a sample of severely and profoundly deaf children who use sign language as their primary means of communication when compared to: (a) a matched sample of hearing children (Maller, 1996) and (b) the hearing standardization sample (Maller, 1997). UNIT items were found to be invariant across deaf and hearing standardization samples (Maller, 2000). State-of-the-art DIF research appears to be nonexistent for other intelligence tests, regardless of the recommendation of Standard 7.3 on the removal of test items that exhibit DIF. Thus, the UNIT is recommended for use with deaf examinees.

RECOMMENDATIONS

Published intelligence tests rarely, if ever, have conformed to the *Standards for Educational and Psychological Testing* (AERA, APA, & NCME, 1999) when used with deaf and hard of hearing people. Practitioners are urged to concern themselves with the potential unintended social consequences of test use for countless deaf and hard of hearing individuals, such as Michael, the young man wanting to attend Gallaudet, or Denise, who may or may not have been in need of gifted education. Certainly tests are needed to identify deaf or hard of hearing individuals who may need special services. However, the routine use of intelligence tests for "hearing impaired" service eligibility determinations may be unnecessary and even harmful to deaf and hard of hearing individuals.

Regardless of the larger question of the unnecessary practice of administering routine intelligence tests to deaf people, the ethical issue of using tests that either do not have the necessary psychometric evidence, as outlined in the *Standards,* or that have evidence of test or item bias must be of utmost concern to practitioners. Practitioners must carefully weigh all decisions regarding test use and test adaptations. As part of these determinations, test users are encouraged to consult test manuals and the extant research regarding the psychometric properties of the test when used with deaf and hard of hearing individuals. Unfortunately, the majority of intelligence test manuals do not provide sufficient evidence regarding how these instruments function when administered with this population, thus putting practitioners in a precarious situation. Specifically, practitioners usually must deviate from standardized procedures in order to adapt to the testing needs of deaf and hard of hearing examinees.

As discussed by Braden (2003), construct-irrelevant variance may be introduced into the test scores of deaf examinees based on testing modifications (e.g., signed administrations). Therefore, practitioners should be aware of how various factors can influence test scores and, thus select, administer, and interpret test scores appropriately. For this reason, many clinicians administer only nonverbal or performance tests to deaf examinees, although some of these measures have been shown to exhibit item bias (see Maller, 1996; 1997). Thus, psychometric evidence is needed for nonverbal and performance tests, not only verbal tests.

Independent research and professional recommendations have identified the ways that intelligence tests function and can be used for deaf people. Encouraging results have been reported on the technical properties of the UNIT when administered to deaf people (Maller, 2000; Maller & French, 2004). Braden (2003) provides professional recommendations on WAIS-III test accommodations (via ASL) for deaf examinees. Further research is needed regarding the psychometric properties of the ASL version of the WAIS-III, as well as other newer tests such as the WISC-IV. The WISC-IV manual completely ignored deaf and hard of hearing examinees, and thus practitioners are strongly discouraged from using it with deaf people.

Practitioners may need to administer an intelligence test when a deaf or hard of hearing person is suspected of having special needs, as opposed to testing all deaf and hard of hearing people in need of services with no suspected special cognitive needs, which is what happens at present. Practitioners are encouraged to seek training in psychometrics and read published research to become informed consumers of tests.

Furthermore, test publishers are urged to recognize that psychometric evidence is needed when they recommend their tests to be used with deaf or hard of hearing individuals, or when they realize that it is common practice to use their test to assess deaf or hard of hearing individuals.

Finally, practitioners, test publishers, and researchers interested in the deaf and hard of hearing population all must be concerned with potential unintended social consequences of intelligence test scores, as described at the outset of this chapter. When a test lacks the necessary evidence, as per the *Standards,* that it measures what it claims to measure, it is not recommended for use, regardless of how much it may *seem* to measure *something*.

REFERENCES

American Educational Research Association (AERA), American Psychological Association (APA), & National Council on Measurement in Education (NCME). (1999). *Standards for educational and psychological testing.* Washington, DC: AERA.

Anderson, R. J., & Sisco, F. H. (1977). *Standardization of the WISC-R Performance Scale for deaf children* (Office of Demographic Studies Publication Series T, No. 1). Washington, DC: Gallaudet College.

Binet, A., & Simon, T. (1905). Méthodes nouvelles pour le diagnostic du niveau intellectual des anormaux. *L'Année Psychologique, 11,* 191–244.

Birch, A., Stuckless, E. R., & Birch, J. W. (1963). An eleven year study of predicting school achievement in young deaf children. *American Annals of the Deaf, 103,* 236–240.

Bollen, K. A. (1989). *Structural equation modeling with latent variables.* New York: Wiley.

Bracken, B. A., & Barona, A. (1991). State of the art procedures for translating, validating and using psychoeducational tests in cross-cultural assessment. *School Psychology International, 12,* 119–132.

Bracken, B., & McCallum, S. (1998). *Universal Nonverbal Intelligence Test.* Chicago: Riverside Publishing.

Braden, J. P. (1984). The factorial similarity of the WISC-R performance scale in deaf and hearing children. *Journal of Personality and Individual Differences, 5,* 405–409.

Braden, J. P. (1985). WISC-R deaf norms reconsidered. *Journal of School Psychology, 23,* 375–382.

Braden, J. P. (1989). The criterion-related validity of the WISC-R Performance Scale and other nonverbal IQ tests for deaf children. *American Annals for the Deaf, 134,* 329–332.

Braden, J. P. (1994). *Deafness, deprivation, and IQ.* New York: Plenum Press.

Braden, J. P. (2003). Accommodating clients with disabilities on the WAIS-III and WMS. In D. Tulsky (Ed.), *Clinical interpretations of the WAIS-III and WMS-III* (pp. 451–486). San Diego: Academic Press.

Braken, B., & McCallum, S. (1998). *Universal Nonverbal Intelligence Test.* Chicago: Riverside Publishing.

Brown, L., Sherbenou, R. J., & Johnson, S. K. (1990). *Test of Nonverbal Intelligence (2nd ed.): Examiner's manual.* Austin, TX: Pro-Ed.

Byrne, B. M. (1998). *Structural equation modeling with LISREL, PRELIS, and SIMPLIS: Basic concepts, applications, and programming.* Mahwah: Lawrence Erlbaum.

Camilli, G., & Shepard, L. A. (1994). *Methods for identifying biased test items.* Thousand Oaks, CA: Sage.

Ceci, S. J. (1996). *On intelligence.* Cambridge, MA: Harvard University Press.

Drossman, E. R., & Maller, S. J. (2000). [Review of Comprehensive Test of Nonverbal Intelligence]. *Journal of Psychoeducational Assessment, 18,* 293–301.

Du Toit, J. M. (1954). Measuring intelligence of deaf children. *American Annals of the Deaf, 99,* 237–251.

Feuerstein, R. (1980). *Instrumental enrichment: An intervention program for cognitive modifiability.* Baltimore, MD: University Park.

Gardner, H. (1993). *Frames of mind.* New York: Basic Books.

Geisinger, K. F. (1994). Psychometric issues in testing students with disabilities. *Applied Measurement in Education, 7,* 121–140.

Gibbins, S. (1989). The provision of school psychological assessment services for the hearing impaired: A national survey. *Volta Review, 91,* 95–103.

Glutting, J. J., McGrath, E. A., Kamphaus, R. W., & McDermott, P. A. (1992). Taxonomy and validity of subtest profiles on the Kaufman Assessment Battery for Children. *Journal of Special Education, 26,* 85–115.

Goetzinger, C. P., & Rousey, C. L. (1957). A study of the Wechsler Performance Scale (Form II) and the Know Cube Test with deaf adolescents. *American Annals of the Deaf, 102,* 388–398.

Gordon, R. P., Stump, K., & Glaser, B. A. (1996). Assessment of individuals with hearing impairments: Equity in testing procedures and accommodations. *Measurement and Evaluation in Counseling and Development, 29,* 111–118.

Gorsuch, R. L. (1983). *Factor analysis.* Hillsdale, NJ: Lawrence Erlbaum.

Hammill, D. D., Pearson, N. A., & Wiederholt, J. L. (1997). *Comprehensive Test of Nonverbal Intelligence.* Austin, TX: PRO-ED.

Hiskey, M. S. (1966). *The Hisky-Nebraska Test of Learning Aptitude Manual.* Lincoln, NE: Author.

Holland, P. W., & Thayer, D. T. (1988). Differential item performance and the Mantel-Haentzel procedure. In H. Wainer & H. I. Braun (Eds.), *Test validity* (pp. 129–145). Hillsdale, NJ: Lawrence Erlbaum.

Holland, P. W., & Wainer, H. (1993). *Differential item functioning.* Hillsdale, NJ: Lawrence Erlbaum.

Holt, J. A., Traxler, C. B., & Allen, T. E. (1992). *Interpreting the scores: A user's guide to the 8th edition of the Stanford Achievement Test for educators of deaf and hard of hearing students.* Washington, DC: Center for Demographic Studies, Gallaudet University.

Horn, J. L., & Cattell, R. B. (1966). Refinement and test of the theory of fluid and crystallized general intelligence. *Journal of Educational Psychology, 57,* 253–270.

Jastak, S., & Wilkinson, G. S. (1984). *Wide Range Achievement Test-Revised administration manual.* Wilmington, DE: Jastak Associates.

Kamphaus, R. W., Petoskey, M. D., & Walters Morgan, A. (1997). A history of intelligence test interpretation. In D. P. Flanagan, J. L. Genshaft, & P. L. Harrison (Eds.), *Beyond traditional intellectual assessment: Contemporary and emerging theories, tests, and issues* (pp. 32–47). New York: Guilford Press.

Kaufman, A. S., & Kaufman, N. (1983). *Kaufman Assessment Battery for Children.* Circle Pines, MN: American Guidance Service.

Kaufman, A. S. (1994). *Intelligent testing with the WISC-III.* New York: Wiley.

Konold, T. R., Glutting, J. J., McDermott, R. A., Kush, J. C., & Watkins, M. M. (1999). Structure and Diagnostic Benefits of a Normative Subtest Taxonomy Developed from the WISC-III Standardization Sample. *Journal of School Psychology, 37,* 29–48.

Kostrubala, C. E., & Braden, J. P. (1998). *The American Sign Language translation of the WAIS-III.* San Antonio, TX: The Psychological Corporation.

Lavos, G. (1962). WISC psychometric patterns among deaf children. *Volta Review, 64,* 547–552.

Mackinson, J. A., Leigh, I. W., Blennerhassett, L., & Anthony, S. (1997). Validity of the TONI-2 with deaf and hard of hearing children. *American Annals of the Deaf, 142,* 294–299.

Maller, S. J. (1991, August). *Cognitive assessment of deaf children: Current issues and future trends.* Paper presented at the annual meeting of the American Psychological Association, San Francisco.

Maller, S. J. (1994). *Validity and item bias of the WISC-III with deaf children.* Unpublished doctoral dissertation, University of Arizona, Tucson, AZ.

Maller, S. J. (1996). WISC-III Verbal item invariance across samples of deaf and hearing children of similar measured ability. *Journal of Psychoeducational Assessment, 14,* 152–165.

Maller, S. J. (1997). Deafness and WISC-III item difficulty: Invariance and fit. *Journal of School Psychology, 35,* 299–314.

Maller, S. J. (1999, April). *The validity of WISC-III subtest analysis for deaf children.* Paper presented at the annual meeting of the American Educational Research Association, Montreal.

Maller, S. J. (2000). Item invariance in four subtests of the Universal Nonverbal Intelligence Test across groups of deaf and hearing children. *Journal of Psychoeducational Assessment, 18,* 240–254.

Maller, S. J. (2001). Differential item functioning in the WISC-III: Item parameters for boys and girls in the national standardization sample. *Educational and Psychological Measurement, 61,* 793–817.

Maller, S. J. (2003). Intellectual assessment of deaf people: A critical review of core concepts and issues. In M. Marschark & P. Spencer (Eds.), *Handbook of deaf studies, language, and education* (pp. 451–463). New York: Oxford University Press.

Maller, S. J., & Braden, J. P. (1993). The criterion validity of the WISC-III with deaf adolescents. *Journal of Psychoeducational Assessment Monograph Series Advances in Psychoeducational Assessment: Wechsler Intelligence Scale for Children: Third Edition* (pp. 105–113).

Maller, S. J., & Ferron, J. (1997). WICS-III factor invariance across deaf and standardization samples. *Educational and Psychological Measurement, 7,* 987–994.

Maller, S. J., & French B. F. (2004). Universal Nonverbal Intelligence Test factor invariance across deaf and standardization samples. *Educational and Psychological Measurement, 64,* 647–660.

Maller, S. J., & McDermott, P. A. (1997). WAIS-R profile analysis for college students with learning disabilities. *School Psychology Review, 26,* 575–585.

Meredith, W. (1993). Measurement invariance, factor analysis, and factorial invariance. *Psychometrika, 58,* 525–543.

Messick, S. (1989). Validity. In R. Linn (Ed.), *Educational measurement* (3rd ed., pp. 13–103). New York: American Council on Education: Macmillan.

McDermott, P. A., Fantuzzo, J. W., & Glutting, J. J. (1990). Just say no to subtest analysis: A critique on Wechsler theory and practice. *Journal of Psychoeducational Assessment, 8,* 290–302.

Miller, M. S. (1984). Experimental use of signed presentations of the verbal scale of the WISC-R with profoundly deaf children: A preliminary report of the sign selection process and experimental test procedures. In D. S. Martin (Ed.), *International symposium on cognition, educational and deafness, working papers, Vol. 1* (pp. 167–185). Washington, DC: Gallaudet University.

Moores, D. F. (1982). *Educating the deaf* (2nd ed.). Boston: Houghton Mifflin.

Myklebust, H. R. (1964). *The psychology of deafness: Sensory deprivation, learning, and adjustment* (2nd ed.). New York: Grune & Stratton.

Nunnally, J. C., & Bernstein, I. H. (1994). *Psychometric Theory* (3rd ed.). New York: McGraw-Hill.

Phelps, L., & Branyan, B. J. (1988). Correlations among the Hiskey, K-ABC Nonverbal scale, Leiter, and WISC-R Performance scale with public-school deaf children. *Journal of Psychoeducational Assessment, 6,* 354–358.

Phelps, L., & Branyan, B. J. (1990). Academic achievement and nonverbal intelligence in public school hearing-impaired children. *Psychology in the Schools, 27,* 210–217.

Pinter, R. (1924). Results obtained with the Non-Language Group Test. *Journal of Educational Psychology, 15,* 473–483.

Pinter, R., Eisenson, J., & Stanton, M. (1946). *The psychology of the physically handicapped.* New York: Grune.

Pinter, R., & Paterson, D. G. (1915). The Binet Scale and the deaf child. *Journal of Educational Psychology, 6,* 201–210.

Porter, L. J., & Kirby, E. A. (1986). Effects of two instructional sets on the validity of the Kaufman Assessment Battery for Children Nonverbal Scale with a group of severely hearing impaired children. *Psychology in the Schools, 23,* 37–43.

Ray, S. (1979). Adapting the WISC-R for deaf children. *Diagnostique, 7,* 147–157.

Ray, S., & Ulissi, S. M. (1982). *An adaptation of the WPPSI for deaf children.* Northridge, CA: Steven Ray Publications.

Reynolds, C. R. (1982). The problem of bias in psychological assessment. In C. R. Reynolds & T. B. Gutkin (Eds.), *The handbook of school psychology* (pp. 178–208). New York: John Wiley.

Rosenstein, J. (1961). Perception, cognition, and language in deaf children. *Exceptional Children, 27,* 276–284.

Roid, G. H., & Miller, L. J. (1997). *Leiter International Performance Scale-Revised.* Wood Dale, IL: Stoelting.

Rosnowski, M., & Reith, J. (1999). Examining the measurement quality of tests containing differentially functioning items: Do biased items result in poor measurement. *Educational and Psychological Measurement, 59,* 248–269.

Sattler, J. M. (2001). *Assessment of children* (4th ed.). San Diego: Jerome M. Sattler Publishers.

Sireci, S. G., Bastari, B., & Allalouf, A. (1998, August). *Evaluating construct equivalence across adapted tests.* Paper presented at the annual meeting of the American Psychological Association, San Francisco, CA.

Stinnett, T. A., Havey, J. M., & Oehler-Stinnett, J. (1994). Current test usage by practicing psychologists: A national survey. *Journal of Psychoeducational Assessment, 12,* 331–350.

Sullivan, P. M., & Burley, S. K. (1990). Mental testing of the hearing impaired child. In C. R. Reynolds & R. W. Kamphaus (Eds.), *Handbook of psychological and educational assessment of children* (pp. 761–788). New York: Guilford.

Sullivan, P. M., & Montoya, L. A. (1997). Factor analysis of the WISC-III with deaf and hard of hearing children. *Psychological Assessment, 9,* 317–322.

Sullivan, P. M., & Schulte, L. E. (1992). Factor analysis of WISC-R with deaf and hard-of-hearing children. *Psychological Assessment, 4,* 537–540.

Sullivan, P. M., & Vernon, M. (1979). Psychological assessment of hearing impaired children. *School Psychology Digest, 8,* 271–290.

Thurlow, M. L., Ysseldyke, J. E., & Silverstein, B. (1995). Testing accommodations for students with disabilities. *Remedial and Special Education, 16,* 260–270.

Vernon, M. (1976). Psychological evaluation of hearing impaired children. In L. Lloyd (Ed.), *Communication assessment and intervention strategies.* Baltimore, MD: University Park Press.

Vernon, M., & Brown, D. W. (1964). A guide to psychological tests and testing procedures in the evaluation of deaf and hard-of-hearing children. *Journal of Speech and Hearing Disorders, 29,* 414–423.

Vonderhaar, W. F., & Chambers, J. F. (1975). An examination of deaf students' Wechsler Performance subtest scores. *American Annals of the Deaf, 120,* 540–543.

Wechsler, D. (1944). *Measurement of adult intelligence* (3rd ed.). Baltimore, MD: Waverly Press.

Wechsler, D. (1974). *The Wechsler Intelligence Scale for Children—Revised.* New York: The Psychological Corporation.
Wechsler, D. (1991). *The Wechsler Intelligence Scale for Children—Third Edition.* New York: The Psychological Corporation.
Wechsler, D. (1997). *The Wechsler Adult Intelligence Scale—Third Edition.* San Antonio, TX: The Psychological Corporation.
Wechsler, D. (2003). *The Wechsler Intelligence Scale for Children—Fourth Edition.* San Antonio, TX: Harcourt.
Wechsler, D. (2003). *WISC-IV technical and interpretative manual.* San Antonio, TX: Harcourt.
Wilhoit, B. E., & McCallum, R. S. (2002). Profile analysis of the Universal Nonverbal Intelligence Test standardization sample. *School Psychology Review, 31,* 263–281.
Wolf, T. H. (1973). *Alfred Binet.* Chicago: University of Chicago Press.

Section III   *Administrative Issues*

Equity in Testing Deaf and Hard of Hearing Individuals—Legal Considerations

Rosaline Hayes Crawford

A spectrum of laws supports individuals with disabilities and protects them from discrimination based on their disability. The three primary federal laws that affect individuals with disabilities are the Individuals With Disabilities Education Act (IDEA), Section 504 of the Rehabilitation Act of 1973 (Section 504), and the Americans With Disabilities Act of 1990 (ADA).[1] The thrust and impetus of these laws is inclusion: providing individuals with disabilities the opportunity to participate in the mainstream of American life, throughout education and into the workplace, allowing them to be independent and productive members of society to the best of their *abilities*.

Although these laws apply to individuals with disabilities generally, this discussion focuses on individuals who are deaf or hard of hearing—individuals who are substantially limited in the major life activity of hearing. Benefits to be gained from early and higher education are presumed, and it is assumed that the ultimate goal following childhood into adulthood is independence and self-sufficiency through gainful employment whenever possible. Each of these life stages may be impacted by the presence of a disability. More importantly, the impact on an early stage of life, such as infant language acquisition and communication, may be presumed to impact later stages, such as formal education and other opportunities.

This chapter begins with a discussion of recent legislation enacted to promote early identification and intervention for deaf or hard of hearing infants. This section also discusses the need to identify children with multiple disabilities, such as deaf or hard of hearing children who have learning disabilities, the provision of special education and related services, and the requirement for modifications in early education testing. Those individuals who are identified early as having a disability or disabilities are more likely to have diagnostic evaluations and receive special education services. These evaluations and services may help guide the provision of modifications and auxiliary aids and services (accommodations) in the context of high-stakes testing leading to postsecondary education, certification, professional licensure, and employment.

The next section presents an overview of Section 504 and the ADA, laws that prohibit disability discrimination in contexts beyond early education. A detailed description of who is protected by these laws is provided, with the suggestion that, as a result of a hearing loss, an individual may also be restricted or limited in speaking, learning, reading, writing, or other major life activities. The last section reviews the ADA regulations that specifically address testing related to employment, postsecondary education, certification, and professional licensing, as well as the challenges faced by testing entities and deaf or hard of hearing test-takers.

EARLY IDENTIFICATION AND INTERVENTION

With the passage of Title VII of the Children's Health Act of 2000, and the establishment of early hearing detection and intervention programs, it is expected that children with hearing impairments will be identified very early and receive intervention services shortly after birth, well before they reach school age.[2] Title VII established the following national goals:

1. hearing screenings for all babies born in hospitals before leaving the birthing facility;
2. hearing screenings for all babies not born in hospitals within the first three months of life;
3. appropriate evaluations by three months for all newborns and infants suspected of having hearing loss to allow appropriate referral and provisions for audiologic rehabilitation as well as medical and early intervention before the age of six months;
4. linkage to statewide systems of intervention and rehabilitative services for newborns and infants with hearing loss; and
5. public policy based on applied research and the *recognition that newborns, infants, toddlers, and children who are deaf or hard of hearing have unique language, learning, and communication needs.*[3]

Title VII has helped to establish the newborn and infant hearing screening, evaluation, and intervention systems and programs that exist now in a majority of states and the District of Columbia. Federal agencies, including the Centers for Disease Control and Prevention (CDC) Early Hearing Detection and Intervention (EHDI) program, coordinate and collaborate with states and the private sector to develop and monitor state EHDI programs. They provide technical assistance and data management that can be used for applied research, program evaluation, and policy development.

It is expected that state EHDI programs will identify newborns and infants with hearing loss and link them to state programs developed under the IDEA. The purpose of the IDEA is "to ensure that all children with disabilities have available to them a free appropriate public education that emphasizes special education and related services designed to meet their unique needs and prepare them for employment and independent living."[4]

Part C of the IDEA specifically addresses early intervention services and individualized family service plans (IFSPs) for infants and toddlers (under three years of age) with disabilities.[5] Infants and toddlers with disabilities are described as those who are experiencing developmental delays or who have a diagnosed physical or mental condition which has a high probability of resulting in developmental delay. Early intervention is critical for deaf and hard of hearing infants and toddlers who have unique language, communication, and learning needs. Limited access to language and communication in the environment also limits incidental learning opportunities. These early needs may be met when these children have an accessible visual language, communication, and learning environment—where the primary mode of communication is American Sign Language (ASL). Other intervention strategies, such as hearing aids, cochlear implants, and auditory and speech therapy, can be and often are employed. However, even with early detection and intervention, delayed and/or limited access to language in the environment can have a lifelong impact on a deaf or hard of hearing child's ability to acquire, learn, and use that language. Oral languages have a sound-based phonological structure generally represented or symbolized in print. Developing literacy skills is especially challenging for a deaf or hard of hearing child who has limited access to the target language in its spoken form; often, the child must find alternate means for deciphering and internalizing the phonological code for that language. There are many strategies used by educators and deaf and hard of hearing children to achieve the literacy skills necessary for education, independence, employment, and professional practice.[6]

The key to literacy starts with early detection and intervention and is fostered through special education and related services provided under Part B of the IDEA.[7] Under Part B, a "child with a disability" is defined as one who by reason of hearing, speech, language, visual, or orthopedic impairments, or because of mental retardation, autism, traumatic brain injury, serious emotional disturbance, other health impairments, or specific learning disabilities, needs special education and related services.[8] "Special education" is instruction specially designed to meet the unique needs of a child with a disability.[9] "Related services" include "developmental, corrective, and other supportive services . . . as may be required to assist a child with a disability to benefit from special education, and includes the early identification and assessment of disabling conditions in children."[10] Special education and related services form the basis of a "free appropriate public education," are provided by the state, meet the standards of the state education agency, include an appropriate education in that state, and conform with the required individualized education program (IEP).[11]

The definitions under the regulations implementing the IDEA have an interesting twist. A "handicapped person" is defined as one who "has a physical or mental impairment which *substantially limits* one or more major life activities."[12] For purposes of public education services, a handicapped person is "qualified" if he or she is of regular school age, or of an age mandated by state law, or to whom a state is required to provide a free appropriate public education.[13] Notwithstanding these definitions, a public elementary and secondary education program must provide a "free appropriate public education to each qualified handicapped person who is in [its] jurisdiction, *regardless of the nature or severity of the person's handicap.*"[14]

It appears that, under the IDEA and the implementing regulations, the touchstone for the child is the presence of a physical or mental impairment that impacts the provision of education services such that the child needs specially designed instruction and/or support services, as required, to benefit from instruction. It appears that the measure of the impact on the child's education determines the child's need for special education and related services.[15] State educational agencies have been tasked with the responsibility to conduct a "full and individual initial evaluation," with parental consent, of a child suspected of having a disability to determine whether the child has a disability and to determine the educational needs of that child.[16]

Under the IDEA, the term "specific learning disability" is defined as "a disorder in one or more of the basic psychological processes involved in understanding or in using language, spoken or written, which disorder may manifest itself in imperfect ability to listen, think, speak, read, write, spell, or do mathematical calculations."[17] Under this definition, all children with hearing loss manifest specific learning disabilities. However, the term "disorder" is further defined to include conditions such as "perceptual disabilities," but not learning problems that are "primarily the result of visual, hearing, or motor disabilities, of mental retardation, of emotional disturbance, or of environmental, cultural, or economic disadvantage."[18] This definition suggests that children with hearing disabilities have *learning problems,* therefore, the need for special education services. But the need to identify children with hearing disabilities who also have *learning disabilities,* which may require other or different special education or support services, seems to be precluded by the definition itself.

According to the National Center for Education Statistics, more than 2,789,000 children with learning disabilities now receive services in federally supported elementary and secondary education programs, representing 46% of all such children with disabilities and nearly 6% of all children enrolled.[19] Based on these figures, an estimated 6% of children with hearing loss are likely also to have specific learning disabilities that are *not* primarily the result of their hearing loss. The effects of delayed and/or limited access to a spoken language due to a hearing loss, particularly when the environment does not provide a fully accessible alternative first language, such as ASL, may result in language deprivation contributing to difficulties in literacy skill development and learning problems. Language deprivation is not only devastating in and of itself but may further exacerbate an existing learning disability. Deaf or hard of hearing children who have specific learning disabilities must be identified and their needs appropriately addressed. Early identification of children with multiple disabilities is critical to the provision of appropriate education and support services and the development of literacy skills necessary for education, independence, employment, and professional practice.

In accordance with the IDEA, the educational needs of the child are identified and made part of that child's IEP. The child's IEP is developed by an "IEP team," which includes the child's parents, regular and/or special education teachers, a representative of the public agency, an individual who is able to interpret the instructional implications of evaluation results, other persons as requested by the parent or agency, and, if appropriate, the child.[20] The IEP must include the child's present levels of educational performance, annual goals, and short-term objectives; special education, related services, supplementary aids and services, and program modifications that will be provided to the child; and transition services beginning at the age of 14.[21] The IEP must also include a statement of the modifications, if any, to be made in the administration of state- or districtwide assessments (testing) of student achievement.[22] As will be discussed further below, these modifications are considered when evaluating future requests for accommodations in the context of testing or assessment.

Public attention has been drawn to student assessment and testing by the passage of the No Child Left Behind Act of 2001 (NCLB).[23] NCLB mandates school accountability by requiring states to implement challenging standards for proficiency in reading, math, and science.[24] The purpose of NCLB is "to ensure that all children have a fair, equal, and significant opportunity to obtain a high-quality education and reach, at a minimum, proficiency on challenging State academic achievement standards and state academic assessments."[25] Each state is responsible for developing standardized tests, built upon approved research-based instruction, to assess students' progress towards the NCLB standards.[26] NCLB does not require states to consider the needs of special education students or universal design elements in the development of these standardized tests. Further, under NCLB, alternative assessments for children with special needs are expected to be very limited. Unfortunately, the interface between NCLB and IDEA is, as yet, unclear. It is expected, however, that modifications for testing identified in a child's IEP will be applied to state assessments made under NCLB.

A deaf or hard of hearing high school graduate may have some understanding about testing, assessments, and the accommodations that he or she needs to have an equal opportunity to demonstrate his or her competency and proficiency. Unfortunately and for many reasons, many deaf or hard of hearing students do not. This understanding, generally, is also limited because of deaf and hard of hearing peoples' insufficient exposure to the testing that leads to postsecondary education, certification, or professional licensing. Further assessment of deaf or hard of hearing test-takers, forms of testing, and alternative assessments may be necessary to determine appropriate accommodations. In other words, modifications made for early education testing may or may not be appropriate for other forms of testing leading to postsecondary education, certification, or professional licensing.

It is important to understand that Section 504 and/or the ADA, not the IDEA, apply to postsecondary education, employment, certification, and professional licensing entities. Discussion of Section 504 and the ADA, next, begins with a brief overview of these laws and a more detailed description of who is protected by these laws. Specific provisions in the ADA related to examinations are then explored with respect to deaf and hard of hearing test-takers.

SECTION 504 AND THE ADA

Section 504 prohibits discrimination on the basis of disability in federal and federally funded programs and activities, which includes virtually all state and local government operations, public and private colleges and universities, and many private entities.[27]

The ADA was enacted "to provide a clear and comprehensive national mandate for the elimination of discrimination against individuals with disabilities" along with clear, strong, and consistent standards enforceable by the federal government through the invocation of congressional authority.[28] The ADA specifically incorporates the standards established under Section 504.[29] Notwithstanding the laudability of the effort to provide consistency, the ADA is divided into titles and sections according to a variety of contexts and applications. Delegation of authority to various agencies to promulgate regulations has resulted in some regulatory and interpretive inconsistencies between agencies and among the courts.

Title I of the ADA prohibits discrimination because of disability in the context of employment and applies, generally, to employers who have 15 or more employees.[30] The major exceptions to this provision are the United States and state governments.[31] Under this title, a "qualified individual with a disability" is one who, "with or without reasonable accommodation, can perform the essential functions of the employment position that such individual holds or desires."[32]

Title II of the ADA prohibits discrimination by reason of disability from participating in or receiving the benefits of the services, programs, or activities of a public entity, which includes state and local governments.[33] Under Title II, a "qualified individual with a disability" is one who "with or without reasonable modifications . . . or the provision of auxiliary aids and services, meets the essential eligibility requirements for the receipt of services or the participation in programs or activities provided by a public entity."[34]

Title III of the ADA prohibits discrimination on the basis of disability "in the full and equal enjoyment . . . of any place of public accommodation" defined as private entities whose operations affect commerce, including places of education.[35] For purposes of Title III, covered entities are prohibited from imposing or applying eligibility criteria that screen out or tend to screen out individuals with disabilities, unless the criteria can be shown to be necessary.[36] Covered entities are also required to make reasonable modifications and provide auxiliary aids and services to individuals with disabilities, unless such would result in a fundamental alteration or, in the case of auxiliary aids and services, such would result in an undue burden.[37]

DISABILITY DEFINED

At the most basic level, the scope of the class of individuals covered under Section 504 and the ADA is different than the one prescribed for special education services under the IDEA.[38] The term "disability" is similarly defined under Section 504 and the ADA as follows:[39]

> . . . with respect to an individual
> (A) a physical or mental impairment that substantially limits one or more of the major life activities of such individual;
> (B) a record of such an impairment; or
> (C) being regarded as having such an impairment.[40]

The focus of this discussion is on individuals who have an "actual" disability, as described under subsection (A), rather than having a "record of" or being "regarded as" having a disability. Understanding the definition of "disability" is important because it defines who is protected under the ADA. The name or diagnosis of the physical or mental impairment is not enough to be considered an "actual" disability if the impact of that impairment on one or more major life activities is variable among people with that impairment.[41] Identifying oneself as deaf, hard of hearing, or hearing impaired is not enough. The law requires the determination of the existence of a disability on a case-by-case individual basis.[42] The "physical or mental impairment" must "substantially limit" at least one "major life activity."

For deaf or hard of hearing people, the physical or mental impairment is a "hearing impairment," described in terms such as a "conductive" or "sensorineural" hearing loss, affecting one or both ears. However, other physical or mental impairments may also exist in a single individual and impact learning, reading, writing, or other major life activities, beyond the impact of the hearing loss on those other major life activities.

The term "major life activities" is defined as "functions such as caring for oneself, performing manual tasks, walking, seeing, hearing, speaking, breathing, learning, and working."[43] By its terms, the list of major life activities is illustrative rather than exhaustive. In a recent case, the Supreme Court stated that major life activities "refers to those activities that are of central importance to daily life" or "to most people's daily lives."[44] The Equal Employment Opportunity Commission (EEOC) Interpretive Guidance suggests that major life activities are "those basic activities that the average person in the general population can perform with little or no difficulty."[45] *A hearing loss may impact more than the major life activity of hearing.* As discussed earlier, a hearing loss, especially one that is present at or near birth, can impact an individual's ability to acquire, learn, and use an oral language. As such, and as a result of a hearing loss, an individual may be restricted or limited in speaking, learning, reading, writing, and other activities that are of central importance to most people's daily lives.[46]

The term "substantially limits" is not defined in the ADA. U.S. Department of Justice (DOJ) guidelines for Titles II and III of the ADA provide that, to be considered a substantial limitation, the "individual's important life activities are restricted as to the conditions, manner, or duration under which they can be performed in comparison to most people."[47] The regulations promulgated by the EEOC under Title I define "substantially limits" to mean "(i) Unable to perform . . . or (ii) Significantly restricted as to the condition, manner or duration under which an individual can perform a particular major life activity as compared to . . . the average person in the general population . . . ."[48] The Supreme Court has concluded that the word "substantial" "clearly precludes impairments that interfere in only a minor way with the performance of [a major life activity] from qualifying as disabilities."[49] The fact that the "condition, manner or duration under which an individual can perform a particular major life activity" is *different* than "the average person in the general population" is also not determinative.[50] The ADA requires individuals claiming protection "to prove a disability by offering evidence that the extent of the limitation in terms of their own experience . . . is substantial."[51] Furthermore, in 1999, the Supreme Court also concluded that, "if a person is taking measures to correct for, or mitigate, a physical or mental impairment, the effects of those measures—both positive and negative—must be taken into account when judging whether that person is 'substantially limited' in a major life activity and thus 'disabled' under the Act."[52] The Court went on to say that the determination of disability "depends on whether the limitations an individual with an impairment *actually* faces are in fact substantially limiting."[53]

Following the Supreme Court's 1999 decisions, the degree of scrutiny involved in the determination of whether an individual has a disability has increased. More frequently, it seems that an individual who undertakes mitigating measures may not have an "actual" disability.[54] Questions have also arisen concerning which mitigating measures to consider and their relevancy to the major life activity alleged to be limited.[55] For example, speechreading (also called lipreading) may mitigate the impact of a hearing loss on the major life activity of communicating, to some degree in some circumstances, but it has no impact on hearing. Today, an individual with a hearing loss who uses hearing aids or other personal devices and who has virtually normal hearing in a wide range of contexts and environments may not be considered as having a disability covered by the protections of Section 504 and the ADA. However, an individual with a hearing loss, even if he or she uses hearing aids or other personal devices, may be substantially limited in the major life activity of hearing as evidenced by an audiogram, speech discrimination test results, and personal experience.

The case of *Bartlett v. New York State Board of Law Examiners* is an interesting case involving dyslexia, a mental impairment, decided after the Supreme Court's 1999 decisions.[56] Despite her limitation and with accommodations, Bartlett had earned a Ph.D. and a law degree. She requested and was denied accommodations for the New York bar examination. She took and failed the bar examination four times, after which she filed suit under the ADA and Section 504. The New York State Board's expert on learning disabilities did not believe that Bartlett had dyslexia or a reading disability, primarily because of Bartlett's performance on two subtests. Just before she took the bar examination for the fifth time, the parties agreed that she would receive *some* of the accommodations she sought; but despite these accommodations she failed again.

The Court of Appeals noted that "a reading disability is not quantifiable merely in test scores. . . . [D]iagnosing a learning disability requires clinical judgment . . . [and] as much as the Board would like to find an easy test discriminator for a reading disability in its applicants, such a test does not exist."[57] The Court of Appeals noted that "[it] is not enough that Bartlett has average skills on 'some' measures if her skills are below average on other measures to an extent that her ability to read is substantially limited."[58] The Court of Appeals remanded the case to the district court to determine whether the condition, manner, or duration of Bartlett's reading amounts to a substantial limit rather than only a mere difference in her reading in comparison to most people.[59]

The Court of Appeals also analyzed whether Bartlett was substantially limited in the major life activity of working. Although the Board argued that Bartlett's impairment excludes her from only one type of job (practicing attorney), the Court of Appeals stated that "exclusion from the practice of law is a significant restriction relative to the class of jobs utilizing a law degree."[60] The Court of Appeals remanded the case to the district court to determine whether Bartlett's "inability to practice law results from her reading impairment, rather than from other factors [such as her education, experience, or innate ability] that might prevent her from passing the bar."[61] The Court of Appeals noted that "Bartlett need not prove that she would have passed the bar examination 'but for' the denial of accommodations . . . [but] may be able to show that the denial of accommodations was a substantial factor preventing her from passing the exam."[62]

Bartlett's struggle to demonstrate the impact of her impairment on the major life activities of reading and working may provide guidance for deaf or hard of hearing test-takers.

For purposes of the discussion that follows, it is assumed that the test-taker has a hearing impairment that substantially limits the major life activity of hearing, taking into account the effect of those measures the individual takes to correct for or mitigate the hearing impairment. Such an individual has a disability as defined under Section 504 and the ADA. In addition, that individual may be able to show the impact that his or her hearing impairment, especially one that is present at or near birth, has on that individual's ability to acquire, learn, and use an oral language, and on that individual's ability to read, write, or work. Such a showing may be necessary in the context of certification and professional licensing testing.

ADA REQUIREMENTS FOR TESTING

Public policy mandates the inclusion of individuals with disabilities, as independent and productive members of society to the best of their *abilities,* in all facets of American life. This public policy is articulated in the preamble to the ADA and in other federal and state laws. Professionals with disabilities are also role models to us and to our children, with or without disabilities. They possess unique experiences, knowledge, and perspectives that can enhance professions that educate, serve, and/or lead others. For example, a vocational rehabilitation counselor who is deaf or hard of hearing, who understands the challenges faced by a deaf or hard of hearing client who is seeking employment, may be better prepared and able to assist those clients.

In addition to the mandate for inclusion of individuals with disabilities, certification and professional licensing entities have obligations to legislative and regulatory bodies, professional organizations, and to the public. Those obligations can be met with respect to individuals with disabilities who are otherwise qualified for certification and professional licensing testing. Certification and professional licensing entities need to ensure that the selection and administration of an examination accurately reflects what the examination purports to measure, generally, and specifically with respect to the individual test-taker who has a disability.

The regulations for Title I of the ADA, which prohibit disability discrimination in employment, specify nondiscriminatory administration of tests:

It is unlawful . . . to fail to *select and administer tests* concerning employment in the most effective manner *to ensure that,* when a test is administered to a job applicant or employee who has a disability that impairs sensory, manual or speaking skills, *the test results accu-*

rately reflect the skills, aptitude, or whatever other factor of the applicant or employee that the test purports to measure, rather than reflecting the impaired sensory, manual or speaking skills of such employee or applicant (except where such skills are the factors that the test purports to measure).[63]

In the context of testing, Section 309 of Title III of the ADA, specifically and further prescribes the following:

Any person that offers examinations or courses related to applications, licensing, certification, or credentialing for secondary or post-secondary education, professional, or trade purposes shall offer such examinations or courses in a place and manner accessible to persons with disabilities or offer alternative accessible arrangements for such individuals.[64]

The regulations state that testing entities must ensure that the "examination is selected and administered so as to best ensure that . . . the examination results accurately reflect the individual's aptitude or achievement level or whatever other factor the examination purports to measure. . . ."[65] This provision mirrors the regulatory language for employment testing ("to select and administer tests . . . to ensure that . . . the test results accurately reflect the skills, aptitude, or whatever other factor . . . the test purports to measure").[66]

Whether it is postsecondary education, employment, certification, or professional licensing, the testing entity should identify the aptitude, achievement level, or other factor that the examination purports to measure. Once the factors to be measured are identified, the testing entity must select and administer tests in an accessible manner that accurately reflects those factors. The regulations specifically prescribe that "[r]equired modifications to an examination may include changes in the length of time permitted for completion of the examination and adaptation of the manner in which the examination is given."[67] Some examinations may be designed to evaluate an individual's reading and/or writing skills. Such tests cannot be given in ASL,[68] since then the test would not be evaluating the individual's ability to read or write. However, many tests are designed to measure the individual's knowledge of the material being tested, or factors other than literacy skills. In such cases, the test can be administered in ASL and may be a better indicator of the individual's actual knowledge or skills. It is also possible to have hybrid tests, which evaluate an individual's literacy skills and other factors.

Testing entities may establish reasonable requirements for advance notice, appropriate documentation of the disability, and the modification, auxiliary aids, or services required.[69] For example, an individual with a hearing loss may obtain, at his or her own expense, an evaluation and report by an appropriate professional, such as an audiologist. Documentation of the accommodations required often appears as the recommendations of the professional who conducted the evaluation and prepared the report documenting the disability.

Evidence that the requested modification or auxiliary aids or services were provided in other testing situations may be sufficient as well as convenient for the test-taker and the testing entity. For example, the College Board provides a quick checklist of elements that are required in order for a Scholastic Aptitude Test (SAT) test-taker to be "eligible" for accommodations: (1) The student must have a disability that necessitates testing accommodations; (2) have appropriate documentation on file at school that supports the need for the requested accommodations; and (3) *receive the requested accommodations,* due to the disability, *for school-based tests.*[70, 71] As such, getting an accommodation for the SAT seems to depend on having received similar accommodations for tests administered in high school. If a student did not receive extended time on an examination in school, for example, the student would be precluded from that accommodation for the SAT. This policy seems to invite the student and the IEP team to explore and experiment with a variety of accommodations in the school setting to ensure its availability on the SAT. While consideration of earlier accommodations provided may be relevant to ascertaining what worked and what did not, especially when considering a current request, it does not appear appropriate to the determination of eligibility *per se,* or eligibility for a particular accommodation.

It should also be noted that the purpose and use of the SAT or other college admissions test-based criteria differs significantly from certification and professional licensure testing. The SAT is not a "pass/fail" college admissions test: The "less successful" SAT test-taker is not necessarily precluded from higher education.[72] On the other hand, the "unsuccessful" certification or professional licensure test-taker is precluded from practicing in that profession entirely.[73] Further, *preclusion* from professional practice occurs only after the candidate has made a significant personal investment in higher education and has successfully completed an undergraduate education program and typically at least one graduate-level education program. Certification and professional licensure testing, therefore, is high-stakes testing.

The experience of the testing entity and the test-taker make provision of some accommodations commonplace. For deaf or hard of hearing test-takers, accommodations tend to include some means for accessing the auditory/oral portion of the examination (i.e., real-time captioning or qualified sign language interpreter services). Extended time for the written portion of the examination is also fairly common, especially when extended time was provided in other testing situations. The provision of extended time for some deaf or hard of hearing test-takers recognizes the need for extra time to process written English—a language they do not hear well or do not hear at all. The experience with these accommodations may be so commonplace that they are provided to deaf or hard of hearing test-takers as a routine matter.

However, many deaf and hard of hearing test-takers have limited experience with the format of the test most frequently employed for certification and professional licensure—the multiple-choice test. As such, a request for and provision of accommodations based on the test-taker's experience with a different kind of testing situation may not be appropriate for certain certification or professional licensing testing.

Perhaps more importantly, the written language used in multiple choice tests is often presented without sufficient contextual references, clues, or redundancy; is truncated with double negatives and multiple embedded clauses; and is made more complex with answer choices that are very similar. Deciphering this written language requires virtually native language proficiency, generally possessed by individuals with full access to the oral language. When such a high level of written language proficiency is required to decipher a test element, extended time may not be an appropriate or effective modification for a deaf or hard of hearing test-taker. Extended time may not ensure that the examination accurately reflects the individual test-taker's level of professional competency. A better solution is to make the written language on multiple-choice tests more clear and thus more accessible to not only deaf and hard of hearing test-takers, but to all candidates. Additionally, providing an alternative assessment for certification and professional licensing may best ensure an accurate reflection of the individual's abilities.

Challenges arise when the modification is outside the experience of the test-taker or the testing entity. In these cases, appropriate documentation that the modification is required may become critical for the test-taker. Because the requested modification is subject to approval by the testing entity's expert(s), test-takers are advised to provide documentation prepared by comparable expert(s). Timeliness of the request may also be a factor.[74] An individual's case may be stronger if the request for a specific modification is made with the initial request for accommodations and is appropriately documented. First, denial of the requested accommodation can be challenged before the test is taken. Denial of the requested accommodation puts the test-taker in a "fail first" position; failing the test without the requested accommodation. (If the test-taker does not fail, there is no need to request the accommodation again or take the test again.) A failed test-taker may request the denied accommodation again and be in a better position, strategically, to receive the accommodation or challenge the denial further.

When testing challenges are brought to court, dueling experts take center stage, battling most frequently over whether the test-taker has a disability, with courts often deferring to the judgment of the testing entity's experts.[75] The issue of whether the modification requested is appropriate or necessary is rarely reached.[76]

CONCLUSION

Early identification and intervention, along with special education and related services for deaf or hard of hearing students, are important keys to developing language and literacy skills necessary for education, independence, employment, and professional practice. Section 504 and the ADA seek to eliminate discrimination against individuals with disabilities, including deaf or hard of hearing individuals, by mandating modifications and auxiliary aids and services to ensure an equal opportunity to participate in the mainstream of American life. The ADA specifically addresses testing related to employment, certification, and professional licensing.

Certification and professional licensing entities have obligations to legislative and regulatory bodies, professional organizations, and the public. These obligations, and the obligations under the ADA, can be met with respect to deaf and hard of hearing test-takers, by ensuring that the selection and administration of an examination accurately reflects what the examination purports to measure, generally, and specifically with respect to the individual test-taker.

A foundation of specialized data about deaf and hard of hearing test-takers, such as that presented in the other chapters of this book, is necessary to effect change in the development and administration of testing leading to certification and professional licensing. This foundation should also prove useful in the development of appropriate documentation of an individual test-taker's need for and the identification of effective modifications for high-stakes testing.

NOTES

1. 20 U.S.C. §§ 1400–1490 (as amended by Pub. L. 108–446, 118 Stat. 2647, Dec. 3, 2004); 29 U.S.C. § 794; 42 U.S.C. §§ 12101–12213.
2. Pub. L. 106-310, 114 Stat. 1101.
3. *Id.* at § 701.
4. 20 U.S.C. § 1400(d)(1)(A).
5. 20 U.S.C. §§ 1431–1445.
6. *See* "Keys to English Print," *Odyssey,* Fall 2003, Laurent Clerc National Deaf Education Center, Gallaudet University.
7. 20 U.S.C. §§ 1411–1419.
8. 20 U.S.C. § 1401(3)(A).
9. 20 U.S.C. § 1401(25).
10. 20 U.S.C. § 1401(22).
11. 20 U.S.C. § 1401(8).
12. 34 C.F.R. § 104.3(j)(1)(i) (emphasis added).
13. 34 C.F.R. § 104.3(k)(2).
14. 34 C.F.R. § 104.33(a) (emphasis added).
15. A child with a disability may not need specially designed instruction. Instead, the child may need support services to access and/or benefit from regular instruction. Such children may have an IEP under the state's special education program or a "504 plan" that provides necessary services or modifications required under Section 504 of the Rehabilitation Act of 1973.
16. 20 U.S.C. § 1414(a)(1).
17. 20 U.S.C. § 1401(26).
18. *Id.*
19. U.S. Department of Education, National Center for Education Statistics. *Digest of Education Statistics, 2000,* Table 53 at 65, NCES 2001-034, by Thomas D. Snyder and Charlene M. Hoffman. Washington, DC; 2001.
20. 20 U.S.C. § 1414(d)(1)(B).
21. 20 U.S.C. § 1414(d)(1)(A).
22. 34 C.F.R. § 300.347(a)(5)(i). Information about recognized test measurement principles and a description of the legal principles in and framework of nondiscrimination laws and constitutional considerations is provided in "The Use of Tests as Part of High-Stakes Decision-Making for Students: A Resource Guide for Educators and Policy-Makers," U.S. Department of Education, Office for Civil Rights.
23. Pub. L. 107-110, 115 Stat. 1425.
24. In addition, NCLB addresses the qualifications of teaching staff. State standards for teacher certification and evaluation of subject matter competence must meet strict federal requirements.
25. 20 U.S.C. § 6301.
26. NCLB requires students to be tested every year, from third to eighth grade, and once in high school. Testing in reading and math was to begin in 2005, and science in 2007. Public and

charter schools must show improvement in students' scores, with 100% of students expected to be proficient at reading, math, and science by 2014. If improvement is not shown, schools will be subject to increasingly severe consequences.

27. 29 U.S.C. § 794(b).
28. 42 U.S.C. § 12101(b).
29. 42 U.S.C. § 12201(a).
30. 42 U.S.C. §§ 12111(5) and 12112(a).
31. 42 U.S.C. § 12111(5)(B)(1); *Board of Trustees of the University of Alabama v. Garrett*, 531 U.S. 356 (2001) (suits for money damages by state employees under Title I of the ADA are barred by the Eleventh Amendment).
32. 42 U.S.C. § 12111(8).
33. 42 U.S.C. §§ 12131(1) and 12132.
34. 42 U.S.C. § 12131(2).
35. 42 U.S.C. § 12182(a); 42 U.S.C. § 12181(7).
36. 42 U.S.C. § 12182(b)(2)(A)(i).
37. 42 U.S.C. §§ 12182(b)(2)(A)(ii) and (iii).
38. A "child with a disability" is one who, by reason of hearing, speech, language, visual, or orthopedic impairments; mental retardation; autism; traumatic brain injury; serious emotional disturbance; other health impairments; or specific learning disabilities, needs special education and related services. 20 U.S.C. § 1401(3)(A).
39. Under Section 504, an "individual with a disability" is defined as "any person who (i) has a physical or mental impairment which substantially limits one or more of such person's major life activities; (ii) has a record of such an impairment; or (iii) is regarded as having such an impairment." 29 U.S.C. § 706(8)(B).
40. 42 U.S.C. § 12102(2).
41. *Albertson's Inc. v. Kirkingburg*, 527 U.S. 555, 566 (1999) (monocular vision). *See also Toyota Motor Manufacturing, Kentucky, Inc. v. Williams*, 534 U.S. 184, 199 (2002) (carpal tunnel syndrome); and *Bragdon v. Abbott*, 524 U.S. 624, 641–42 (1998) (HIV infection).
42. *Albertson's*, 527 U.S. at 566 ("The Act expresses that mandate clearly by defining 'disability' 'with respect to an individual,' 42 U.S.C. § 12102(2), and in terms of the impact of an impairment on 'such individual,' § 12102(2)(A).").
43. 29 C.F.R. § 1630.2(i); 28 C.F.R. § 35.104 (Disability)(2); 28 C.F.R. § 36.104 (Disability)(2).
44. *Toyota*, 534 U.S. at 197-198. In this case, the "major life activity" at issue was "performing manual tasks." The Court stated that "to fit into this category—a category that includes such basic abilities as walking, seeing, and hearing—the manual tasks in question must be central to daily life. If each of the tasks included in the major life activity of performing manual tasks does not independently qualify as a major life activity, then together they must do so." *Id*. at 197.
45. 29 C.F.R. pt. 1630, App. § 1630.2(i).
46. Reading and writing have been recognized as major life activities by some courts. *See, e.g., Gonzales v. National Board of Medical Examiners*, 225 F.3d 620 (6th Cir. 2000) (reading and writing), and *Bartlett v. New York State Board of Law Examiners*, 226 F.3d 69 (2d Cir. 2000) (reading).
47. 28 C.F.R. pt. 35, App. A, § 35.104 and 28 C.F.R. pt. 36, App. B, § 36.104 (same).
48. 29 C.F.R. § 1630.2(j)(1). The regulations promulgated under Title I provide further guidance regarding substantial limitations in the major life activity of working:

The term "substantially limits" means significantly restricted in the ability to perform either a class of jobs or a broad range of jobs in various classes as compared to the average person having comparable training, skills and abilities. The inability to perform a single, particular job does not constitute a substantial limitation to the major life activity of working. 29 C.F.R. § 1630.2(j)(3).

49. *Toyota,* 534 U.S. at 197.

50. *See Albertson's,* 527 U.S. at 565.

51. *Id.* at 567.

52. *Sutton v. United Air Lines, Inc.,* 527 U.S. 471, 482 (1999).

53. *Id.* at 488 (emphasis in original).

54. *See, e.g., McCleary v. National Cold Storage, Inc.,* 67 F. Supp. 2d 1288 (D. Kan. 1999) (plaintiff uses a leg brace and experiences pain with excessive standing or walking); *Matlock v. City of Dallas,* No. 3:97-CV-2735, 1999 WL 1032601 (N.D. Tex. Nov. 12, 1999) (plaintiff had virtually normal hearing with use of hearing aids); *Samul v. Daimler Chrysler Corp.,* 2000 WL 1480890 (E.D. Mich. Aug. 29, 2000) (plaintiff's medication for a heart condition caused susceptibility to bleed profusely if injured); *Saunders v. Baltimore County, Maryland,* 163 F. Supp. 2d 564 (D. Md. 2001) (plaintiff with medicated asthma claimed only difficulty breathing at place of employment); and *Mayers v. Washington Adventist Hospital,* 131 F. Supp. 2d 743 (D. Md. 2001) (plaintiff with medicated asthma suffered only temporary difficulty breathing at place of employment).

55. *See, e.g., Finical v. Collections Unlimited, Inc.,* 65 F. Supp. 2d 1032, 1039–40 (D. Ariz. 1999) ("Because the analysis of disability focuses on the major life activity alleged to be substantially limited, the relevant mitigating measures are those that affect the claimant's ability to perform that major life activity," rather than their impact on the individual's level of functioning in society or performance of "everyday activities."). *In accord, Bartlett v. New York State Board of Law Examiners,* No. 93 CIV. 4986(SS), 2001 WL 930792 at *31 (S.D.N.Y. Aug. 15, 2001). The court in *Bartlett* also concluded that mitigating measures (i.e., a wheelchair) that permit an individual to *avoid* performing or using a particular major life activity (i.e., walking) are not relevant in the determination of disability. *Id.* at *34.

56. 226 F.3d 69 (2d Cir. 2000).

57. *Bartlett,* 226 F.3d at 79 (citing *Bartlett,* 970 F. Supp. 1094, 1114 (1997)).

58. *Bartlett,* 226 F.3d at 81.

59. *Id.* at 81–82.

60. *Id.* at 83–84.

61. *Id.* at 85.

62. *Id.*

63. 29 C.F.R. § 1630.11 (emphasis added).

64. 42 U.S.C. § 12189. 28 C.F.R. § 36.309(a).

65. 28 C.F.R. § 36.309(b)(1)(i).

66. 29 C.F.R. § 1630.11.

67. 28 C.F.R. § 36.309(b)(2).

68. The ADA Title I regulations specifically lists "appropriate adjustment or modifications of examinations," in its definition of reasonable accommodations. 29 C.F.R. § 1630.2(o)(2)(ii). Further, the EEOC Interpretive Guidance states that "alternative or accessible test modes or formats include the administration of tests . . . via a reader or sign language interpreter." 56 Fed. Reg. 35739 at 35750 (July 26, 1991).

69. 28 C.F.R. pt. 36, App. B, § 36.309.

70. The SAT is administered by Educational Testing Service (ETS) but owned by the College Entrance Examination Board (the College Board), an independent entity.

71. *Services for Students with Disabilities,* at http://www.collegeboard.com/disable/students/html/eligible.html (last visited Oct. 2, 2004) (copy on file with author). Notwithstanding the elements specified on the quick checklist, the College Board does provide an appeal process for students who do not meet any one of the requirements. American College Testing (ACT) outlines eligibility requirements for extended time in chart format that includes: (1) professionally diagnosed disability; (2) appropriate documentation on file at school; and (3) extended time used for tests in school due to disability. *ACT Assessment Test Accommodations for Students with Disabilities: 2004–2005,* at http://www.act.org/aap/disab/chart.html (last visited Oct. 2, 2004) (copy on file with author).

72. It is possible to score so low on the SAT, or other college admissions examination, that an applicant may be perceived as incapable of higher education in that setting or possibly any setting. Postsecondary education admissions decisions, however, are not generally based entirely on such scores.

73. Similarly, in professions that have a tiered licensure process, a test-taker may successfully complete an entry-level license examination, but be precluded from advancing if he or she is unable to pass higher level licensure examinations. Advancement within a profession may be further complicated by limited or inaccessible workshops and other professional development opportunities needed to obtain the knowledge or credentials for higher level licensure.

74. See *Wynne v. Tufts University School of Medicine,* 976 F.2d 791 (1st Cir. 1992) (evidence that other institutions permitted oral exams for dyslexic students was not enough to overcome university's judgment that new request for alternative to written multiple choice biochemistry exam for student with alleged cognitive disability would impose an undue hardship on the academic program; university's judgment was reasonable in light of other accommodations requested and provided to student).

75. See, for example, *Price v. National Board of Medical Examiners,* 966 F. Supp. 419 (S. D. W. Va., 1997) (testimony of defendant's experts that plaintiffs had not submitted sufficient documentation to support the diagnoses of ADHD or specific learning disabilities was more compelling than plaintiffs' experts), and *Gonzales v. National Board of Medical Examiners,* 225 F.3d 620 (6th Cir. 2000) (court relied primarily on the testimony of defendant's experts and concluded that plaintiff could read and write as well as the average person). But see *Bartlett v. New York State Board of Law Examiners,* 226 F.3d 69 (2d Cir. 2000) (lack of deference to the Board's manner of assessing whether plaintiff had dyslexia or a reading disability; deference given to an assessment of reading ability that is based on observations and clinical judgment).

76. *Wynne v. Tufts University School of Medicine,* No. 89-1670 1990 WL 52715 (1st Cir. Apr. 30, 1990), *rehearing en banc,* 932 F.2d 19 (1st Cir. 1991), *affirmed,* 976 F.2d 791 (1992). In 1990, the Court of Appeals for the First Circuit reversed the decision of the district court in favor of Tufts. The 1990 opinion discusses factors the university may assess, multiple-choice tests, and the possibility that different testing formats may assess the same factor. The appeal was heard again by the Court of Appeals and the district court's decision in favor of Tufts was affirmed in part and reversed in part. On remand, the district court again decided in favor of Tufts. The Court of Appeals affirmed that decision in 1992.

Sign Language Interpretation in Testing Environments

Phyllis Rogers

As a professional sign language interpreter, I was once assigned to interpret the written portion of the driving test for a young deaf adult. We met at the Department of Motor Vehicles (DMV), and after an extensive wait, entered the testing area. Although I had long since forgotten most of what was asked on the driver's test, I still had a general sense of the content. (If this had been a test on "Queen Anne-Style Architecture" or "Physical Properties of Suspension Bridges," that would most certainly not be the case.) Content knowledge is just one of many important factors to consider for successful test interpretation.

Much of what I do as an interpreter is guided not only by content knowledge, but also by specific information about the deaf or hard of hearing client. It is helpful for me to know about each person's level of sign language proficiency, educational background, familiarity with the role of an interpreter, and the ways in which he or she might utilize interpreting services during a test. Being able to converse at length with the deaf or hard of hearing individual prior to the testing activity is another critical factor which will enhance the quality of test interpretation.

Interpreters must also consider factors related to the testing protocol and setting. Without advanced preparation, it is not unusual for test administrators to become suspicious of the interpreting process or to suddenly determine that interpreting is "not allowed." Sometimes the testing room, lighting, and other logistical arrangements make interpreting a test more difficult. Sometimes deaf people are themselves unfamiliar with ways in which to utilize interpreting services during tests. My training as a professional interpreter is essential in the application of ethical standards, identification of logistical issues, and cross-cultural mediation to address some of these challenges.

A deaf person can know a lot about driving a car and the rules of the road and still fail a driving test because of the complexities involved in test interpretation. About halfway through this particular test, I could overhear the DMV supervisor ask one of the other employees rather loudly about what the interpreter was doing in the testing area. Soon, he had made his way over to me and announced his question, "Can she read? Because if she can read then she doesn't need you here, so you can just go sit down outside of this area!" Given what I knew about this deaf individual, I dealt with the interruption by explaining my role to the DMV supervisor, stating that I was here to provide interpretation as needed for the written English language on the driver's test as well as for any other spoken interaction between the deaf person and DMV staff. I suggested that if he had any other questions, he would need to address them directly to the client, but she was in the middle of taking her test. Unfortunately, my attempt to mediate at this level was not successful.

"Well I just want to know if she can read or not!" the DMV supervisor barked. By this time, other people taking tests in adjacent booths were beginning to glance in our direction to see what all the commotion was about.

"Would you like to pose this question to her, sir?" I offered.

"Yeah. Just ask her, I don't have all day!" he snorted.

Reluctantly, I tapped the young woman on the shoulder. She had been deeply engrossed in question number 12 and was surprised to see the red-faced DMV supervisor standing behind her.

I signed a short explanation of what had just transpired, including the explicit question about her reading skills and the implicit question of whether or not she needed my services. Unfortunately, that amount of information and the abrupt shift from the test to the interpreting issue was overwhelming for the individual, as it would have been for almost anyone. She responded that she could read, so the DMV supervisor got ready to escort me rather forcibly into another room. Fortunately, as it dawned on her what was happening, the woman then stated that she did need me to sign the questions because she couldn't read all of the words, just some, and the sentences were too long. She was embarrassed to have to say this in a public area, and I was embarrassed for her. Quite a scene had been created.

Eventually we got back to the test; but at that point, my thought process was nowhere near peak level. Predictably, the stress level of the deaf individual also increased. She got the next three answers wrong, and as a result, the computerized test shut down.

Shared with the permission of the deaf candidate, this actual scenario is a poignant illustration of how even one factor, the test administrator's lack of familiarity with the interpreting process, may make the difference between a deaf or hard of hearing candidate passing or failing a test.

Whether it is a spelling test in an elementary school classroom or a high-stakes graduation exam in a high school or a professional exam for a particular field, the answer to "accommodation" is seldom as simple as "plugging in" a sign language interpreter. When the test is geared to determine an individual's knowledge of subject matter or ability to demonstrate a certain skill, rather than an individual's proficiency in English, it makes sense to think about delivering the test content in the test-taker's primary language. However, the accommodation is little understood, for there is much more to interpreting than mere substitution of one language for another.

In fact, professionals distinguish between the cognitive processes of translation and interpretation. In translation, working from one written language to another, translators have the opportunity to consider the source text at length, do research, and perhaps confer with the original author as they craft the written translation. When interpreting, interpreters must consecutively or simultaneously convey the dynamic spoken or signed information of one language into another. The practice of rendering written tests into another language is actually called "sight translation." It involves working from the written form of one language to the spoken or signed form of another language. It is different from either translation or interpretation, requiring different cognitive processes, such as the need for a certain level of reading comprehension skill on the part of the interpreter. *The Interpreters' Edge*, a training package for interpreters, explains that "some interpreters find sight translation more difficult than other modes of interpreting because they have more trouble focusing on the meaning rather than words—the essence of proper interpreting—when the message is written in black and white on a piece of paper (Mikkelson, 1995). A study comparing interpreting, translation, and sight translation found that each process is unique and one no less mentally taxing than another (Agrifoglio, 2004). Sight translation, however, is not usually taught in the interpreter training curriculum, nor is it evaluated as a part of obtaining interpreter certification (except for the Registry of Interpreters for the Deaf Certification for Deaf Interpreters performance examination). Thus, when considering the challenges of interpreting tests, it is important to first recognize that sight translation is virtually unexplored territory within the field of sign language interpreting.

Typically, in a testing setting, interpreters must interpret interaction that takes place at the testing site between test-takers in addition to rendering the test information. This chapter describes eight of the many complicating factors which impact the process of interpretation and of sight translation with ramifications for interpreters, deaf and hard of hearing test-takers, test developers, and test administrators.

LINGUISTIC VARIATION AMONG DEAF AND HARD OF HEARING PERSONS

Deaf and hard of hearing persons vary linguistically in multiple ways. Their sign language usage may be influenced by regional or ethnic dialects. Other factors include age, gender, and personality as well as cognitive, physical, and innate ability. Sign proficiency varies according to the age at which individuals learned to sign, whether or not they could hear and speak before they became deaf, whether or not they came from a deaf family or a hearing family, their educational level, and whether or not they were raised and educated in a community of fluent sign models or were isolated, having little contact with a deaf community. Additionally, both proficiency and style of signing may be influenced by exposure to one or more English-based pedagogical sign systems used in some educational settings. These systems combine features of English and American Sign Language (ASL), which has its own grammar and lexicon, but they may not adequately serve as full language models for either. In many cases, personnel in schools or other programs model signing that is neither rule-governed, accurately produced, or consistent.

Because many deaf people are not exposed to sign language when they are very young, or because their sign models are often marginally fluent or use an inconsistent variety of different sign systems, many deaf people are themselves not fluent in ASL. Faced with limited communication access and in the absence of a solid first-language foundation in either English or ASL, most deaf and hard of hearing individuals grow up experiencing some degree of language deprivation (Berdichevsky & Mounty, 1998) or difficulties with functional communication skills (Karchmer & Allen, 1999). These issues are not magically resolved upon graduation from high school, and interpreters find these same issues in the deaf adult population.

Spoken and written English language skills within the deaf and hard of hearing population also vary greatly, depending on the amount of residual hearing, age of onset, educational and family factors, as well as innate, cognitive, and personality factors. English is an auditory language, developed through interaction with thousands of other people, as well as through media and text, over a lifetime. Deaf individuals typically do not have access to the auditory signal for the spoken language, or to information conveyed through this spoken language in the conversations of those around them, on the radio, or over the subway station intercom. Their exposure to English may come from some lipreading skills, some reading skills, some signed English or cueing systems, or fingerspelling, and this exposure is rarely as complete or as pervasive as it is for people who can hear the language. Some deaf people have compensated remarkably and have excellent English skills, but many deaf people possess incomplete English language skills as well as significant cultural and knowledge gaps because their access to the language is restricted.

For those with some usable hearing, the shape of the audiogram and the range of sounds that are impacted by hearing will affect how an individual is able to use the hearing they have, even with sophisticated hearing aids. Thus, access to spoken language by hard of hearing individuals may vary considerably from situation to situation, depending upon things such as background noise and the number of people speaking or interacting. Children who grew up moderately to severely hard of hearing often miss out on incidental learning and educational and sociocultural experiences tied to hearing. Professionals generally do not advise placement of such children in programs that provide instruction in both ASL and English, even though doing so would provide them with a language foundation they may not get from exposure to English alone. It is not at all unusual, therefore, for persons who grow up hard of hearing to have clear speech, but nonnative patterns of use and understanding of English, and to experience difficulties in school and on standardized tests. Not infrequently, hard of hearing people later learn to sign, either to gain access to educational or social opportunities in signing environments, or because they have lost more hearing, or for both reasons. Thus, in some situations, including testing situations, they may require and request assistance from sign language interpreters.

An interpreter hired to render a test in sign language is faced with the possibility that the deaf or hard of hearing test-taker may prefer English-based signs, ASL, or a mixture of both, or may use a nonstandard form of sign communication. This wide variation in language usage presents many challenges for the interpreter.

LINGUISTIC VARIATION AMONG INTERPRETERS AND COMPETENCY ISSUES

Just as language skills vary within the deaf and hard of hearing population, interpreters also vary greatly in their ASL and English proficiency. They are also diverse with respect to education level, cognitive ability, personality, life experience, and training.

The predominant means by which interpreters are currently trained in the United States is through study in two-year interpreter training programs. There are also four-year and master's degree programs for interpreters. Generally, after completing a program, most individuals continue training and work for several years before they are able to pass the examinations required for minimum certification by the Registry of

Interpreters for the Deaf. Then, many more years of skill development will be needed in order to meet the needs of various deaf and hard of hearing individuals in specific settings.

Anyone who has taken two years of Spanish or French knows full well that two years of study hardly qualifies one to interpret a Scholastic Aptitude Test (SAT) in one's second language. Yet, because of a severe shortage of qualified sign language interpreters nationwide, individuals with only beginning or intermediate sign language skills are working as "interpreters" to fill this void. Sadly, interpreters can be found everywhere who lack language competence, cultural competence, and/or ethical and professional competence. Unfortunately, those who are least informed are also often the least aware of their own deficiencies, and may readily agree to interpret in testing settings for which they are wholly unqualified.

Interpreters who are less than fluent, who have limited experience in the field, little cultural awareness, and lower levels of education will generally be unable to deliver appropriate sight translation for tests because they do not understand the underlying complexities involved. They cannot appropriately assess or accommodate the individual language needs of the deaf test-taker, render the test information accurately, or recognize and effectively negotiate the ethical issues they encounter. Nevertheless, the hiring of interpreters and oversight of the quality of service they provide is virtually unpoliced at this time. Only a few areas of the country currently require that interpreters pass some level of competency testing or meet specific educational requirements to work as interpreters in a particular state. Even when standards are in place, they are usually only for public school educational settings and are typically set to the most minimum criteria (Jones, 2004). Moreover, these standards provide no assurance that even general knowledge assessments, let alone highly specialized subject content, can be interpreted accurately by these individuals. Often overlooked is the fact that interpreting requires proficiency in two languages, not just one. Sometimes the English language and literacy skills of the interpreter are insufficient for the test translation task.

Thus, it is critically important that standards be set for the hiring of interpreters for testing situations and that interpreter selection be given primary consideration. Successful sight translation by interpreters requires background knowledge in test development, an educational level that matches or exceeds the level required of the test, familiarity with the subject matter and the candidate, and the ability to meet the individual's linguistic needs. Deaf or hard of hearing persons taking tests should have substantial input into the selection of the interpreter, and those who struggle with understanding the interpreters should be given the opportunity to retake the test with different interpreters.

TEST LANGUAGE, TEST DEVELOPMENT, AND TEST INTERPRETATION CONSIDERATIONS

Test developers normally consider the English wording of test prompts and responses at length in order to avoid confusion or ambiguity. However, they do not plan for sign language rendition during the test creation process, and wording that is clear in

English may present significant translation challenges. It falls to the interpreter to determine which signs to use and how to produce question prompts and responses in a meaningful way for a given deaf or hard of hearing candidate.

Regional variations in sign language also present challenges. For example, there are at least five signs for the concept of "birthday" and the sign for the concept of "making sure of something" in Texas is very similar to the sign for "honesty/ truth" on the East Coast. Interpreters unfamiliar with the background or preferences of a deaf or hard of hearing candidate may inadvertently render a test item incorrectly.

On the other hand, signs sometimes provide the answers to test questions. The term *necking* in physics refers to a particular shape of pipe. The sign for this term is a clear visual representation of the shape. If the physics test requires a test-taker to define *necking*, and the interpreter produces the ASL sign for that term, the signed translation has provided the answer.

ASL and English are different languages with distinct grammatical systems and lexicons. There may be only 1 sign for 10 English synonyms, and a multitude of ASL signs for a single English word, but the shades of meaning do not correspond between the two languages. The interpreter faces difficulty when a test-taker is required to discriminate between certain English synonyms which are not similarly distinguished in ASL. Another important factor is to recognize that English has a horizontal structure where more information typically implies a longer word, phrase, and sentence because word suffixes, prefixes, tense markers, adjectives, adverbs, and clauses provide the additional details. At a lexical level, English words change grammatical structure through additions of prefixes and suffixes and certain rule-bound internal changes (e.g., *inform* becomes *information, informative, uninformed,* and *informing*). ASL, on the other hand, is said to be a vertical language, where the additional information is frequently incorporated into the sign through a change in formation and/or movement, with simultaneous modifications to the accompanying facial expression and/or body position. Response question prompts which require a deaf individual to distinguish between certain grammatical features in English may be ambiguous when rendered in sign language. Additionally, deaf and hard of hearing individuals as well as interpreters vary in proficiency with respect to these sign inflections, modulations, and nonmanual markers, creating many possibilities for error in test-taking. In *Legal Ramifications of an Incorrect Analysis of Tense in ASL* (Shepard-Kegl, Neidle, & Kegl, 1995) "a deaf plaintiff misunderstood when he was asked 'Did you understand when you were signing the paper at (Company A) that you were borrowing money and agreeing to pay it back?' The plaintiff responded 'yes' because he thought he was being asked if he presently understood the question, but he was not aware that he was being asked if he understood at the time when he was signing the paper."

Every language has rule-governed processes by which new vocabulary is added to the lexicon. There are certain terms which have been coined in the English language for concepts in specific fields of study. Creation of new lexical items requires significant interchange between and among members of a linguistic community. Therefore, these terms may exist in English while they have not yet appeared in the sign language lexicon. Several challenges exist with respect to field-specific vocabulary when interpreting tests. The interpreter has to know the meaning of the English term, be aware of signs which specifically convey the term, know if the deaf individual is familiar with these signs or uses different ones, and also be fluent in use of the grammatical rules for borrowing vocabulary from one language into another. Breakdown in communication can occur at any of these points, impacting testing results. The interpreter may not understand that certain English terms have specific meanings within a field of study. For example, on a social work licensure exam, the word *practice* refers to the activity of doing social work, not to a business, as in *medical practice,* or a skill rehearsal or drill, as in *piano practice.* If the interpreter does not know that there is a difference between *mean, median,* and *mode,* the interpreter may convey all of these terms with a more generic sign for "average." The interpreter may recognize the meaning of the field-specific term, but be unaware of existing sign vocabulary for that term. Without sufficient linguistic exposure in both English and ASL, which is directly related to the subject matter being tested, the interpreter will struggle. Because of inconsistent quality in the fluency skills of educators and interpreters, it is very possible that deaf persons have been taught "invented" signs for field-specific terms in a classroom or training setting. These contrived signs may be conceptually incorrect or violate ASL grammatical principals. Perhaps these signs were created solely for use in an individual classroom and are unknown elsewhere. The interpreter and the test-taker arrive at a testing site, therefore, without a shared vocabulary. If the interpreter uses signs unfamiliar to the deaf candidate, the testing is complicated by the need to negotiate the meaning of signs during the test.

INCIDENTAL LEARNING CONSIDERATIONS

As has already been mentioned, access to the spoken English language and the incidental learning that happens auditorially is typically quite restricted for deaf and hard of hearing persons. Most hearing parents do not sign at home with their deaf children, or if they do, the signing is sporadic and simplistic. Parents and professionals alike often do not realize the extent to which hard of hearing children miss out on incidental learning. General knowledge is usually not taught in school, but rather is acquired incidentally or passively in home and community settings. Yet, for a deaf child, school may be the only setting where there is access to information via teachers who can sign or interpreters. Consequently, general or "common" knowledge content on tests has not necessarily been accessible to many deaf and hard of hearing persons. For instance, a deaf person may have learned the meaning of the word *persevere* but not know what a box spring mattress is, because *persevere* was expressly taught in school, but nobody ever talked about box spring mattresses in that setting.

There are also situations where language used commonly in a particular field is incorporated into the test items even when that language does not occur in textbooks or training manuals. Returning again to testing for social work licensure, the phrase *doorknob syndrome,* used in reference to a client who continues to bring up new issues or concerns when it is already past the time for a session to end, appears on the test. This expression might be known to social workers who have interacted freely with one another in casual spoken-language conversations at work, but not to a deaf or hard of hearing social worker because the item is not typically seen in textbooks.

Interpreters will not always be aware of the subtle ways in which incidental learning impacts deaf and hard of hearing test-takers. Interpreters who are keen enough to discover test items where incidental learning issues impact the response then face weighty ethical decisions about whether to alter the test content. They may consider expanding upon or explaining test content so that they "teach" the piece of incidental learning prior to posing the test question. Or, they may think about substituting part of the information in the test item with something equivalent but which is more likely to be in the category of common knowledge for the deaf or hard of hearing candidate. Parsing out incidental learning issues requires background knowledge of the test-taker, background knowledge in the field being tested, and a close familiarity with the experiences of deaf and hard of hearing learners in schools, in the home, and in many other settings. The more familiar the interpreter is with the test-taker and subject matter being tested, the more likely the interpreter will be able to intercept these difficulties.

INTERPRETER NEUTRALITY AND TEST PREPARATION CONSIDERATIONS

Interpreters are supposed to refrain from influencing, providing opinions, and changing the content, emotions or goals of the message. Professional interpreters strive to maintain clear boundaries, and ethically are charged to minimize their influence to the extent possible, but it is virtually impossible to be present and not influence communication in some way. Roy (2003) states, "Interpreters enter the interaction with all of their deeply held views on power, status, solidarity, gender, age, race, ethnicity, nationality, socioeconomic status (SES), as well as the cultural norms and societal blueprints that encompass the encounter: they use all of these to construct and interpret reality." Interpreters are human beings. They understand information and process information in relationship to their own human experience and knowledge base. Test scores are not always altered because of this influence, but interpreters are undoubtedly a part of the human interchange as well as the linguistic interchange. Their influence may raise test scores for deaf applicants, or lower them.

Part of this influence involves human error. Striving for neutrality can reduce, but not eliminate, human error. A good interpretation in any language will not be perfect, and as Cokely (1995) states, "These interpreter specific factors that may lead to a greater level of miscommunication are perception, memory, semantics and performance. Any error or miscue attributed to one or more of these factors can be significant enough to result in distortion or omission of the original message." Interpreters may make mistakes in several ways. They may misunderstand the test question and what it is asking. They may be unfamiliar with the specificity of certain English terminology, which is essential to a particular field of study. They may err in their assessment of the deaf or hard of hearing individual's level or type of language usage. They may inadvertently sign a prompt in a way that creates ambiguous meaning. They may inadvertently omit something that was tied to the key or correct answer in a multiple-choice time.

Sometimes they can repair their errors if they become aware of them, but repairs take time and force the candidate to sort out two renditions of the same prompt or response.

In any language interpretation, some part of the message will be lost or changed due to cultural and linguistic differences; some will be changed due to human influence, and still more because of human error on the part of the interpreter. These discrepancies occur to a lesser extent when the interpreter and the candidate are highly "compatible" in language usage and fluency and when the interpreter possesses knowledge of the subject matter.

The issue of interpreter quality overlaps the issue of neutrality. An interpreter who lacks sufficient training may be unaware of internal bias and how it impacts and informs interpreting decisions. Worse, interpreters whose salaries depend on the student being in the classroom the following year naturally hope that the student will have success in passing the courses. They face a moral struggle when the deaf or hard of hearing student puts down the wrong answer on a test. All it takes is an inadvertent raised eyebrow by the interpreter, and the student might just erase that answer and choose another. Not all interpreters win this moral battle, particularly when working in isolated settings with little oversight. It is easy to rationalize ethical infractions: "I know the student really knew this answer"; "I've seen this student get that answer right before"; or even "If the student fails the test, then everyone is going to think I'm a bad interpreter." Infractions are more likely to occur when an interpreter is poorly trained in recognizing boundary issues and maintaining proper boundaries. Interpreters who have a stake in test results should refrain from interpreting the test; yet it is often these same interpreters who are most familiar with the test-takers language needs and with the subject-specific signs used for instructional purposes in preparation for the test.

Probably the best way of gaining neutrality and decreasing error is to select highly qualified interpreters for the task and provide them with adequate preparation of the test content. A second recommendation is to have interpreters work in teams whenever possible. This approach provides a check and balance on both boundary and accuracy issues and expands the available background knowledge brought to the sight translation work.

Preparation entails becoming familiar with the deaf or hard of hearing candidate and the test's subject matter. "Just knowing the right words in the other language is not enough," emphasize Seleskovitch and Lederer (1989), using the following example: "North Sea exports of oil have been raised aggressively to help cover the balance of payment and exchequer costs of the strike." Full comprehension of this statement requires background knowledge of the event, specifically understanding the following facts: British coal exports were stopped, foreign currency revenue was lost, and subsidies doubled from one year to the next, impacting public finances. Interpreters must strive to comprehend the complete idea, including implied meaning, prior to interpreting. What may be shared background knowledge among test-takers is not always shared among interpreters. If the interpreter understands the goals of the test and the content of the questions and answers, the interpreter's mental schema equates far better to the test developer's schema. Interpreting judgments will therefore more likely equate to those that align with the goals of the test developers. While the interpreter may not need to know which answer is correct, the interpreter does need to understand the subject matter being tested and the field-specific terminology used in the test.

In preparing to interpret a test, the interpreter must give thought to the translation challenges, incidental learning issues, professional boundaries, linguistic compatibility between interpreter and test-taker, field-specific vocabulary, and content background knowledge. Additionally, the test translation should be fluid and efficient so that the candidate is not unduly burdened with wading through unnecessarily cumbersome interpretations. Consideration of each of these factors takes time, thought, and planning well in advance of the actual test administration. Part of the testing accommodation, therefore, should support and respect the interpreter's preparation needs. Interpreters should have access to training materials associated with the test subject matter, an opportunity to review the actual test, and time to meet with candidates to become familiar with their linguistic needs.

LOGISTICAL AND PROTOCOL CONSIDERATIONS

Certain factors inherent in the testing process pose particular difficulties for interpreters. The most common of these is the time constraint. Interpreting takes time. The process requires an interpreter to read and comprehend the test prompt and response items, contemplate the best translation, and then render the translation in sign language. It takes time for the deaf or hard of hearing individual to read the printed test information, watch the signed translation, and then respond. The amount of time required varies among candidates and interpreters.

Another factor to consider is that a written test is static. The information on a page or on a computer screen can be reviewed, reread, reorganized, and reconsidered. When that same information is delivered in sign language, the information is not static, but dynamic. The candidates will likely need test items to be signed multiple times because they cannot hold all of the information in visual memory in the same way that printed words hold information on a page or screen. Sometimes what they see signed appears to conflict with what they thought they understood from the printed English version, also necessitating the need for repetition.

Permitting repetitions may give too much assistance, particularly if the interpreter only repeats questions after noticing incorrect responses, realizing that an interpretation error might have caused the response error. Yet, forbidding repetitions would unfairly penalize the deaf or hard of hearing candidate for interpreting-related errors. Advance preparation with the test will allow the interpreter to render the translation with less error. Also, the deaf or hard of hearing person can request a repeat prior to selecting an answer. The interpreter can repeat a randomly selected subset of items, or all items, at the end of the test. All of these procedures will extend the testing time.

With the issue of extended time also comes fatigue, both on the part of interpreters and test-takers. The deaf test-taker is faced with numerous tasks during an interpreted test, including negotiating language differences, resolving apparent conflicts between the signed and written form of the question, teasing out professional content and vocabulary with which the interpreter may be unfamiliar, maintaining a rapport with an interpreter, negotiating grammatical differences between ASL and English, dealing with test environment barriers or nonstandard disruptions during the testing process, and taking the test. Additional tasks constitute additional stressors, creating additional fatigue. Interpreters have very similar stressors. Test administrators may want to consider dividing the test into parts and permitting deaf and hard of hearing candidates to take the test with significant breaks in between certain sections in order to reduce the amount of fatigue.

Another challenge has to do with limitations imposed on where the interpreter can sit or how much of the test the interpreter is allowed to see. Computerized tests are typically delivered in rooms which are ill-suited to accommodate two interpreters. Perhaps the interpreters cannot see the computer screen, or the candidate cannot easily view both the screen and the interpreter, or the two interpreters cannot sit in close enough proximity to work as a team effectively.

Limitations on interaction between deaf or hard of hearing persons and the interpreter also interfere with successful test translation. Test administrators should expect discussion to occur between the test-taker and the interpreters. There is frequent need to clarify, to agree on sign vocabulary, and to correct interpreting error. The signed discussion may appear to the casual observer as "cheating," so test administrators need to become comfortable with the idea that certain linguistic agreements must take place during the interpreting process.

NONSTANDARD TEST ADMINISTRATION

When an interpreter is present for almost any kind of test, the test is considered to have been administered in a nonstandard manner. This issue is complex not only because of the lack of norms for a test administered through interpretation and the complexity of the sight translation task, but also because changing any one procedure can open the door for change in other procedures. The uniqueness of the situation sometimes sparks curiosity. It is doubtful that the DMV supervisor routinely interrupts people in the middle of their tests. Test-takers are not routinely asked to describe their literacy skills in a public place. Yet, both of these issues arose because the test was being given in a nonstandard manner.

It is important for test administrators to have a clear understanding of protocol for both the hiring of interpreters and the use of interpreting services during a test. Considerations for selection of interpreters, which includes input from the deaf or hard of hearing test-taker, credentials, educational level, boundaries, subject matter knowledge, and linguistic compatibility, must be thought out well in advance. Procedures for interpreters to go about preparing for the sight translation task must be clearly articulated. Logistical arrangements for seating, lighting, and time extension should be carefully thought out, and protocols should be established for what is and what is not permitted during the test-taking and interpreting process. Test sites may wish to develop written guidelines to address all of these procedures as well as confidentiality and fidelity statements for interpreters to sign prior to rendering the test.

SKILLS AND KNOWLEDGE VERSUS LANGUAGE ASSESSMENT

The tests discussed up to this point are those designed to test a person's skills and knowledge. These tests are written in English and therefore may not provide a true picture of the deaf or hard of hearing individual's knowledge, skills, and abilities. The accommodations of sign language interpreting for these tests may result in a closer approximation, but as this chapter has described, providing such an accommodation can be a complex process. It is quite difficult to avoid testing English skills when the test is written in English.

Other tests are specifically designed to assess an individual's fluency in the English language, such as high school and college entrance and exit exams which test English grammar, vocabulary, and reading comprehension. There is much debate over whether sign language accommodation for these tests is reasonable. To provide interpretation changes the entire purpose of the test. To refuse to provide it may mean that an otherwise bright and high-achieving deaf or hard of hearing person is barred from significant opportunities in both academic and employment areas.

Spanish skills are not assessed through offering a Spanish test with a Chinese interpreter. Similarly, providing a sign interpreter for tests which are designed to test English does not provide information about a deaf or hard of hearing candidate's English skills. However, a deaf person may have a wealth of strategies to cope with English limitations and may be very capable of entering colleges or positions of employment without the level of English skills thought to be necessary. They may have fluent ASL skills which are desperately needed in many specialized fields in order to meet the needs of deaf students or clients. This is a country where educational, medical, legal, social, religious, and business services are offered primarily through spoken English, creating a vicious cycle of limited access for deaf persons. ASL skills should be valued just as much as spoken English skills are valued. Much thought should be given to the purpose of testing English skills and the ramifications of requiring deaf people to demonstrate competence in a language where they experience significantly limited access. Perhaps deaf people who are barred from college entrance, high school diplomas, or licensure in certain professions just because English is not their primary language could demonstrate other competencies which allow them to achieve in spite of English language limitations. There is a need for a much more creative approach to determining the skill sets truly needed for high-stakes entrance and exit exams, particularly where testing of English language competency is concerned, because sign language interpretation will seldom be the appropriate choice for such tests.

These eight critical issues are just some of the factors which impact the success of interpreting in testing situations. Having described the difficulties of interpreting in testing situations, the question becomes whether test translation should be considered at all. When should it be done, and if so, how can it be done most effectively? Several suggestions have been offered to improve the quality of test translation, and acting on these suggestions requires cooperation between interpreters, test developers, deaf consultants, deaf test candidates, and test administrators. The following list summarizes recommendations for best practices in the accommodation of interpreting services for testing.

- Hire well-trained, qualified, fluent and experienced professional interpreters.
- Hire a team of two interpreters.
- Allow for candidate input regarding the selection of interpreters.
- Allow re-testing when interpreting quality is questioned.
- Provide the testing entity and/or test administrator with guidelines and standards addressing interpreting related issues.
- Ensure that professional interpreters engage in self-assessment as to their qualifications, subject matter expertise, linguistic competence, and ethical boundaries.
- Provide interpreters with materials that explain the constructs being measured, samples of tests, and ample time to acquire the necessary subject matter knowledge.
- Allow for interpreter input related to testing protocol and logistics and eliminate potential barriers.
- Arrange a pre-test meeting time for interpreters and candidates to discuss interpreting needs, sign preferences, and subject-specific vocabulary.
- Consider testing in a separate room or area which comfortably accommodates a team of interpreters and the candidate.
- Extend test time and provide breaks between sections of the test to reduce fatigue.
- Provide training for deaf and hard of hearing candidates regarding the role of the interpreter and strategies for using interpreting services during a test.
- Develop a confidentiality and fidelity statement for interpreters to sign, which would address concerns about ethical practices during test translation.
- Review tests and consider alterations when incidental learning factors or difficulties with translation pose undue hardships (or the alternative) for deaf and hard of hearing candidates.
- Address test development and sight translation in testing settings in interpreter training curricula.

Following these suggestions requires advance planning, lengthy consideration and discussion, and additional expense. Alternative measures to assessing deaf and hard of hearing candidates may be a better choice until stronger guidelines are in place, and may be the only reasonable choice for tests designed to assess English language skills.

This chapter has provided some insight into the interpretation process and detailed many reasons why test translation is not an automatic solution to the test-taking process for deaf and hard of hearing individuals. The fact that these challenges exist does not mean that interpreters cannot interpret tests. The deaf individual mentioned in the beginning of this chapter eventually returned to the DMV, took the test using sign language interpreting services, passed, and has been driving accident-free for several years.

More and more frequently, deaf and hard of hearing people are encountering tests which they must pass, for example, to graduate from high school, receive a diploma, enter college, become certified or licensed in a specific profession, or receive a promotion. These tests are created in English for persons who can hear and who have had a lifetime of access to spoken English. This factor alone renders them invalid for most deaf or hard of hearing candidates. Provision of an interpreter may resolve some of the testing challenges for some deaf or hard of hearing individuals, but it also creates other validity and reliability concerns. The interpreting profession strives hard to provide appropriate, accurate, ethical services, and there are many excellent interpreters; but even the highest levels of quality and professionalism will not resolve all of the concerns related to test translation. The decision to provide test translation, therefore, should not be a casual one, and the results of an interpreted test should be viewed with much caution.

REFERENCES

Agrifoglio, M. (2004). Sight translation and interpreting: A comparative analysis of constraints and failures. *Interpreting* 6(1), 43–67.

Berdichevsky, C., & Mounty, J. (1999). Foreign language learning and language development. In H. Markowicz and C. Berdichevsky (Eds.), *Conference proceedings: Bridging the gap between research and practice in the fields of learning disabilities and deafness* (pp. 81–91). Washington, DC: College of Continuing Education, Gallaudet University.

Cokely, D. (1995). The interpreted medical interview: It loses something in the translation. *Reflections*, 3(10).

Jones, B. E. (2004). Competencies of K–12 educational interpreters: Ideal vs. minimum vs. real. In E. Winston (Ed.), *Educational interpreting: How it can succeed*. Washington, DC: Gallaudet University Press.

Karchmer, M., & Allen, T. (1999). The functional assessment of deaf and hard of hearing students, *American Annals of the Deaf*, 144(2), 77.

Mikkelson, H. (1995). Introduction. In *The interpreters' edge*. Spreckles, CA: Adebo. Audiorecording.

Roy, C. (2003). *Analyzing a discourse process: Turn-taking in interpreted interaction*. Lecture series, Interpretation Department, Gallaudet University, Washington, DC.

Seleskovitch, D., and Lederer M. (1995). *A systematic approach to teaching interpretation.* Silver Spring, MD: Registry of Interpreters for the Deaf.

Shepard-Kegl, J., Neidle, C., & Kegl, J. (1995). Legal ramifications of an incorrect analysis of tense. *Journal of Interpretation*, 7(1), 53–70.

Section IV   *Cases From Specific Professions*

Certification Testing for Therapeutic Recreation: Equity, Access, and Preparation

Anne Simonsen

Therapeutic recreation is a discipline that is grounded in the idea of leisure, recreation, and the enhancement of one's quality of life. As such, it is practiced in health care, human service, and community settings. One can find therapeutic recreation professionals in hospitals, rehabilitation centers, long-term care facilities, community recreation and park agencies, group homes, day care programs, and corrections facilities. According to the National Therapeutic Recreation Society (2000),

Therapeutic recreation uses treatment, education, and recreation service to help people with illnesses, disabilities, and other conditions to develop and use their leisure in ways that enhance their health, functional abilities, independence, and quality of life. (National Therapeutic Recreation Society [NTRS], 2000)

Therapeutic recreation is grounded in leisure and recreation, but also has a role as a treatment/therapy modality which can assist an individual in improving his or her function and gaining independence (Sylvester, Voelkl, & Ellis, 2001).

The field of therapeutic recreation has a long history of credentialing. The first Voluntary Registration Plan started in 1956 and included three levels of mastery; it continued to be used until 1969 (Carter, Van Andel, & Robb, 2003). In 1969, the National Therapeutic Recreation Society (NTRS) revised the plan to include six levels of mastery (Carter et al., 2003). However, registration in therapeutic recreation remained voluntary, and there was no examination for entry into the profession.

In 1981, as a way to meet the National Commission for Health Certifying Agencies' requirement that the credentialing board had to be separate from the professional organization, the National Council for Therapeutic Recreation Certification (NCTRC) was formed (Carter et al., 2003). According to Connolly (1998a), "NCTRC's mission is to protect the consumer of therapeutic recreation services by promoting the provision of quality services offered by the NCTRC certificants" (p. 404). Professionals in therapeutic recreation acknowledge that NCTRC is *the* certification authority for the field (Connolly, 1998a). Although many jobs in therapeutic recreation require that the incumbent be certified as a Certified Therapeutic Recreation Specialist (CTRS), the NCTRC certification is voluntary, and only a few states have any kind of restrictive practice laws that limit who can work in therapeutic recreation. However, no one can use the CTRS credential unless she or he has passed the CTRS examination and maintained his or her credential by completing the appropriate continuing professional development activities and paying the necessary fees.

After an extensive job analysis project under the auspices of the NCTRC, the Educational Testing Service (ETS) was contacted to prepare a national exam. The exam was offered for the first time in November 1990 (Carter et al., 2003). A great deal of controversy surrounded the exam because there was no "grandparenting" provision for therapeutic recreation professionals who were already certified. Everyone, regardless of prior certification status, had to take the exam and pass it by November 1995 in order to retain his or her certification as a CTRS. This requirement meant that more than 9,000 persons who were already CTRSs had to take and pass the certification exam as any new applicant would; no one was exempt. Since the first examination in 1990, the NCTRC has completed additional job task analyses and revised the exam. Although the exam began in written, paper-and-pencil form, it became a computer-based mastery exam in 2001 (Carter et al., 2003).

At the same time that the NCTRC was developing an exam that was specific to therapeutic recreation, the National Certification Board (NCB) of the National Recreation and Park Association (NRPA) was developing its own test for certification of the recreation generalist or what is now known as the Certified Park and Recreation Professional (CPRP) examination (Carter et al., 2003). This exam was administered for the first time in 1990 and became computer-based in 2001 (Carter et al., 2003). Only one deaf graduate of the Recreation and Leisure Studies Program at Gallaudet University has taken this exam, and the NCB allowed this person to have a sign language interpreter during the examination. The interpreter, an individual who had minimal understanding of the discipline, did not sign every question and answer. The interpreter was available only to clarify the words if the test-taker had some difficulties understanding the stem and/or answer choices. Unfortunately, the individual did not pass the exam and chose not to retake it.

Both certification exams have been designed for the entry-level practitioner, and both exams are touted as being appropriate for the new graduate with a bachelor's degree. Both certification exams pose the same challenges to persons who are deaf and hard of hearing. Both exams have eligibility requirements related to coursework, internships, and graduation from university programs that candidates must meet prior to taking the exam. In addition, both credentialing plans are voluntary national programs, and both require that individuals holding the certification must update and document continued education and development and complete re-certification within a specified period of time—every five years for the CTRS credential and every two years for the CPRP credential (Carter et al., 2003).

However, even though there are similarities related to the purpose and development of both certification examinations, the focus of this chapter is on the CTRS exam governed by the NCTRC. This is the examination which most graduates of the Gallaudet University Recreation and Leisure Studies Program choose to take.

THE IMPACT OF THE CTRS EXAM ON DEAF TEST-TAKERS

In 1991, one of the first graduates of the Therapeutic Recreation Program at Gallaudet University applied for and was granted eligibility to take the CTRS exam. At the time of application, this individual had been working in therapeutic recreation for approximately one year. Eligibility to take the CTRS exam was granted. However, an individual must not only be eligible to take the CTRS exam, but also must pass the exam before receiving the CTRS credential (Connolly, 1998b). This individual prepared to take the exam by reviewing the materials and textbooks from college therapeutic recreation courses and using any exam preparation materials that were available. Unfortunately, this person did not pass the exam that first time but was resolved to take the exam as many times as necessary to obtain the CTRS credential. When NCTRC sent the exam results, information concerning areas of weakness was provided so that the test-taker could concentrate on improving the score in these areas. Each time a person applies to take the exam, she or he has to pay the appropriate fee. This process becomes expensive if one takes the exam multiple times, and one must pass the exam within five years or re-apply for eligibility and pay the eligibility application fee again. This individual took the exam a second time in 1992, and did not pass once again.

During this same time period, faculty in the Recreation and Leisure Studies Program at Gallaudet University learned of three other deaf or hard of hearing individuals who had graduated from therapeutic recreation programs at "traditional hearing" universities and who had not passed the CTRS exam. An awareness began to grow that deaf and hard of hearing therapeutic recreation professionals might be having difficulty passing the CTRS exam. Conversations with deaf and hard of hearing test-takers and faculty in other professional preparation programs at Gallaudet led the Recreation and Leisure Studies Program faculty to surmise that difficulty with the certification exam might be related to the use and understanding of English and the nature of standardized tests. It was at this point that faculty in the Recreation and Leisure Studies Program at Gallaudet first attended meetings of what was then called the National Task Force on Equity in Testing Deaf Professionals. Conversations with other faculty and practitioners in related health and human service disciplines helped make it clear that persons who were deaf and hard of hearing were experiencing a pattern of difficulty passing standardized certification/licensure exams in many professions. From these conversations arose the question "What can be done to alleviate this problem and make it possible for graduates from the Recreation and Leisure Studies Program to pass the CTRS exam?"

One of the answers to this question was to work with the NCTRC to try to develop a fair and equitable way of testing deaf and hard of hearing candidates. Overtures were made to the NCTRC board, and discussions ensued about alternative testing methods. Some methods that were suggested included onsite/live sign language interpretation of the test questions, videotaped interpretation of the test questions, extended examination time, and different (i.e., lower) cutoff scores for deaf and hard of hearing test-takers. Although discussion continued, NCTRC was only willing to consider granting extended time to candidates when the request was verified by a college/university administrator or health care professional.

Another answer to the question involved providing more preparation for deaf candidates, which was specific to the content of the CTRS exam immediately prior to their taking the test. This preparation was possible and doable, and the individuals who had already taken the CTRS exam, as well as other Therapeutic Recreation Program graduates who were planning to take the exam, requested that Gallaudet develop a course of this nature. One of the main reasons for this request was that the CTRS credential was required for them to obtain and/or keep their current jobs in therapeutic recreation. Since a "critical mass" of potential CTRS test-takers was interested, the faculty at Gallaudet University designed a therapeutic recreation review course which was offered in fall of 1993.

As an aside, there is often a lack of privacy in the Deaf community—many members of the community know the business of other members. This phenomenon has been called "the small community" effect (Gutman, 2002). For good or ill, the fact that the first CTRS test-taker had not passed the exam two times became common knowledge among the therapeutic recreation students and other therapeutic recreation graduates. Information of this nature can be destructive and self-defeating—and become a self-fulfilling prophecy. The self-talk/scenario goes something like, "If _____ cannot pass the CTRS exam, and _____ has taken it two times, then I will have a lot of difficulty with the CTRS exam and probably will not be able to pass it, so why should I try? I don't really want a job in therapeutic recreation anyway, so I don't need the CTRS certification." This self-limiting conversation affects individuals as well as the group. It was imperative, therefore, to decrease the effect of a few persons' not passing the CTRS exam and increase the self-confidence of all therapeutic recreation students and graduates. They had to believe they would be able to pass if they were given the appropriate tools to do so. To this end, the therapeutic recreation review course was designed to focus on the WHAT, content areas that had been identified by the NCTRC and were addressed in the study guides, or cognitive training, and the HOW, those emotional and mental responses that would assist test-takers to increase the probability of passing, or affective training.

The therapeutic recreation review course was offered at Gallaudet University for the first time in November 1993. Six individuals who were eligible to take the CTRS exam attended; two of the six were graduates of the Gallaudet program who had previously not passed the CTRS exam. The course started on a Saturday and ended on the following Friday. There was a total of 36 scheduled hours for either classroom/didactic work or discussion/participation. The topics for the course followed the CTRS exam outline in the *NCTRC Candidate Bulletin* (1993). Additional topics included "test-taking skills" and vocabulary related to therapeutic recreation, health care, and human services. The course instructors were committed to meeting the communication needs of all the participants, which required using whatever method succeeded in "getting the point across."

The goals of the therapeutic recreation review course were multifaceted. The primary goal was to prepare graduates to take the CTRS exam; other goals included: (1) to assess the knowledge that students retained after graduation, which was related to the practice of therapeutic recreation; (2) to assist graduates in retaining and increasing the knowledge that is necessary to function appropriately in their jobs as therapeutic recreation professionals; and (3) to collect data related to what knowledge majors in the therapeutic recreation option already have, what additional knowledge is required, and how best to impart this knowledge to them. The fee for the course covered the instruction and materials that were distributed to the attendees.

Three of the six therapeutic recreation review course participants took the CTRS exam immediately following the completion of the course. All of them took the exam at the same test site in the same room, with extended time and an interpreter for test directions only. One of the three, the individual who had taken and not passed the exam two times previously, passed. The others did not. When the course participants were asked about the most valuable part of the course on an evaluation form, their responses indicated that studying vocabulary and discussion with colleagues were the activities that helped them the most. Most of the participants felt that the workshop needed to be held every year and that the sharing of resources and skills was very important.

As a result of the "success" of the 1993 therapeutic recreation review course, another one was held in November 1994. This course was held during the weekend, starting on a Friday evening and ending on a Monday evening. Ten individuals attended the 1994 therapeutic recreation review course. Nine of them were graduates of the Gallaudet University Therapeutic Recreation and Leisure Studies Program, and one individual, also deaf, was a graduate of another university. The group was diverse with respect to educational background (both mainstream and schools for the deaf), degree and onset of deafness, and membership in both deaf and hearing families. Most of them were between 25 and 30 years of age and had worked for at least one year postgraduation. It was possible for them to work in therapeutic recreation prior to passing the CTRS exam because they were eligible to take it as a result of the graduation requirements for the therapeutic recreation option in the Gallaudet Recreation and Leisure Studies Program.

All of the attendees were encouraged to purchase the two CTRS exam study guides that were available in 1994. In addition to the study guides, university faculty members created a packet with a five-page vocabulary list and additional information, which was sent to all the participants prior to the start of the course itself. The topics were indicated in the CTRS exam outline in the 1994 *NCTRC Candidate Bulletin*. The course schedule was reduced to 29 hours. All of the participants took a multiple-choice pre-test that had more than 200 questions. Permission was obtained from the publishing companies to use questions from the two study guides and rearrange them for the pre-test and post-test. When the pre-tests were corrected, the scores ranged from 53.1% to 85% of the questions being answered correctly. As a result of the pre-test scores, several categories were identified, which seemed to give the test-takers/participants the most problems. These topics included assessment, evaluation, documentation, and diagnostic groups. Each of these content categories was addressed in detail during the course. At the completion of the review for each of these content categories, a short multiple-choice test was given to the participants related to the specific content area. At the completion of the course, all but one of the participants were given a post-test, which was the same test as the pre-test. Scores on the post-test ranged from 75.8% to 96.1% of the questions being answered correctly. In addition to receiving detailed information related to therapeutic recreation content, course participants also received written and oral/signed information concerning test-taking strategies. This information was infused throughout the course and was interspersed with content information. The evaluations indicated that vocabulary and group discussion were again considered the greatest strengths of the course. In addition, participants indicated that taking tests repeatedly was helpful in reducing their test anxiety. Four of the therapeutic recreation review course participants passed the CTRS exam in November of 1994, and two others passed it in May of 1995. Of the four who passed the CTRS exam in November 1994, three were first-time test-takers, and the other was taking the test for the second time.

Until recently, the therapeutic recreation review course had not taken place at Gallaudet University since 1994. Review courses were offered two times between 1994 and 2002, but not enough people registered. A therapeutic recreation review course was held early in 2004, and several graduates who planned to take the CTRS exam within the next year attended. The few graduates from the Therapeutic Recreation Program at Gallaudet University, who have taken the CTRS exam in the past few years, have done so on their own. They have studied with colleagues at their worksites and with other CTRS candidates. Three graduates of the Therapeutic Recreation Program have passed the CTRS exam in the past few years. One graduate has taken the test two times and has not passed. One graduate, who had let the certification lapse, took the test immediately after it became computer-based and did not pass—even though this individual had been working in therapeutic recreation as a CTRS for several years. These test-takers requested and received extended time. According to deaf and hard of hearing test-takers, the extra time allows them to be able to read each question and all possible responses carefully, so that they understand all the nuances of what is being asked. Most of the graduates of the Therapeutic Recreation Program have opted not to take the CTRS exam. In fact, most of them have not even completed the *NCTRC Candidate Bulletin* and applied for eligibility to take the CTRS exam, even though they have been continually encouraged to do so by Therapeutic Recreation Program faculty. They are working in nonclinical settings where the CTRS credential is not required, or they are using their background in therapeutic recreation and working in a related human service field. It appears that without a therapeutic recreation review course available to graduates, most of them do not pursue the CTRS credential.

LESSONS LEARNED

Many lessons can be learned from this story. Some of them are related to the politics of working with professional credentialing boards and how to influence decisions related to testing and exam management. Others are related to the education of the general public, the profession, the faculty who create the curriculum, and the courses within the curriculum. Still others are related to student competencies and outcomes. Finally, lessons are also related to the curriculum itself, the purpose driving the curriculum, and how the curriculum impacts the success of graduates' taking and passing a credentialing exam. What have been the problems and the barriers?

Probably the biggest problem in therapeutic recreation certification testing is that a person is declared competent or not competent to receive the CTRS credential based on this single measurement. This measurement has an enormous effect on the life of the test-taker as it determines whether or not an individual gains entry into the profession of therapeutic recreation.

Another concern is related to changing the test from a paper-and-pencil format to a computer-based, mastery exam format. Some test-takers find computer-based testing to be daunting, especially if they do not use computers on a daily basis and are unfamiliar with the technical skills needed to move through the test itself. The mastery exam format does not allow an individual to go back through the entire test once a particular section is finished. This method of testing in itself can create undue anxiety for persons who perceive themselves as poor test-takers.

In addition, the majority of the questions that are used in this type of standardized, credentialing test require the test-taker to regurgitate facts, analyze information, and apply this information to situations that are presented in the test itself. This feature can be problematic in a profession where face-to-face contact between the individual and the practitioner/professional is at the heart of professional practice. It appears that individuals often choose therapeutic recreation as a career *because* it is based on face-to-face interaction and not on written tasks, although that tendency is becoming less prevalent as the need for documentation increases. How can a written exam possibly measure a person's disposition and readiness to work with others and facilitate positive outcomes? It is also not uncommon for an individual to be able to do well in the classroom yet fail in the real-world setting, as well as the reverse.

Finally, the exam is timed, and the only apparent reason for this seems to be this is the tradition that has been established in the standardized testing industry. However, the job tasks inherent in therapeutic recreation (unless it is an emergency situation) all take longer than a few seconds or minutes to accomplish. Assessing clients, writing treatment/activity plans, and implementing and evaluating programs all take considerable time to do well. Administrative tasks such as preparing budgets, dealing with personnel, and establishing policy are generally long-term projects. There is little in the practice of therapeutic recreation that demands a professional to complete something *post haste*. Why then is it necessary for the exam to be timed, when having it not timed would eliminate the need for "extended time requests"?

Additional considerations are as follows:

1. In an ideal world, a credentialing exam should be only one of several measures of expertise in a total competency assessment system. This system would include an interview, a videotape of the person working with clients, a self-assessment related to perceived competence, a professional portfolio that includes evaluations of the individual's performance during internships and previous employment, and a content-based test, including written multiple-choice, short-answer, and essay questions and/or a face-to-face exam, all related to the body of knowledge in the profession.
2. Another problem was having instructors of deaf and hard of hearing candidates becoming actively involved with the NCTRC too late in the examination development and implementation process. If professionals who are deaf and hard of

hearing themselves, or who are hearing allies familiar with the learning and testing needs of the population, do not get involved with the credentialing board/decision-makers at the outset, then any suggestions for test revision after that point are most likely going to be met with resistance. The CTRS exam was developed in the late 1980s, and the first certification exam in therapeutic recreation was given in November 1990. The Therapeutic Recreation Program at Gallaudet University began in 1987, and the first person who graduated from it took the CTRS exam in 1991. This timing was too late in the exam design and implementation process to request that major changes be made in the ways in which competence was to be determined, the test was to be constructed, and accommodations were going to be provided. Intra-professional politics, information, and connections are at the core of this problem.

3. Lack of understanding of deafness and hearing loss is another major problem. Educating the profession about persons who are deaf and hard of hearing is crucial. In therapeutic recreation, persons who experience hearing loss have always been considered clients, not practitioners—the service recipients instead of the service providers. Looking at persons who are deaf and hard of hearing, who have graduated from therapeutic recreation programs, and who are eligible to take the CTRS exam requires, at the very least, a change in attitude and perception on the part of hearing decision-makers. Although changing attitudes is not an easy process, they can be changed by a combination of education and exposure to persons of equal status (Anthony, 1969; 1972; Kisabeth & Richardson, 1985; Swisher, 1986). Unfortunately, the small number of therapeutic recreation professionals who are deaf or hard of hearing does not allow this reorientation to occur on a widespread basis. Most therapeutic recreation professionals who have worked with individuals who are deaf and hard of hearing have done so when the hearing loss is accompanied by other challenges, such as mental retardation and other developmental disabilities. In fact, the concept of deafness as nonpathological is not even considered by most therapeutic recreation professionals. It is important to understand this mindset when dealing with equitable testing, especially when testing is controlled by persons who have little or no experience with individuals who are deaf and hard of hearing. Too often, hearing professionals suggest different and lower cutoff scores for persons who are deaf and hard of hearing. This suggestion is often based on the mistaken assumption that deaf and hard of hearing persons cannot achieve the level that is expected of hearing persons. This solution is not acceptable under any circumstances, but especially if one is interested in maintaining high quality, equality, and equity. The CTRS exam scores obtained by deaf candidates who did not pass ranged from 1 point to 14 points below the cutoff score. In subsequent testings, the individuals in all of the above categories passed. Some candidates needed only a second testing, while others needed four additional testings. The only consistent pattern was that as individuals took subsequent exams, their scores improved. Again, it would be a good idea to use multiple measures to assess the competence of everyone. If that is too cumbersome and not easily instituted, then additional or supplemental

measures may be used for those who score within a specified number of points from the cut score. These additional or supplemental measures could include observations of the person at work (bearing in mind confidentiality considerations), a face-to-face examination, additional questions that are in a short-answer or essay format, and a professional portfolio.

4. Graduates of therapeutic recreation programs who do not pass the exam inadvertently serve to perpetuate the assumptions and myths that people in the profession already have about this group. Deaf and hard of hearing students who major in therapeutic recreation have to develop the competencies that are necessary to practice. They must realize that the responsibility to learn and develop expertise lies on their shoulders, as well as on those of the program's faculty members. One of the competencies that students need is the ability to use and understand English, which means developing a personal and professional vocabulary and the ability to understand and use standard academic/professional English grammatical constructions. It also requires writing understandably, comprehending written English, and using higher level cognitive skills (e.g., applying, analyzing, synthesizing, and evaluating). Students must be predisposed to learning and must be able to take advantage of the academic environment that is present at a college/university. However, to do so, candidates must have the necessary educational background so that they are at the appropriate level of readiness when they arrive at the college/university. This area is the responsibility of the elementary, middle, and high schools, as well as colleges and universities.

5. In cases where numerous test-takers from a single college/university do not pass the exam, therapeutic recreation professionals perceive the curriculum and the content of the courses at such an institution as lacking rigor. Often, the attitude is that if the curriculum were rigorous, the candidates would pass the CTRS exam; but there is not a direct cause-and-effect relationship here. However, the college/university curriculum has to be stringent enough that students can work at the level expected of a beginning professional when they are on the job, meaning that the courses and the content within each course must meet the required national standards. This expectation can be a challenge at any college/university, but it can be especially so at Gallaudet University where all information and communication is visual. Obtaining all information via vision is extremely tiring and can leave one exhausted after attending several classes in one day. This process increases the chance of missing some crucial fact or nuance, since only sight is being utilized. It may mean that for students to develop adequately and appropriately as professionals, they need to attend more classes and/or take more credits. It may mean that the faculty who develop the curriculum need to focus more intently on the essential skills and less on the desirable skills. It may also mean that the way the courses are taught needs to be changed so that students have more opportunities to relate theory to the hands-on experiences that support it. This feature would include making sure that in addition to presenting content competently in sign language, faculty write, use, and fingerspell the appropriate professional terms and vocabulary so that students are familiar with them before

they take the certification or licensure exam. It may mean that faculty have to provide students with many different types of experiences so that they truly understand the content and the character expected of the therapeutic recreation professional. Finally, it may mean that members of university faculties need to advise their deaf and hard of hearing graduates to work in the profession for at least one year before taking the CTRS exam—as a way to put their university classroom learning into practice and further develop as a professional beforehand. When graduates are fortunate enough to have either a formal or informal mentor who is a CTRS, especially one who is deaf or hard of hearing, they may have an increased chance of passing the exam on the first try. In fact, those students who have passed the CTRS exam on the first try, without a review course, seem to be older students with a strong academic focus, who have come back to school after working for a number of years and know they want to major in therapeutic recreation.

As a result of the efforts of the past few years and the increased ability of some deaf and hard of hearing test-takers to now pass the exam, awareness of the problem of equitable testing in therapeutic recreation has noticeably increased. Has the problem been solved? No. However, identifying the problem has made people aware of some of the issues involved when deaf and hard of hearing professionals, in order to receive a professional credential, are required to pass an exam that is embedded in written English. The credentialing board and therapeutic recreation professionals are now aware that deaf and hard of hearing test-takers can pass the CTRS exam. They are aware that there are professionals who are deaf and hard of hearing who are Certified Therapeutic Recreation Specialists, and they are doing excellent work in their chosen field. The credentialing board is now more aware of the need for extended time—as a means to reduce heightened anxiety so that the full meaning of the question/stem and the possible answers/responses can be evaluated adequately by the test-takers within a multiple-choice exam format. Deaf and hard of hearing therapeutic recreation students and graduates are aware of the importance of passing the CTRS exam for entry into the profession. Gallaudet's program is also aware that the curriculum must clearly meet certain standards so that graduates can qualify to take the certification exam and pass it.

SUGGESTIONS FOR SUCCESS IN THE FUTURE

Can success for deaf and hard of hearing test-takers be guaranteed when they take the CTRS exam? No, of course not, because it cannot be guaranteed for anyone taking the exam, whether deaf, hard of hearing, or hearing. However, some specific ways that success for deaf and hard of hearing test-takers may be increased by efforts of professionals who are interested in working on behalf of deaf candidates, in any profession, follow:

- Get involved immediately if development of a professional certification and/or licensure exam is under consideration by any national professional organization.

Being involved early has the potential to be much more effective than being involved mid-stream or close to the end.

- Assist in the process of actual test development and the writing of test items by joining the appropriate professional committee or task force. Be politically astute. Explain, or get someone who can, how to write test items so that they are not confusing for persons who are deaf and hard of hearing. (This explanation will actually help every test-taker.) Discuss what accommodations seem to be "reasonable" for deaf and hard of hearing test-takers and obtain some advice in this area. What might be feasible for one profession may not be for another.

- Discuss alternative methods for assessing professional competence. Eliminating a certification or licensure exam may not be the best solution. However, having the exam be only one of several measures makes competence assessment much more fair and can ultimately lead to a more balanced and accurate evaluation.

- Evaluate the professional preparation curriculum. Does it help students learn the knowledge and skills necessary to practice the profession? Does it assist the student in developing the character necessary and required to practice the profession? How can the curriculum be improved? Obtain feedback from employers, internship supervisors, program graduates, current students, program faculty, and faculty in other disciplines who teach students in the professional preparation program. It is imperative that the curriculum be on a par with all other professional preparation curricula, but it must take into consideration the specific learning environment necessary for deaf and hard of hearing students to be successful.

- Work with the feeder schools and school systems that send students to the college/university program. Deaf and hard of hearing students need more experience with formal, standardized testing. Consider what academic, study, and personal skills are absolutely necessary for students to have, so that they are ready to engage in a professional preparation program at the baccalaureate degree level.

- Educate the profession as a whole concerning deafness and hearing loss and their relationship to candidates' demonstration of professional competence. Offer workshops and make presentations at professional conferences to increase awareness and potentially change attitudes and behavior.

- Work with students in the professional preparation program so that they understand the importance not only of doing well in their classes but also of gaining and retaining the knowledge and skills that they learn. Assist them in understanding the impact that this mastery will have on the rest of their lives. Offer test preparation/review courses as indicated and teach not only the necessary content and knowledge but also test-taking skills. Encourage students to have confidence in their abilities to pass the exams.

- Never give up! Continue to work and advocate for equitable testing for deaf and hard of hearing test-takers.

CONCLUSION

It is clear that the controversy surrounding how best to assess and evaluate competency for therapeutic recreation professionals, especially those who are deaf and hard of hearing, has not been resolved. Of the between 15,000 and 16,000 "actively certified" CTRSs (Riley, 2003), probably only about 25 are deaf and hard of hearing. This number is small compared with the population as a whole. Granted, there are not many deaf and hard of hearing individuals who qualify to take the CTRS exam. Yet the pass rate for those taking it is only about 40%, and it decreases to 30% when it is the first time that a deaf or hard of hearing individual has taken the exam—a significant difference when compared with the 70–78% pass rate for the entire population of CTRS test-takers from May 2002 through May 2003 (NCTRC, 2003, Fall).

The NCTRC recently published certification standards changes. By December 31, 2007, the number of required therapeutic recreation courses in any professional preparation program was to be increased from three to four (NCTRC, 2003, Fall). Although this change may seem insignificant, it is not. For small programs, like the one at Gallaudet University, this change will be difficult at best; it is not likely that the number of candidates majoring in therapeutic recreation will be sufficient to sustain the number of therapeutic recreation-specific courses required for graduates to meet the certification eligibility requirements and to sit for the CTRS exam.

One individual who took the CTRS exam to re-certify did not pass the exam, and therefore, did not get re-certified even though this person had been working in the profession for several years. The frustration experienced from this result led to this individual's leaving the therapeutic recreation job and subsequently, the profession. Another graduate took the CTRS exam two times, not passing either time. This individual expressed it well by saying, "I know in my heart, I'm a good specialist in [therapeutic recreation], and I understand the population and patients/clients on many levels. . . . I gained a feeling of security (and) readiness for the exam. . . . I failed twice. I thought maybe this isn't the field for me." (Confidential personal communication, September 27, 2003). This individual has left the therapeutic recreation field and is in graduate school in another discipline. Is there anything sadder for a profession than losing good and qualified people because of testing procedures, which have such potentially disparate and devastating impacts? Not if this profession is to survive.

REFERENCES

Anthony, W. A. (1969). The effects of contact on an individual's attitudes toward disabled persons. *Rehabilitation Counseling Bulletin, 12*(3), 168–170.

Anthony, W. A. (1972). Societal rehabilitation: Changing society's attitudes toward the physically and mentally disabled. *Rehabilitation Psychology, 19*(3), 117-126.

Carter, M. J., Van Andel, G. E., & Robb, G. M. (2003). *Therapeutic recreation: A practical approach*, (3rd ed.). Prospect Heights, IL: Waveland Press.

Connolly, P. (1998a). Health care credentialing. In F. Brasile, T. Skalko, & J. Burlingame (Eds.), *Perspectives in recreational therapy: Issues of a dynamic profession* (pp. 384–388). Ravensdale, WA: Idyll Arbor.

Connolly, P. (1998b). NCTRC credentialing. In F. Brasile, T. Skalko, & J. Burlingame (Eds.), *Perspectives in recreational therapy: Issues of a dynamic profession* (pp. 404–412). Ravensdale, WA: Idyll Arbor.

Gutman, V. (Ed.). (2002). *Ethics in mental health and deafness.* Washington, DC: Gallaudet University Press.

Kisabeth, K. & Richardson, D. B. (1985). Changing attitudes toward disabled individuals: The effect of one disabled person. *Therapeutic Recreation Journal, 19*(2), 24–33.

National Therapeutic Recreation Society. (2000). *Definition statement.* (Rev. ed.), Ashburn, VA.

Riley, B. (2003, October). *National Council for Therapeutic Recreation Certification (NCTRC) annual certificants' meeting.* National Recreation and Park Association Annual Congress, St. Louis, MO.

Swisher, A. L. S. (1986). *The efficacy of two continuing education approaches in changing attitudes toward disabled persons and attitudes toward the therapeutic recreation profession.* Unpublished doctoral dissertation, University of Maryland, College Park.

Sylvester, C., Voelkl, J. E., & Ellis, G. D. (2001). *Therapeutic recreation programming: Theory and practice.* State College, PA: Venture Publishing. The NCTRC newsletter. (2003, Fall). *Copy Editor,* 7.

GRE Performance and the Deaf Community

Charlene Sorensen

This chapter focuses on Deaf community experiences, perspectives, and concerns related to performance on the Graduate Record Examinations (GRE). The GRE is administered by the Educational Testing Services under the direction of the Graduate Record Examinations Board, which is affiliated with the Association of Graduate Schools and the Council of Graduate Schools. The study on which this chapter is based arose as an incidental activity resulting from a National Science Foundation (NSF) grant-funded project at Gallaudet University. One of the outcomes of this project was the recognition of serious concerns among deaf and hard of hearing individuals regarding the general GRE and a statistical evaluation of their performance on a series of practice exams that confirmed poor performance on the exams regardless of academic ability. Strategy workshops were developed and provided in sign language for potential test-takers. All participants used sign language for communication purposes at school and at the workshops. The members of the Deaf community who participated in the workshops included deaf and hard of hearing individuals who attended Gallaudet University. The concerns of the students regarding the GRE, the identified problems encountered during test-taking, the impact of the training on scores, and inferences regarding the competitiveness of student scores after the workshops are documented in this chapter.

THE BEGINNINGS

At Gallaudet University, a small liberal arts university where most of the undergraduate students are deaf or hard of hearing, a pilot program for preparing students for the GRE was instituted as an incidental aspect of an NSF grant project called Focus On Reaching Women in Academics, Research and Development in Science, Engineering and Mathematics (FORWARD in SEM), HRD-97-14729. This grant project was conducted by four co-principal investigators: Dr. Rachelle Heller at the George Washington University (GWU), Dr. Catherine Mavriplis at GWU, Dr. Charlene Sorensen at Gallaudet University, and Dr. H. David Snyder at Gallaudet University. The purpose of the project was to prepare underrepresented groups for advanced studies in the fields of science, engineering, and mathematics. The special foci of this project were women, minorities, and deaf or hard of hearing individuals.

The original grant project, FORWARD in SEM, had five components for preparing individuals to pursue advance degrees: A mentoring network, a workshop called FORWARD to Graduate School, a research competition, course materials that enhanced access to the information by deaf and hard of hearing participants, and a linked seminar course. The seminar course was one of the most illuminating for identifying obstacles to the Deaf community in pursuing advanced degrees in science, engineering, and mathematics.

The seminar course was offered to expose students to graduate-level research expectations and proposal writing/scientific publication, as well as, by default, to look at the admission requirements for graduate school, including course work, research experience, the admission essay, and entrance exam requirements. The seminar was offered as a multidisciplinary, interactive, linked course with GWU. The purpose of this course was to promote student research on topics such as environmental issues, where anyone in the fields of science, engineering, or mathematics could participate—with each person bringing their strengths and knowledge base to the table to assist in solving a problem. The end result was to produce a research proposal suitable for submission to a funding agency.

During the pilot seminar, Gallaudet University also undertook the additional task of determining the needs of deaf or hard of hearing students who wished to enter graduate programs in science, engineering, and mathematics, as well as the obstacles that students would have to overcome. Statistically, few members of this population are currently pursuing advanced studies in these fields. The goal for the seminar was to not only have students work on research areas, but also to address important issues regarding barriers to accessing higher education. A desired outcome was to assist students in advocating for their admission into the graduate schools of their choice.

During the first of these seminar courses, students began to share their concerns about going to graduate school. Although we identified a variety of expressed concerns (e.g., "Interpreters do not normally know advanced technical vocabulary needed in graduate school," "No one I know has gotten into graduate school," and "I have never been at a school with hearing people before and do not know if I would be accepted"), no concern occurred as frequently as concerns about GRE scores. The GRE is used by many graduate schools as a primary instrument to screen student skills, and individuals who consistently score low on the GRE test are at a significant disadvantage for gaining admissions as well as financial assistance.

This concern over standardized testing for admission (specifically the GRE) was consistent among all participants in the seminar at Gallaudet and was later discovered to be a concern for many deaf and hard of hearing students regardless of their major field. Even students who had high grade-point averages were extremely worried that this exam could be an obstacle to their educational goals. It was not seen as simply a challenging exam; it was seen as a barrier to graduate school. Students expressed concern over their performance often before they had attempted the exam or even a practice exam. Several students had decided not to go to graduate school because they were convinced that they could never "pass" the test. More than a few students, when exposed to test questions, believed that the testers were trying to trick them to prevent them from going to graduate school.

Although students who are worried about the GRE can seek workshops to assist in preparation, our students also complained that the workshops available to hearing students were not helpful to them. Obtaining sign language-interpreted GRE review courses outside the university was difficult and rarely possible. Even having the material interpreted did not truly offer equal access to the same amount of material and interaction: The lag time between instruction and interpretation often makes asking questions difficult, quick group discussions are difficult, etc.

After much dialogue, it was obvious that, for deaf candidates, the GRE does represent a significant barrier to graduate school—both due to the students' concerns over even attempting the test and, as later discovered, their actual performance on the exam. The concerns of the students gave birth to the GRE preparation workshops presented at Gallaudet University in sign language.

THE GRE

A description of the GRE may be useful at this point. There are a variety of tests under the GRE heading: the general examination and many subject area tests. Students applying for graduate programs are most often required to take the general examination. At the time of the initial workshops, the exam included three multiple-choice parts: verbal, quantitative, and analytical. The content of each of these sections is described later in this chapter. Since that time, the format has changed to two multiple-choice sections, verbal and quantitative, and an analytical writing component. In addition, separate and specific GRE subject area tests are offered by Educational Testing Service (ETS; e.g., biology, chemistry, engineering, psychology, etc.). Many science, engineering, mathematics, and technical (SEMT) graduate programs require such a subject area test in addition to the general exam. The pilot program at Gallaudet, however, focused only on the general exam as it was most commonly required, and some of the strategies learned regarding the general test might be applied to more area-specific tests as well.

PRE-WORKSHOP CONSIDERATIONS AND NEEDS ASSESSMENT

We, the grant co-principal investigators from Gallaudet University, decided that part of the seminar could be an optional series of weekend GRE preparation sessions. During the first semester, the preparation was for the seminar students only. During the following semester, workshops were made available to all science, engineering, mathematics, or technology students. Afterwards, students exhibited such great interest in attending these workshops that they were opened to students at Gallaudet University who majored in any subject area. These workshops were to provide exposure to various types of test questions, test-taking strategies, and a brief review of the basic information with which students struggled most, and they were to be conducted in sign language. The workshops continued for three-and-a-half years—the length of the grant project. Due to popular demand, they were re-started in spring 2004 and will be offered in the spring for subsequent years through Gallaudet University's summer and Saturday programs.

Although the test was paper-based when the GRE workshops began, it became a computer adaptive test soon afterwards. The workshops were then altered to match the changes in the GRE as they occurred.

Before starting the workshops, students were informally questioned regarding their concerns on the content of the exams. Students' concerns were specific and showed much self-awareness as well as at least a superficial knowledge of what would be required on the verbal and mathematical portions of the GRE. Their concerns on the specific sections are described below. Students also felt they had limited strategies for the question types on the test and expressed concern over understanding the questions and connotations within the questions and answers. These concerns are not unrealistic. Studies have shown that the impeded access to English for deaf and hard of hearing individuals often makes the "language of standardized tests" especially difficult for members of this population, whether or not a given individual uses American Sign Language (ASL) or English as their primary language, or communicates using a sign system that combines features of both languages. The term *primary* is used rather than *first language* because many deaf individuals have hearing parents and/or may have been exposed only to English growing up. However, the language they currently use most or understand best on a day-to-day basis is American Sign Language. Access to English and English phraseology, especially as presented on multiple-choice standardized tests, is especially limited. Specifically, the fragments or question stems as well as the manner in which English is presented on standardized tests make it more difficult for the students to derive concepts or vocabulary from context. In short, performance on standardized tests shows that the average deaf person scores lower on standardized tests than hearing persons (Allen, 1994; Holt, 1994). Students are well aware of this fact. Their concerns about scoring too low were realistic, based on the results from the pre- and post-test.

When questioned about their concerns on the verbal section, students had a sense that their struggles arose from the differences between an auditory language like English and a visual language like ASL, and from their difficulty in accessing the former. As our project faculty evaluated performance on this portion of the test, we concurred with many of the students' concerns and perceived barriers. These issues included: (1) In English, many words can often be used to describe one concept; but in signed languages, one sign may used to describe many words. The opposite is also true. In short, there is not a one-to-one correspondence between languages. This situation means that deaf readers/test-takers often know only the most frequently used meanings of English words that have multiple meanings. With the limited access to the questions due to the "language of standardize tests," recognizing the other meanings from context did not occur. (2) Students often knew that there was some secret to breaking down words based on their sounds or spelling, but the concept of doing so was not natural to some of them since word parts are not a significant part of their primary signed language. (3) Students found it difficult to identify the connotations of words used in the hearing world.

Students were also concerned about the required mathematics sections. Statistically, deaf students often perform below their hearing peers on standardized tests in this area, and students were aware of this fact (Allen, 1994; Holt, 1994). They had less confidence in their math ability on standardized tests than on any of the other tests—even among students who had high grades in their math and science courses.

Students did not have a strong opinion regarding the analytical section, possibly because they were not as familiar with this portion as they were with the other portions. After exposure to questions of this nature, they were baffled as to where to begin to unravel what was being asked as well as how to assess the validity of each answer.

In addition to the content of the exam, the students were also concerned about graduate schools pre-judging them if their scores were flagged for having received special accommodations such as interpreters or extended time. They also had concerns that graduate schools would not give them a chance if they had special needs. ETS has, for a long time, made provisions for special populations in testing situations; for those who are deaf and hard of hearing, the provisions available include extended time and the provision of a sign language interpreter for the test's instructions only. Over the course of the pilot program, conversations were held with a representative from ETS who was familiar with the special-needs accommodations. Since 2001, ETS no longer flags the scores of candidates who have had special accommodations and instead only states that the test was taken under "nonstandard conditions."

After preliminary discussions, pre-tests, and follow-up conversations, several facts became clear and gave guidance as to how to set up workshops for each of the sections of the test. Faculty members working with the project were given the basic concepts that are covered on the different sections of the exam, so that they could review the material with students. The following strategies also needed to be reviewed regarding any multiple-choice test: (1) Eliminating one or more answers will increase one's odds of getting the question correct; (2) understanding the instructions before one arrives will allow one to focus time and energy on the questions; (3) making connections and visualizing as much as possible without wasting time is the goal—probably the most significant goal—as we also need to incorporate visualizing and understanding the question with the limited comprehension issues mentioned above; and (4) practice with example tests will lead to a better performance and better understanding of the nature of the test itself.

THE WORKSHOP

The preparation program was set for a series of weekends since it was often difficult to find common times during the academic week. The goals for the program were:

1. To see the current status of students who may be taking the GRE in the future. From this, we would learn better the true barriers to the students and where to focus and divide our time and effort for the strategy workshops.
2. To provide strategy sessions and workshops conducted in sign language to improve preparation for the test.
3. To see the outcome/improvement of students after preparing for the GRE via strategy sessions/workshops.

Originally the sessions ran for nine weeks with three hours each Saturday morning. The sessions were divided as follows:

- Week 1: Orientation and pre-test
- Week 2: Vocabulary building
- Week 3: Analogies and antonyms
- Week 4: Reading comprehension
- Week 5: Basic math/algebra/geometry review
- Week 6: Word problems
- Week 7: Logical and analytical thinking
- Week 8: Post-test
- Week 9: Follow-up and feedback

Each workshop included a basic review, a strategy review, and group problem-solving time. Students were exposed to different types of questions, strategies for answering questions, and the logic behind the questions, and they also practiced the art of "process of elimination." Workshops were led by instructors from Gallaudet University who teach their courses in sign language, who themselves have good test-taking skills, and who are knowledgeable in their field. The analytical section was taught by the principal investigators of the project. Research and education association materials were used for the paper-based portion. Copies of the GRE Powerprep tool were purchased to use when the test became computer-based. (In the next section, the results of the pre-tests and the impact of the training sessions are described.)

Eventually, the workshops were reduced in duration from nine weeks to four, and each session increased in length from three hours to five and a half as a result of feedback from faculty and students regarding the number of weekends involved. As will be described later, the results after the shortened sessions were more varied than after the nine-week time frame.

GRE PRE-TEST PERFORMANCE

The possible score range on each section of the GRE is 200–800. The pre-test scores were extremely low. Over the course of the three and a half years of the pilot program, the mean scores for the deaf students on the pre-tests were as follows: verbal 343.1, quantitative 385.0, and analytical 386.5. These scores are for those students participating in the workshops from the third semester and beyond. During the first two semesters, only the amount by which each student's score changed was retained. Once the principal investigators realized the positive impact that the sessions were having, the specific pre- and post-test scores were documented. The number of participants whose specific scores were recorded/retained was 52. Pre-test and post-test data presented in this chapter use these 52 data points only.

For ease in understanding the performance level, percentages may be helpful. Compared with the national averages, the above average scores for this group of students translated into an average of at or below the 22nd percentile in each category (meaning that 22% of the population scored at or below this average and 78% scored above this level). The scores reported are from students spanning all academic areas (humanities, sciences, social sciences, etc.) who had good academic grade performance in their coursework. For many students, the low scores were not only discouraging but also debilitating. Almost all students expressed frustration and disbelief at their low scores—only 9 of the 52 had any section above the 60th percentile, and only 4 had any section above the 75th. Overall, 82.7% of all students fell at or below the 50th percentile. Only 2 students of the entire 52 (3.8%) scored above the 50th percentile in every category. Test score comparisons to others in their specific fields of study as well as the national average were provided to the students. Again, these were quite discouraging to the students. Many students left the pre-test with the attitude of "Why bother?" or "Maybe I need to try doing some more on my own before I even try this GRE strategy workshop, so I won't embarrass myself," etc. Thirty-three of the 52 students, 63.5%, did not return for any of the other workshops and therefore had no strategy training. However, in spite of the discouragement, some students were still motivated to continue the strategies training. Since most scores were low, it is not clear that the slightly lower scores were the primary reason for not returning for the workshops. Those who did not return had an average score of 326.0 for the verbal, 368.5 for the quantitative, and 366.4 for the analytical; they scored at or below the 18th percentile. For those who were willing to return for the workshops, their scores were 372 for the verbal, 415.3 for the quantitative, and 422.6 for the analytical section; they scored at or below the 28th percentile.

GRE WORKSHOP RESULTS

During the workshops, we continued to get confirmation that many of the issues were seemingly deaf-specific and not necessarily knowledge-specific. In all content areas, students felt there was not always enough information in the stem of the multiple-choice item to be able to obtain a visual image of what was being asked or described. After much practice, students found that putting every answer with the question stem gave them a better picture of the question being asked, but this took additional time.

For the verbal part, the lack of familiarity with English vocabulary was significant. Because a single sign may represent the concepts of several English synonyms, students often did not recognize a specific word. But when the concept was signed, they were able to thoroughly describe or discuss the relationships and meanings. The first strategy was to enable students to understand the written vocabulary by reviewing how to break down words into "word parts" or morphemes. A majority of students involved in our workshops struggled with Latin or Greek root words, prefixes, or suffixes. Although some deaf individuals have been taught how to break down words and do it well, the majority of our students were not comfortable with the skill. When initially reviewing word parts, students could produce only a limited number of words when given a word part (e.g., give four words that have *ab-* as their prefix). When asked if a word was made of parts or if it was a gestalt (i.e., could not be divided into two or more meaningful subunits), students struggled with how to divide the word by parts or even syllables. For them, the strategy used by hearing persons of orally sounding out the words was generally not much help. Thus, students tried to remember rules for where to divide words, such as those regarding double consonants or vowels. They needed to learn the word parts and then look for those parts within words. Often, hearing people will have a clue about the meaning of a word because parts of that word "sound" like parts of the words that they already know. For the deaf person, this "clue" is not as evident. They must recognize the part visually and match it to a definition. After reviewing a few examples and learning the lists of word parts, many of the students developed a sense of whether a word was composed of several parts or was a gestalt. Determining what the parts meant was still a slow process. Once students determined that a word was made of parts they had learned, they felt better equipped to answer the questions. Also, it helped them feel less like the words they encountered or thought they knew had hidden meanings or connotations only known in the hearing world.

Additional strategies to help students with the verbal portion of the exam included a review of the parts of speech, a description of the instructions, a method of eliminating most probably wrong answers, creating sentences to find relationships, and understanding embedded clauses. With questions containing antonyms and analogies, where only words and not sentences were provided, students did well after learning to make sentences and relationships before trying to answer the questions. Again, vocabulary was the biggest limitation in this portion of the exam.

Students also had concerns about how to answer the mathematics parts. In more than one case, a student was frustrated with the part of the exam where one marks "A" if column "A" was larger, "B" if column B was larger, "C" if A and B are equal, and "D" if you cannot determine which is larger. Students translated the instructions to mean mark "D" if you cannot decide (determine) the answer. Note that DECIDE and DETERMINE are signed in the same way. In those cases, students marked "D" if they were not immediately sure of the answer. Their rationale was that those questions would not count against you. This problem was simply remedied by explaining what was meant by choice "D."

Other needs in the math workshops included a review of the basic math rules, strategies for eliminating answers, quick calculations with rounding to 10s, etc., determining how the language gives clues to the mathematical functions, and the use of 0, 1, -1, 0.1, and -0.1 in trying to determine relationships between x and y. The students had typically tried only one value for problems where relationships between x and y were being evaluated and therefore chose the wrong answer. Though this is a problem any test-taker could experience, it was found consistently among our participants. A lack of familiarity with standardized math tests may contribute to this consistency.

Finally, most students were unfamiliar with the analytical portion of the GRE and lacked strategies for attacking such questions. For this section, students were encouraged to draw pictures to turn the sentences into visual concepts. They were shown a variety of types of questions and recommendations for what types of diagrams would be beneficial.

GRE POST-TEST PERFORMANCE

Of the students who returned for the strategy workshops, significant improvement occurred in their scores when the material was discussed over the nine-week period. When strategy courses were provided over nine weeks, all students improved from between 100 and 350 points. (These data are from the first two semesters where only the change in total scores was noted and retained.) Although this change is quite significant, it still left students in the below-50th percentile area, which is not sufficient for entry into competitive graduate programs.

For the four-week sessions, the data became more varied. An increase of more than 50 points was noted for 47.3% of the students, 26.3% essentially scored the same in their pre-test scores and post-test scores, and 26.3% decreased. Two students only came for the pre-test and post-test without participating in the workshops; their scores dropped by more than 100 points.

Because four factors came into play when changing from the nine-week to the four-week sessions, it cannot be concluded which one had the greater impact on the reduced numerical benefit of the workshops. The factors were: (1) The four-week workshops were opened to all majors for these sessions, (2) the longer time spans per session were admittedly difficult for the students, (3) the shorter amount of total time on each test section reduced the content of the sessions, and (4) missing a single session had greater impact. Missing one or more sessions was common for both the nine-week program and the four-week program. Mandatory attendance was difficult because the series was free and voluntary. As three of the four factors discussed above deal with changing from nine shorter sessions to four longer sessions, it becomes important to determine the optimal number of sessions and length of session times. Students who were surveyed felt that the four weeks were too few—they needed time to process the material and practice it. However, students also felt they would be less inclined to commit nine weekends of a semester to the workshops. Students also identified a preference for having the sessions offered as a "college course" over a one- or two-semester period.

PERCEPTIONS OF THE WORKSHOP AND CONTINUING EFFORTS FOR OVERCOMING THE GRADUATE SCHOOL OBSTACLES

Overall, students reported that the workshops were helpful in that they were exposed to the kinds of questions they would have on the GRE, learned to understand the instructions better, and came to believe that they could improve if enough effort was put into their studies. However, because they were still not scoring competitively, students were also informed to advocate for themselves in applying to schools. Students were encouraged to reference the National Task Force on Equity in Testing Deaf and Hard of Hearing Individuals website to show that deaf individuals statistically do less well on standardized tests than their hearing counterparts (See http://gri.gallaudet.edu/TestEquity/index.html). It is important that graduate admissions officers understand these issues so that they have better indicators of performance and do not screen out high-potential students. Several students have advocated for themselves in this way and have successfully entered graduate school.

A member of ETS is on that task force and has been significantly helpful in facilitating changes in some of the test questions, thus securing greater equity for deaf test-takers. To work with ETS to improve the accessibility of their tests for students who are deaf and hard of hearing is a continuing goal.

For the continuing workshops, the number of sessions will be kept to four. This reduction greatly increases the attendance and makes the series cost-effective; in addition, a fee will be charged for the workshops, possibly resulting in more consistent attendance at the sessions. Future data will include tracking scores along with attendance. Students will also be encouraged to take the workshops for a full year before they take the exam.

LESSONS LEARNED REGARDING THE DEAF COMMUNITY AND GRE PERFORMANCE

The test preparation workshops were beneficial for a variety of reasons: increased student self-confidence, improvement of student comprehension of the test questions and answer choices, improved student strategies, and increased awareness of how to self-advocate. However, there is still great concern about equal access to graduate education for deaf and hard of hearing individuals. Although it is true that students improved significantly (especially during the nine-week programs), the majority of students still scored far below the 50th percentile. This fact makes them less than competitive for admission into programs as well as for financial support.

Schools do use multiple tools to assess a student's admission request, but the GRE often plays a significant role. The use of this tool may make equity in access impossible for deaf and hard of hearing individuals. Consideration of a separate scale of competitiveness for deaf individuals may be helpful if the GRE is used at all as a tool for assessing readiness for graduate school, but development of such a scale would take time. A more immediate approach is educating graduate admissions officers about the performance levels and issues that are known regarding the Deaf community and the GRE at the time of application. (Note that students are often hesitant to point out their deafness during the application process. Their concern is that they will be discriminated against due to the school's financial responsibility for interpreting costs and/or the department's unfamiliarity with a deaf individual's capability because the department may not have had deaf students before.) That education can happen through materials such as this book, publications in journals, and presentations at professional conferences. However, this educating of graduate admissions officers can also occur, and usually first occurs, via students who are applying to individual programs. This is why the preparation workshops must be accompanied by preparing students to advocate for admissions, even if their scores are not competitive. Since the beginning of the workshops, a few students have applied to and entered graduate school. Those who reported back stated that personal contact with their future department chairs, re-application, and requests for reconsideration were necessary. Furthermore, students felt somewhat more empowered to do and request the above because they had learned about studies, as well as the task force, that exist to strengthen their case for decreasing the dependence on a standardized test score when assessing a deaf and hard of hearing student's ability to do graduate work.

REFERENCES

Allen, T. E. (1994). Who are the deaf and hard-of-hearing students leaving high school and entering postsecondary education? *American Annals of the Deaf, 139*(4).

Holt, J. (1994). Classroom attributes and achievement test scores for deaf and hard of hearing students. *American Annals of the Deaf, 139*(4).

Maximizing Access to Licensure for Deaf and Hard of Hearing Social Workers

Teresa V. Mason and Judith L. Mounty

Early studies on the testing of individuals from diverse ethnic groups reported that "minority group children suffer intellectual deficits when compared with their 'more advantaged' peers" (Cole & Bruner, 1971, p. 868). One might suggest that today's testing procedures are more refined, better developed, and more rigorously studied. While that suggestion may be true, evidence suggests a continuation of differential testing patterns among individuals from various cultural and ethnic groups (McDowell, 1992). This chapter addresses the use of standardized tests, specifically for social work licensure, with those candidates who are deaf and hard of hearing.

GENERAL USE OF STANDARDIZED TESTS

In the social sciences, standardized testing is used in the United States for a number of reasons. Test scores in the United States are the vehicles for access to most educational and employment opportunities (McDowell, 1992; Olmedo, 1981). Test scores are used as guidelines for academic placements, college admissions, and course grades. In clinical studies, researchers use standardized instruments to conduct studies that help broaden the knowledge base and improve upon existing technologies by measuring individual or group differences. Social scientists use reliable and valid measures to conduct research about clinical disorders, treatment approaches, and medication effectiveness (Olmedo, 1981). Policy decisions are sometimes based upon the results of studies using standardized instruments. Overall, professionals in the social sciences area view standardized tests as helpful tools for accomplishing productive, scholarly goals.

However, we can identify situations where standardized instruments normed for majority members are unable to fulfill their function. Most mainstream test instruments are targeted by English-speaking test makers for English-speaking test-takers. Candidates from diverse cultural, ethnic, and linguistic backgrounds may perform differently on standardized tests that are normed for members of the majority culture. Thus, the data gleaned from these tests may not accurately reflect measurement goals and the true mastery demonstrated by candidates.

In a study cited by Oquendo (1996), researchers found that Spanish-speaking patients were seen as less psychotic when evaluated in English compared with being evaluated in Spanish. Similarly, the results of a study by Dikert (1988) showed that staff members at inpatient mental health programs for the deaf have more positive attitudes toward deaf patients than staff members serving the general (hearing) population.

Inaccurate results from such tests may distort the reality of the individuals taking those tests and may have potentially harmful implications.

In summary, standardized tests are widely used in the United States. Test scores are often the keys to many opportunities, such as employment and education. Research findings suggest that many standardized tests are culturally and linguistically biased in favor of the majority culture and language. Members with diverse cultural and linguistic backgrounds may have difficulty with such tests. This difficulty may inadvertently compound an already disadvantageous situation and lead to further oppression of and discrimination against marginalized groups.

SOCIAL WORK LICENSURE

As in other fields, the profession of social work has used licensing examinations to protect the public from harm caused by incompetent professionals (American Educational Research Association, American Psychological Association, & National Council on Measurement in Education, 1985; 1999; Association of Social Work Boards, 2001). The Association of Social Work Boards (ASWB) was established in 1979 to regulate the profession of social work. At that time, only 23 states and Puerto Rico had laws regulating the profession. Since then, the rest of the states have adopted similar legislation. The organization's membership now includes 52 jurisdictions, including Puerto Rico, the United States Virgin Islands, and several Canadian provinces. The organization also educates its members, students in the field, and other interested parties on social work regulations.

All ASWB members use a set of examinations developed by and maintained by ASWB. The existence of a central entity allows boards to learn from one another and work together to further their goal of protecting the public through professional regulation. This entity can also help its members explore and seek solutions to problems and challenges (ASWB, 1999; 2001; 2002). The ASWB mission statement reads: "The mission of the Association of Social Work Boards is to assist social work regulatory bodies in carrying out their legislated mandates, and to encourage jurisdictional efforts to protect a diverse public served by social workers who are regulated through common values, ethics, and practice standards. The Association will help to foster public and professional understanding of the value, competency, and accountability of regulated social workers" (ASWB, 2002).

As of 2001, ASWB examinations are used in 49 states, the District of Columbia, the Virgin Islands, and the Canadian province of Alberta. Only California, which has its own licensing examination, and the United States territory of Puerto Rico do not use the ASWB examinations. However, each jurisdiction uses examination data differently and has its own set of criteria for awarding licenses, including degrees required, types of licensure (one to four), years of work, and number of required hours of supervision. Some states award licenses only after a particular number of years of work, and only at the advanced or clinical levels. Other states require tests and award licenses for social workers, persons with bachelor's degrees, and those just completing their master's degrees.

EXPERIENCES OF DEAF AND HARD OF HEARING SOCIAL WORKERS SEEKING SOCIAL WORK LICENSURE

Anecdotal reports by consumers and their advocates have long indicated that deaf and hard of hearing graduates of social work programs experience barriers related to licensure. Some consumers and agency administrators requested assistance from the National Task Force on Equity in Testing Deaf and Hard of Hearing Individuals, which one of the authors (Mounty) co-chairs. The Gallaudet University Department of Social Work, its students and graduates, and the ASWB work in concert with the task force. However, until now, there had been no research conducted to examine the problem. Mounty designed a multiple-choice written survey with the goal of gathering information from deaf and hard of hearing social workers and social work program graduates. Although exact terms may vary from jurisdiction to jurisdiction, one must possess a valid license to call oneself a social worker. In that regard, some of the respondents might be unlicensed and therefore unable to use this professional title.

The survey was divided into five sections: background information, current employment, educational preparation for social work practice, professional development, and licensing. To ensure that the questions were written in understandable English, it was reviewed by undergraduate and graduate students in the Gallaudet Department of Social Work. A small pilot study was also conducted, and improvements were made to the survey based on participant feedback. The study was approved by the Gallaudet University Institutional Review Board, and the survey was distributed at professional conferences and meetings and was posted at the website for the National Task Force on Equity in Testing Deaf and Hard of Hearing Individuals. Additional participants were identified by word of mouth. The study was still in progress at the time this book went to press, but a summary of preliminary findings based on descriptive statistics and qualitative analyses of 36 completed surveys is presented.

The respondents were primarily Caucasian females, 75% of whom identified themselves as deaf rather than, for example, hard of hearing or late-deafened. More than 85% of the respondents had a master's degree in social work, and of those, close to half also had a bachelor's degree in social work. Most currently work full-time in a field related to social work (83%) with deaf or hard of hearing individuals (78%). Of the 36 respondents, the largest number (14) have between 4 and 10 years of experience with 9 having less than 4 years experience, and 13 having more than 10 years of experience.

Fifty percent of the respondents have a license to practice social work in one or more jurisdictions. Of the 15 participants who specified which type of license they have, 8 are licensed at the clinical level. Eleven jurisdictions—10 different states and Canada—were represented. Some respondents obtained licenses before ASWB set up its current national testing system, and several jurisdictions do not participate in that system. Sixty-nine percent of the respondents reported having taken a licensing exam one or more times. Six people have taken an exam twice, three people have taken one three times, two people have taken an exam four times, and one has taken an exam six times. Not surprisingly, the highest-level examination, required in most jurisdictions to practice independently, bill for third-party payment, do administrative work, and obtain grants or contracts, was the one most often taken repeatedly. Note that not being able to become licensed at the higher levels limits opportunities for leadership and professional advancement and essentially prohibits a social worker from providing training and supervision for other social workers.

The reasons for not having a license included not having passed a test and not having the required licensure. Anecdotal reports suggest that many deaf and hard of hearing graduates of social work programs avoid having to take licensure tests because they are afraid of failing. In this small sample, only a few respondents gave this reason. More than 55% of the respondents work in human service agencies with deaf and hard of hearing clients or in school programs with deaf and hard of hearing students, holding positions that draw on their social work training but that do not require them to take a standardized test for licensing or certification.

The findings of this study reinforce a point often made throughout this text, namely that standardized tests are challenging for deaf and hard of hearing candidates at least in part because of inordinately complex syntax, unfamiliar and infrequently used word meanings, and idiomatic or figurative language tied to the experience of unhampered access to spoken as well as written English. In other words, the issue is one of access. Deaf and hard of hearing individuals who grow up in English-only environments, as well as those exposed to both languages, are hampered in accessing English because it is a language designed to be heard. This challenges a myth, born of misunderstanding, that deaf individuals who have difficulty with standardized tests necessarily have American Sign Language (ASL) as their first or native language. Individuals who acquire ASL at an early age either have culturally Deaf parents or attend a school for deaf students where they are exposed to ASL-using adults and peers.

Over half of the respondents in this study were mainstreamed for high school. Most of the others attended either a school for deaf students (28%) or a program for deaf students housed at a school for hearing students (18%). The totals exceed 100% because several individuals selected more than one option. Responses to questions about language and communication used while growing up suggest that most respondents grew up in English-speaking environments and that less than half of them had early exposure to ASL or signing while growing up. Yet, about 60% of the respondents indicated that they currently sign, and about 50% say that they use ASL as one of their languages, suggesting that while it is not a native language, it is useful and important in their adult lives, very likely because it can be fully accessed.

Sixty-four percent of the respondents indicated that additional criteria should be utilized to determine eligibility for certification for deaf or hard of hearing candidates who do not pass social work licensing tests. Making the English on the tests more clear and providing specially designed preparation courses are the two things that many respondents thought would most help other deaf and hard of hearing candidates pass the licensure tests. Comments on the surveys also suggest that access to English on the test is seen as a core issue in unsatisfactory test performance for those seeking social work licensure. Responses to a question about professional development after completing a degree indicated that lack of access to workshops and training may also be contributing to difficulties with testing and licensing for social work candidates.

RECOMMENDATIONS FOR MAXIMIZING ACCESSIBILITY FOR SOCIAL WORK LICENSURE

Despite the numerous barriers that deaf social workers may face when taking the social work licensing exam, there are potential solutions. First, effective solutions require recognition that there are difficulties that deaf test-takers face when taking a licensing exam in a language that is often not fully accessible or truly native. Second, test administrators and/or state officials must be willing to study the problem and recommend changes. Third, a willingness to invest money, time, and energy is essential for creating an equitable testing environment for deaf test-takers. Finally, deaf test-takers must be willing to make their needs known to test administrators so that accommodations may be granted. Below are several examples of potential solutions to some accessibility problems.

- Specially designed preparation courses. Research in other professions (see Simonsen, this text) suggests that candidates may benefit from a course or workshop series provided in the candidates' most accessible language by professionals knowledgeable in the field and with the test, and familiar with the kinds of problems many deaf and hard of hearing persons encounter with standardized tests.

- Practice tests. The Americans With Disabilities Act (ADA) stipulates provision of practice and preparation materials to those with disabilities. The ASWB provides a sample practice test; however, multiple practice tests for deaf test-takers may be helpful. Currently, prospective test-takers may purchase review materials and practice test packages from one or more independent entities, none of which are under the auspices of ASWB. However, these tests may or may not accurately represent the content and format of the items on the actual ASWB tests.

- Use of complementary or alternative criteria or data. Multiple measures of social work knowledge and skills possessed by deaf and hard of hearing candidates may provide a more accurate picture of skills. For example, a candidate's portfolio may include graduate school grade-point average, graduate school instructor recommendations, employer/supervisor evaluations, work samples, and recommendations from colleagues. In this way, a portfolio that captures a holistic view of a candidate's skills may be more useful for employers to make hiring decisions using a single measure.

- Creation of an interactive exam in which a deaf and hard of hearing social candidate is interviewed by a test administrator with an interpreter. The test would allow a constructed response or short answer by the candidate. This type of test may be more expensive to develop and score. However, this variation in testing may also be more equitable.

- Administration of the test using a sign language interpreter. In some cases, a candidate's knowledge, skills, and values may be better reflected on an exam when a sign language interpreter signs the test questions. In this way, the exam is administered in the test-taker's *primary or preferred* language and may not be as vulnerable to misinterpretation as when one must make sense of the question from a second, less-accessible language. Interpreters used for translation of the social work licensure exam must have adequate training. Interpreters must be well-versed in social work terminology and concepts in order to present an accurate translation of the concepts being measured. However, this option may be quite complicated because translation of instruments may affect construct validity (Crowe, in press). Rigorous field-testing of a translated instrument, along with back-translation, is needed prior to using it in "live" testing situations.

- Creation of a standardized, sign language version of the social work licensure exam. Creating alternate versions provides candidates with more than one option for taking the exam. For example, a signed version of the licensing exam may also have closed-captioning with the English version of the question on the screen. In addition, the data gathered from alternative versions of the exam can be used to create normative data about this population.

CONCLUSION

The challenges that deaf and hard of hearing social workers encounter in standardized tests for licensure are shared by deaf and hard of hearing professionals in other fields, and by deaf and hard of hearing test-takers in general. A central issue is the tendency to use complex English constructions without the contextual information that characterize face-to-face communication in the classroom and professional settings. The language of standardized testing is unique and even more decontextualized than textbook language. Unfortunately, many deaf and hard of hearing individuals have not had equal access to the language in order to use "self-talk" strategies to parse the English and unlock the intended meaning or purpose of the item. Multiple meanings and idiomatic lexical items that are not vital to the content being measured compound the problem. Inequities in access to knowledge and experience, both general and discipline-specific, also contribute to the challenge.

The regulation of social workers is important for protecting the interests of clients. Yet, the use of high-stakes tactics for determining who should be licensed may cause deaf and hard of hearing social workers to be a population at risk. The unique and special role of social workers as agents for change makes it especially important for deaf and hard of hearing social workers to assume leadership roles for advocating needed changes in their own community, as well as fill the all-important role of serving deaf and hard of hearing clients.

REFERENCES

American Educational Research Association, American Psychological Association, & National Council on Measurement in Education. (1985; 1999). *Standards for Educational and Psychological Testing.* Washington, DC: American Psychological Association.

Association of State Social Work Boards. (1999). *Are we there yet? The first 20 years of an association visionary journey.* Culpepper, VA: Author.

Association of Social Work Boards. http://www.aswb.org/members.shtml. Retrieved August 31, 2002.
Association of Social Work Boards. (2001). *Social work laws and regulations: A comparison guide.* Culpepper, VA: Author.
Cole, M., & Bruner, J. S. (1971). Cultural differences and inferences about psychological processes. *American Psychologist, 26,* 867–876.
Crowe, T. (in press). Cross-cultural translation: American Sign Language as an example. *American Annals of the Deaf.*
Dikert, J. (1988, May/June). Examination of bias in mental health evaluation of deaf patients. *Social Work,* 273–274.
McDowell, C. (1992). Standardized tests and program evaluation: Inappropriate measures in critical times. *New Directions for Program Evaluation, 53,* 45–54.
Mounty, J. (2003). Testing and licensing of deaf social workers. Unpublished paper.
Olmedo, E. L. (1981). Testing linguistic minorities. *American Psychologist, 36,* 1078–1085.
Oquendo, M. A. (1996). Psychiatric evaluation and psychotherapy in the patient's second language. *Psychiatric Services, 47,* 614–618.

New Hurdles: The Impact of Recent Federal Mandates on the Assessment of Deaf and Hard of Hearing Teachers and Teacher Candidates

Paul S. Singletary

Few educators or laypersons would quarrel with the goals of two recent federal mandates that affect teacher education: Title II of the Higher Education Act of 1998, and the No Child Left Behind Act of 2001. It is doubtful that anyone would argue with the underlying premises that (a) teacher education can and should be improved, or that (b) every child deserves a highly qualified teacher in the classroom. However, *how* one goes about achieving these goals has been a source of controversy over the years, as well as fodder for political campaigns. Today, deaf and hard of hearing teachers and teacher candidates, as well as administrators of schools and programs that serve deaf and hard of hearing students, are being "caught in the crossfire" between (1) federal and state legislators and parents, who are demanding better teachers in the classrooms, and (2) accrediting bodies and state departments of education, who are responding to this pressure by forcing school districts and teacher preparation programs to raise standardized test score requirements for teachers and teacher candidates.

GOALS AND REQUIREMENTS OF THE TITLE II OF THE HIGHER EDUCATION ACT (1998)

In October 1998, Congress responded to public pressure to improve the quality of teachers in the classroom by passing Title II of the Higher Education Act. According to the *Reference and Reporting Guide for Preparing State and Institutional Reports on the Quality of Teacher Preparation, Title II, Higher Education Act,* one of the law's key provisions is that higher education institutions must report—to their state education agency and to the general public—the pass rates of their program completers' performance on required state teacher licensure tests. Another provision of the Title II mandate is that state education agencies are to establish satisfactory and unsatisfactory levels of performance on the state teacher licensure tests for the institutions of higher education in their jurisdiction. Those institutions whose overall performance rate is less than satisfactory will be labeled "at risk" and given technical assistance and a chance to improve. Failure to improve overall performance to a satisfactory level (as determined by the state) will result in a label of "low performing" for that institution (National Center for Education Statistics, 2000).

Under the Title II mandate, each state education agency must develop a procedure by which "low-performing" institutions that do not improve their overall performance rates on required teacher licensure tests will lose state approval of their teacher preparation program. Furthermore, these low-performing institutions not only are to be declared ineligible for any funding for professional development activities awarded by the U.S. Department of Education, but they are also to be prohibited from accepting or enrolling any student that receives aid under Title IV of the Higher Education Act in the institution's teacher preparation program (National Center for Education Statistics, 2000).

FURTHER ACTION BY THE FEDERAL ACCREDITATION OVERSIGHT PANEL

In 2002, the National Advisory Committee on Institutional Quality and Integrity (NACIQI), the federal accreditation oversight panel for the U.S. Department of Education, demanded that if the National Council for Accreditation of Teacher Education (NCATE) wanted to retain its federal recognition as a national accrediting body, NCATE would have to require 80% pass rates on state teacher licensure tests at both the program and institutional levels as a requirement for NCATE accreditation. Threatened with the loss of its authority for carrying out its mission, NCATE had little recourse but to comply with this demand, even though representatives from NCATE's partner, the American Association of Colleges for Teacher Education (AACTE), had expressed "substantive concerns with the implementation of the new policy on use of licensure test results" (Schumann, 2003, p. 2). NCATE's Unit Accreditation Board bowed to NACIQI pressure in March 2003 by ruling that beginning with fall 2003 accreditation site visits, an institution will not be able to meet NCATE's Standard I: Candidate Knowledge, Skills and Dispositions, unless 80% or more of its program completers pass the required state licensure content examinations for that institution's state. This ruling is very serious considering that, under the current NCATE evaluation system, *all* standards must be met for an institution to be fully accredited. According to the NCATE guidelines, the required content tests include state licensing exams in academic content areas such as English, mathematics, French, music, early childhood education, special education, and elementary education. In addition, content tests include state licensing exams for other professional school personnel such as school counselors and administrators (NCATE, 2004, January 5).

GOALS AND REQUIREMENTS OF THE NO CHILD LEFT BEHIND ACT (2001)

Unlike Title II of the Higher Education Act, which requires teacher preparation programs to meet pass-rate standards for state licensure tests, the No Child Left Behind Act (NCLB) targets the performance of individual teachers. Although many of the provisions of NCLB deal with academic standards and the testing of students, one key provision focuses on requirements that teachers must meet to obtain or keep their jobs. According to NCLB, because recent studies indicate that teacher quality plays a paramount role in student achievement, all teachers in core academic areas must be "highly qualified" by the end of the 2005–2006 school year. *Highly qualified* is a specified term under this mandate, and its requirements include (1) possession of a bachelor's degree, (2) full state certification and licensure as defined by the state, and (3) demonstrated competency, as defined by the state, in each core academic subject he or she teaches (U.S. Department of Education, 2003, pp. 11–13).

Beginning with the 2002-2003 school year, under NCLB all new teachers must demonstrate competency by passing (a) for new elementary teachers: a rigorous state test on subject knowledge and teaching skills in reading or language arts, writing, mathematics, and other areas of the basic elementary school curriculum, or (b) for new middle and high school teachers: a rigorous state test in every subject they teach. Experienced teachers already employed must either meet the requirements for new teachers, or they may demonstrate their competency through a state evaluation that meets NCLB guidelines, known as a "high, objective, uniform state standard of evaluation" (HOUSSE). The U.S. Department of Education's *NCLB Teacher Toolkit* has one section that is extremely important to teachers of deaf and hard of hearing students, and that is the section on how the No Child Left Behind Act applies to special education teachers (U.S. Department of Education, 2003, p. 21):

If a teacher teaches any core academic subject, then under NCLB he or she must be highly qualified. However, special educators who do not directly instruct students in a core academic subject or who provide only consultation to highly qualified teachers of core academic subjects in adapting curricula, using behavioral supports and interventions or selecting appropriate accommodations do not need to meet the highly qualified requirements. (Note: Teachers must also take into account the Individuals with Disabilities Education Act [IDEA] requirements for special education teachers.)

"PASS THE TESTS OR ELSE."

Two Congressional mandates and intense pressure from the U.S. Department of Education's federal accreditation oversight panel have all developed the same message for those who wish either to enter or remain a member of the teaching profession, and for the postsecondary institutions that wish to train them: "Pass the state licensure tests, or else." The common thread from these three sources of federal intervention seems to be that ensuring teacher quality is one of the highest priorities, and that the primary measure of teacher quality must be (by law) scores on teacher licensure tests.

CRITICISMS OF THE USE OF STATE TEACHER LICENSURE TESTS AS A SOLE MEASURE OF TEACHER COMPETENCY AND THE QUALITY OF TEACHER PREPARATION PROGRAMS

Although the U.S. Department of Education and the voting majority in Congress in recent years all seem to be convinced that the performance of teacher candidates on state licensure tests should be used to sanction teacher preparation programs and to weed out certain would-be teachers, researchers and higher education specialists are not of the same mind. Not only do some educational researchers believe that the tests themselves lack validity, but others in higher education believe that the tests discriminate against racial and ethnic minorities, persons whose native language is not English, and persons with disabilities.

CHARGES THAT STATE LICENSURE TESTS USED AS SINGLE MEASURES ARE NEITHER VALID NOR ADEQUATE

In 2001, R. Clarke Fowler, an associate professor in the School of Education at Salem State College in Massachusetts, examined the effectiveness of teacher licensure tests in Massachusetts. His conclusion:

Thus the question is not whether current efforts to improve schools of education will resolve our educational ills—they won't. Rather, the question is whether the mechanisms that policy makers are using to improve schools of education—more certification tests, higher cut scores, and severe penalties for institutions that fail to meet specific pass rates—will deliver the increased accountability and better teachers that policy makers have promised. . . . My experience in Massachusetts indicates that this test-and-punish approach will not deliver on either promise. (Fowler, 2001, p. 11)

A similar conclusion was reached that same year, when a preliminary report, entitled *Testing Teacher Candidates: The Role of Licensure Tests in Improving Teacher Quality* (2001), which was subsequently published in 2003, raised serious issues about the validity of using performance on state licensure tests as an accountability tool for measuring the quality of teacher preparation, or as a requirement for licensure. However, unlike Fowler's article, which was written by one educator, this other report was the product of the 17-member Committee on Assessment and Teacher Quality which was convened by the National Research Council, at the request of the U.S. Department of Education, to conduct a 20-month study of the validity of teacher licensure tests as a measure of teacher quality. Some of the conclusions reached by this group of assessment experts (Committee on Assessment and Teacher Quality, 2001, pp. 165–171) represent direct challenges to the validity of the punitive sanctions required by Title II of the Higher Education Act and NCLB:

- On whether or not test scores alone are an adequate measure of teacher quality: "Because a teacher's work is complex, even a set of well-designed tests cannot measure all of the prerequisites of competent beginning teaching. Current paper-and-pencil tests provide only some of the information needed to evaluate the competencies of teacher candidates."

- On the appropriateness of using teacher licensure tests as an accountability tool: "By their design and as currently used, initial teacher licensure tests fall short of the intended policy goals for their use as accountability tools and as levers for improving teacher preparation and licensure programs. The public reporting and accountability provisions of Title II may encourage erroneous conclusions about the quality of teacher preparation [emphasis added]."

- On whether or not comparing institutional pass rates is an adequate way to judge the quality of teacher education programs: "Although the percentage of graduates who pass initial licensure tests provides an entry point for evaluating an institution's quality, simple comparisons among institutions based on their passing rates are difficult to interpret for many reasons. These include the fact that institutions have different educational missions and recruiting practices, their students have different entry-level qualifications, teacher education programs have different entry and exit testing requirements, and programs have different procedures for determining the institutional affiliations of their candidates. By themselves, passing rates on licensure tests do not provide adequate information on which to judge the quality of teacher education programs."

- On whether or not comparing passing rates across states is appropriate: "Simple comparisons of passing rates across states are misleading. Many states use different tests for initial licensure or set different passing scores on the same tests. . . ."

- On whether or not data from a variety of sources are more valid: "To fairly and accurately judge the quality of teacher education programs, federal and state officials need data on a wide variety of program characteristics from multiple sources. . . ."

- Two of the Committee on Assessment and Teacher Quality's recommendations:

    – "States should not use passing rates on initial licensure tests as the sole basis for deciding whether their teacher education programs are low performing."

    – "The federal government should not use passing rates on initial licensure tests as the sole basis for comparing states and teacher education programs or for withholding funds, imposing other sanctions, or rewarding teacher education programs."

Canadian educators, who have studied the use of teacher test scores in the U.S. education system in order to draw comparisons with Canadian educational testing issues, have also questioned the validity of teacher tests as a measure of teacher quality. According to a position paper posted on the Canadian Teacher Federation's website:

Despite the rhetoric about testing as a means to improve teacher quality, paper-and-pencil tests cannot assess the complex knowledge and abilities required for effective teaching. The Elementary Teachers' Federation of Ontario, in a position paper on teacher testing, notes that "key elements of teaching, like classroom management, rapport with students, developing a collaborative learning environment, and the ability to communicate with parents, cannot be assessed in a written test. . . ."

Over the years, U.S. litigation has served to raise important issues of test validity and reliability. The Massachusetts-based National Center for Fair and Open Testing (FairTest) reports that teacher tests are not valid instruments for assessing teacher quality because there is no correlation between the test score and teacher performance on the job—in other words, tests cannot predict (Canadian Teacher Federation, 2000, p. 1).

In the article cited above, the Canadian Teacher Federation quotes from an American study that analyzed the validity of the Educational Testing Service's Praxis examinations for teachers. The authors of this study concluded that:

educators need to reconsider their rationale and policies regarding basic competency testing for teachers. The fact is that after more than a decade of teacher testing, research has failed to demonstrate any significant relationship between basic competency tests and other measures of program success, including success in teaching.... Any rationale for teacher competency testing that assumes predictive validity is probably misleading. (Dybdahl, Shaw, & Edwards, 1997, pp. 248–265)

CHARGES THAT STATE LICENSURE TESTS ARE BIASED AGAINST MINORITIES

Not only are there serious questions about whether teacher licensure tests measure what they purport to measure, but some educators also believe that these standardized tests are biased against minorities and pose a serious challenge to increasing diversity in the field of teaching. The National Research Council's Committee on Assessment and Teacher Quality study found that:

The lower passing rates for minority teacher candidates on current licensure tests pose problems for schools and districts in seeking a qualified and diverse teaching force. (Mitchell, Robinsons, Plake, & Knowles, 2003, p. 167)

FairTest agrees with this charge of bias against minority teacher candidates:

According to FairTest, competency tests have kept thousands of minority teacher candidates—Black, Latino, American Indian and others—out of U.S. elementary and secondary classrooms. Test bias and the use of cut-off scores result in lower pass rates for minority candidates than for white candidates, a factor which contributes to the mismatch between student diversity and the composition of the teaching force. Paradoxically, as the proportion of U.S. students from minority groups increases, the proportion of teachers from minority groups is declining. (Canadian Teachers' Federation, 2001, p. 4)

BIAS IN STANDARDIZED TESTS FOR DEAF AND HARD OF HEARING EXAMINEES

Test bias and the use of cutoff scores result in lower pass rates for deaf and hard of hearing teacher candidates as well. Although very little quantitative research has been conducted to date on how well deaf and hard of hearing examinees perform on teacher licensure tests per se, empirical evidence, and research on how deaf examinees in the elementary and secondary schools fare on general standardized tests, suggest that teacher licensure tests do pose unique challenges for deaf and hard of hearing examinees that are not faced by other test-takers.

One major hurdle for deaf and hard of hearing examinees is that teacher licensure tests are all written in English. That this poses a problem is not necessarily because many deaf examinees are users of American Sign Language (ASL) as a primary language. Dr. Judith Mounty, director of the Center for ASL Literacy at Gallaudet University and co-chair of the National Task Force on Equity in Testing Deaf and Hard of Hearing Individuals, points out that a lack of full access to the English language would be true regardless of whether ASL or English was the first language the child was exposed to in the home (Mounty, August 19, 2004, personal communication).

Dr. Carol Traxler (2002), research scientist at the Gallaudet Research Institute and co-chair of the National Task Force on Equity in Testing Deaf and Hard of Hearing Individuals, explains why. A part of the challenge with language access is that a deaf person never has full access to the nuances of an auditory language that new hearing speakers of a language can absorb even passively (Gallaudet University, 2002). For this reason, the challenges faced are not always the same as the ones faced by hearing native speakers of other auditory languages who take tests in English. Traxler identifies four fundamental flaws that are cited by experts in the licensure testing for deaf test-takers:

1. Insufficient context in the stem of multiple choice items for a person not fluent in English.
2. Time restrictions on the examination may cause an unfair disadvantage for test-takers whose native language is not English, and who therefore must spend a longer amount of time understanding the questions being asked on the test [Note: this pitfall can be avoided when extended time is granted as a test accommodation].
3. Inappropriate content of some items (for example, items about music and rhyme).
4. Use of unnecessary English language idioms and common words with multiple meanings (such as "cotton to" used as a verb meaning "to take a liking to," or infrequently used, unfamiliar words that require users of English as a second language to take longer to decode).

Mounty (2004) has identified the following factors as examples of how test construction and the wording of test items can be biased against deaf and hard of hearing examinees. These factors may occur in isolation or sometimes in combination to adversely affect test scores:

- The overall style of language used in testing is very specialized. Compared with the general test-taking population, both hearing non-native speakers of English and deaf and hard of hearing test-takers may find these atypical or specialized uses of the language more challenging. Often deaf and hard of hearing persons who do not have difficulty reading and understanding other written material, including course textbooks, magazines, newspapers, or adult-level fiction, are stymied by the items on standardized tests.

- The problem may be the use of vocabulary that is not often used in everyday conversation or written material. Note that we are not discussing discipline-specific or specialized vocabulary. Rather, this concern relates more to the choice of a low-frequency meaning of a word that has multiple meanings, some of which occur with higher frequency in English and are more familiar to deaf, hard of hearing, and non-native users of English.

- Sometimes test developers choose grammatical constructions that make the item more difficult to decode, or contain extremely long sentences with multiple embedded subordinate clauses to conserve space and/or time. Long and complex sentences may make an otherwise easy item more difficult, because the English must be decoded before the context can be processed. For someone who does not have native competence in English, this strategy may pose an unmanageable and unfair processing and memory load.

- Some constructions are difficult and confusing for all candidates, but may present an unfair additional challenge to non-native users of English and deaf and hard of hearing candidates. For example:
    - "Which of the following is not a reason to promote an employee?" (At the very least, the word *not* should be underlined.)
    - Items which give four of five statements and then ask which are true (e.g., A only; A, B, C; B only; C only; B and C only;
    - All of the above; None of the above, etc.)

Gallaudet University is the world's leading liberal arts university for deaf and hard of hearing persons. Although its M.A. in Deaf Education program prepares hearing, deaf, and hard of hearing students to be teachers of the deaf, its B.A. in Education program enrolls almost exclusively deaf or hard of hearing students. In any given year, often a great majority of students who are seeking an *initial* license in either program are either deaf or hard of hearing. For this reason, and because Title II institutional reports are supposed to only report test scores from program completers who are seeking an initial teaching license, the Gallaudet University Title II pass rates should theoretically be a fairly accurate indication of how well deaf and hard of hearing students fare on the required state licensure tests for the District of Columbia. During the first two report years under Title II legislation, the Gallaudet University pass rates for those program completers seeking an initial license hovered around 40% (Gallaudet University, 2002). The fact that the majority of these program completers were deaf or hard of hearing strongly suggests that deaf and hard of hearing examinees during those years were having a difficult time passing the Praxis tests, which are teacher licensure tests required by the District of Columbia and more than 30 other state educational jurisdictions.

THE MAINE CENTER ON DEAFNESS SURVEY

Other than the previously mentioned Gallaudet University Title II pass rates, until recently most of the evidence that deaf examinees fare poorly in comparison to test-takers in general on teacher licensure tests has been anecdotal. Even though there exist studies of how well deaf students at the K–12 level perform on standardized tests in comparison with non-deaf students, further research is needed on how well postsecondary and professional-level examinees who are deaf or hard of hearing fare in comparison with their hearing counterparts.

In the summer of 2003, the Maine Center on Deafness (MCD) undertook such a research project. The goal of this study was to determine if deaf teacher candidates for licensure in states other than Maine were encountering the same problem as Maine's deaf teacher candidates for licensure: difficulty in passing the required state licensure tests, the Praxis tests published by the Educational Testing Service. What prompted this survey was that in Maine, some deaf teachers had been hired under an emergency Targeted Need Certificate, but although they had passed the required college coursework, they were unable to pass the required Praxis tests within the given time frame. In the summer of 2003, Beth Gallie, a lawyer for the MCD, and her assistant Jessica Emmons, designed and conducted a telephone survey to identify the extent to which deaf candidates for teacher licensure in other states or jurisdictions were experiencing difficulties in passing their required licensure tests. Many of the schools for the deaf that Gallie and Emmons contacted were located in 25 states or jurisdictions (i.e., the District of Columbia) that required the Praxis tests for teacher licensure. Of these 25 jurisdictions where Praxis was required, the schools in 16 (or 64%) of the jurisdictions said that their deaf teachers were having problems passing required Praxis tests.

The MCD survey results also show that deaf teachers at schools for the deaf had problems passing the required teacher licensure tests in two states that required tests other than the Praxis series. And in two other states, although teacher licensure tests were required for hearing teachers, these tests were waived for deaf teachers if they could demonstrate competency by passing certain courses, so there is no measure as to whether or not the deaf teachers there were having problems passing the required tests. In yet another state, in 2003 deaf teachers were required to take the Praxis tests, but they were not required to pass them, and so again there was no indication as to whether or not the Praxis tests would have posed a problem for deaf teachers if they had been held to the same standards as other (i.e., hearing) teachers. And in yet another state, whether or not deaf teachers performed well on the Praxis was clouded by the fact that requirements differed for hearing and deaf teachers: Deaf teachers were not required to take the reading and writing sections of the *Praxis I Pre-Professional Skills Test* (PPST) that was required of hearing teachers.

Although the MCD survey had some limitations, it was a very important undertaking because for the first time, it offered a study that documented that a significant number of deaf examinees have difficulty passing required standardized state licensure tests.

Importance and Limitations of the MCD Survey

While the MCD survey results successfully demonstrated that employed deaf teachers in schools for the deaf in at least 16 states or jurisdictions were experiencing difficulty in passing the Praxis tests, this survey did not address (a) the performance of deaf teacher *candidates* for licensing or certification who had not yet found jobs, or (b) how well deaf teachers in the mainstream schools of those states fared on these tests. Furthermore, it should be noted that the MCD survey report of the deaf teachers' performance was based not on actual score reports, but on the perceptions of school administrators (principals, superintendents, or program directors) of how well their teachers fared. While these undoubtedly were highly informed opinions, these perceptions may not have been exact. The same qualifications can be given regarding survey responses from the nine states or jurisdictions using Praxis tests, which reported that their deaf teachers did not have problems passing the tests.

Another word of caution in interpreting the MCD survey results is that the required tests vary from state to state, and so it may well be that the difficulty of passing these tests also varies from state to state. Even in states that use the *same* test series (i.e., the Praxis series), it is up to each state to determine its own cutoff scores, and these minimum scores can and do vary from state to state. For example, the passing scores required for teacher licensure on the PPST in reading vary from a high of 178 in Virginia (although this can be avoided if the examinee achieves a composite score of at least 532) or 177 in Vermont and for the Department of Defense Dependent Schools, to a low of 170 in three states—Nebraska, Mississippi, and Montana (Educational Testing Service, 2003, September).

However, in spite of some limitations, the Gallie and Emmons MCD survey is extremely important as a "pioneer effort" in documenting how well deaf and hard of hearing examinees fare on teacher licensure tests. Furthermore, enough data in the survey are available to establish without question that deaf examinees face a real challenge when it comes to passing required state licensure tests for teachers. It is hoped that this survey will inspire future research in this area, because the need for it has been clearly established.

FUTURE IMPACTS: "WHERE DO WE GO FROM HERE?"

As we have seen, current evidence—whether in the form of survey results, Title II pass rates, or anecdotal reports from teachers and administrators in the field—clearly indicates that many deaf and hard of hearing teacher candidates face serious challenges in passing required standardized tests for teacher licensure, and like examinees from other minority groups, they do not fare as well on these tests as hearing test-takers. But not only do teacher *candidates* face these challenges; experienced deaf and hard of hearing *teachers* in the field, who may have thought they had succeeded in passing their state licensure requirements, are now faced with the fact that because of NCLB, they may not be finished with their licensure testing after all. These teachers may discover that in order to keep their jobs in special education, they must now pass additional subject matter content tests that are required under NCLB to prove that they are "highly qualified" teachers. It does not matter if they have glowing track records and years of experience and commendations as excellent teachers; under NCLB, no teacher of core academic subjects is immune, and if their previous licensure tests were in special education and not specific to the subject matter courses that they are now teaching, they may now be required to take new tests to keep their jobs.

As for teacher education programs that are specially developed for deaf and hard of hearing students, what are they to do to meet the new challenges posed by Title II and NCLB? Will they have to raise entry requirements to ensure that their graduates pass the state licensure examinations, thus decreasing enrollment? Or should they keep entry requirements as they are now, but try to avoid loss of accreditation because of low pass rates by formally including standardized test preparation courses in their curriculum? And even if institutions add these test preparation courses, is there any guarantee that this will fully address the problem?

We have seen an abundance of evidence, including opinions from many experts in the fields of teacher education and assessment, that claim (a) that standardized teacher licensure tests fall far short of the goals for which they are now being used, or as many would say, for which they are being misused or abused; (b) that they discriminate against minority test-takers; (c) that they do not measure what they purport to measure, namely teacher quality; (d) that they are inadequate and misleading when used in isolation; (e) that comparing pass rates across institutions and states is like comparing "apples and oranges"; and (f) that the current tests (used alone) should not be used either to judge teacher quality or the quality of teacher preparation programs. If all or even any part of the above list is true, is there *any hope* that Title II and/or NCLB will be repealed in the near future?

Not according to David Imig, former president and CEO of the American Association of Colleges for Teacher Education (AACTE), who wrote that is "unlikely that the law will be changed. The law remains one of the few accomplishments of the Congress and it remains a favorite of both Republicans and Democrats" (Imig, 2004, pp. 1–2).

CONCLUDING REMARKS: WHERE DO WE GO FROM HERE?

If David Imig's prediction and reasoning are on target that NCLB is here to stay, one can also assume likewise that Title II requirements will not go away any time soon. Where does this law leave prospective and current deaf and hard of hearing teachers, as well as the institutions and programs that prepare them? Obviously, institutions, teachers, and teacher candidates have little choice but to face these challenges "head on," despite the existence of strong legitimate challenges to the validity and fairness of these federal mandates. In light of the extremely high stakes involved, one or more of the following outcomes is conceivable:

- To protect their national accreditation and state program approval, postsecondary institutions could be forced to raise the entrance and/or exit requirements to their teacher preparation programs, thus raising the bar for access into the teaching profession for deaf, hard of hearing, and hearing persons. If it is true that teacher licensure tests pose an even greater challenge for deaf and hard of hearing examinees, then this could result in reducing the number of deaf and hard of hearing teachers in the field.

- Title II and NCLB requirements could force changes in the curricula for teacher preparation programs by forcing them to include text preparation courses, in addition to promoting the practice of "teaching the test" in college classrooms.

- Test preparation workshops for teachers who are already in the field, but who are being forced to take additional tests under NCLB, may become crucial as schools are threatened with the loss of teachers in their ranks who might not be able to otherwise pass these tests.

- Deaf and hard of hearing teachers and teacher candidates, and/or their advocates, could decide to challenge Title II and NCLB requirements in the courts, especially if they find a way to document satisfactorily that the tests are invalid, or that they unfairly discriminate against persons from racial and/or ethnic minorities, and against persons with disabilities.

It is difficult to predict which, if any, of the outcomes may come to pass, but one thing is clear: The Title II and NCLB mandates have created new hurdles that will have a serious impact for years to come, not only on deaf and hard of hearing teachers and teacher candidates, but also on the postsecondary institutions that prepare them.

REFERENCES

Canadian Teacher's Federation. (2001, May 17). Limitations of teacher testing. *CTF Action Update*. Retrieved on September 6, 2004, from http://www.ctffce.ca/en/action/2000/testing.htm.

Dybdahl, C. S., Shaw, D. G., & Edwards, D. (1997). Teacher testing: Reason or rhetoric. *Journal of Research and Development in Education, 30*(4), 248–254. As quoted in Canadian Teacher's Federation (2001, May 17). Limitations of teacher testing. *CTF Action Update*. Retrieved on September 6, 2004, from http://www.ctf-fce.ca/en/action/2000/testing.htm.

Educational Testing Service. (2003, September). *Understanding your Praxis scores 2003–2004*. Retrieved September 6, 2004, from http://ftp.ets.org/pub/tandl/09706PRAXIS.pdf.

Fowler, R. C. (2001, June 18). What did the Massachusetts teacher tests say about American education? (Electronic version, p. 11) *Phi Delta Kappan, 82*(10), 773–780. Retrieved on September 6, 2004, from www.pdkintl.org/kappan/k0106fow.htm.

Gallaudet University. (2002, April). Contextual statement. *Title II institutional report*. Washington, DC: Author.

Gallie, B., & Emmons, J. (2003, Summer). Unpublished survey. Portland, ME: Maine Center on Deafness.

Imig, D. G. (2004, June 1 revision). Contextual scan. (Electronic version). American Association of Colleges for Teacher Education. Retrieved on September 6, 2004, from http://www.aacte.org/Members_Only/june04scan.pdf.

Mitchell, K., Robinson, D., Plake, B., & Knowles, K., eds. (2001). *Testing teacher candidates: The role of licensure tests in improving teacher quality* (163–172). Washington, DC: National Academy Press.

Mounty, J. (2004). Standardized testing: Considerations for testing deaf and hard of hearing candidates. *Issue Brief: National Task Force on Equity in Testing Deaf Persons*. Retrieved on September 6, 2004, from http://gri.gallaudet.edu/TestEquity/stantest.html.

National Center for Education Statistics. (2000). Appendix A: Statutory provisions Title II, Sections 207 and 208 of the Higher Education Act. *Reference and reporting guide for preparing state and institutional reports on the quality of teacher preparation, Title II, Higher Education Act*. Washington, DC: U.S. Department of Education.

National Council on Accreditation of Teacher Education. (2004, January 5). The use of pass rates in NCATE accreditation. *News briefs*. Retrieved from September 6, 2004, from http://www.ncate.org/newsbrfs/Use_of_Test_Scores_spring_2004.pdf.

Schuhmann, A. M. NCATE's New 80% Policy. *AACTE Briefs, 24*(6), 2.

Smith, M. C. (2004, January/February) Taking stock in 2004: Teacher education in dangerous times. *Journal of Teacher Education, 55*(1), 3–7.

U.S. Department of Education, Office of the Deputy Secretary (2003). *No child left behind: A toolkit for teachers,* (11–13). Washington, DC: Author.

Section V *Summing Up*

Summary and Recommendations

Judith L. Mounty and David S. Martin

When we review the numerous chapters by well-qualified authors in this book, including their penetrating analyses and proposals for needed directions in the field of assessing adults who are deaf or hard of hearing, we see a wide variety of messages. Yet, we also see some commonalities and, by inference, a number of long overdue recommendations, policies, and practices. Let us look first at a synthesis of these various analyses.

1. It is critically important for professionals who are deaf or hard of hearing to meet and maintain established standards, both to demonstrate that they are at least equally capable of professional work when compared with hearing peers, and for protection of clients and students. Thus, no one is calling for permanently waiving assessments or lowering expectations for prospective professionals who are deaf or hard of hearing—just the opposite.
2. Though high standards must be maintained, the means of assessing HOW deaf and hard of hearing candidates meet those standards is the critical question. In chapter after chapter in this book, a variety of authors in different ways have indicated how, with few exceptions, most assessment mechanisms at this time have inherent inequities built into them when applied to persons who are deaf or hard of hearing.
3. It may help to require the same assessments of all prospective professionals, deaf or hearing, but provide reasonable accommodations to make up for some inherent inequities in the assessment instruments.
4. Several fundamental choices are available to the assessment developer and, by extension, to the assessment administrator.
   a. Carefully analyze the content and format of existing assessment instruments and make appropriate changes that will render them more equitable for all candidates, without changing the form of testing (e.g., paper-and-pencil or computer-delivered written test).
   b. Similarly analyze and revise the blueprint and test development guidelines used to generate items for a specific test so that new/subsequent items and or forms of the test are more accessible for all candidates.
   c. Develop and administer alternative forms of assessment under certain conditions on the basis that no matter what accommodations and adaptations are made to existing instruments, they may not be truly equitable in their current form; thus, other measures must be used in lieu of or in addition to a given standardized test—sometimes referred to as multiple measures.

Whichever options or combination thereof is elected by assessment authorities in given cases will continue to be a function of the purpose for which the test is being used or the professional entities involved. But certainly all options must be openly explored in all cases.

Regardless of the variety of techniques, we must bear in mind that the core issue is usually the candidate's ability to adequately *access the language* of whatever assessment is being required. Thus, all efforts need to be centered on ways to optimize accessibility—and thereby "level the playing field." Some of the inequities in assessment for persons who are deaf or hard of hearing are the result of inequities in the curriculum that has led to their preparation for a given assessment—including the curriculum that candidates experienced from the time of entry into formal schooling. Thus, addressing these inequities, which is beyond the direct scope of this book, is a critical piece of the puzzle. Compared with hearing peers, deaf and hard of hearing adults generally also have significantly fewer opportunities for continuing education and professional skills training, including preparation for entry or advancement in their chosen profession.

Let us look now at recommendations for future action, which would be the most desirable end result of anyone reading and thinking about the content of this book. The following recommendations are proposed:

1. We must continue to embark on wider and deeper research related to assessing deaf or hard of hearing persons. A call for private and public funding of such efforts seems appropriate, yet difficult because deafness is a low-incidence phenomenon. More efforts must be expended in this direction.
2. Continuing examination of laws and regulations of both state licensure agencies and professional certification bodies must take place. A long educative process was needed in order to demonstrate to officials in several professions (as described in the fourth section of this book) that special considerations are critical when assessing prospective professionals who are deaf or hard of hearing. However, this effort is far from finished: *Every* professional group must now be given this information and this analysis of the problems and solutions when assessing deaf or hard of hearing candidates.
3. University programs which prepare students for fields requiring professional licensure or certification must become much better informed about the needs of deaf and hard of hearing candidates and about ways of ensuring that they indeed do have full access to the knowledge and skills in the preparation program; otherwise, the most equitable assessments will still result in failure for these candidates because they will truly lack the requisite knowledge and/or skills.
4. Additional opportunities for test preparation must be provided to deaf or hard of hearing candidates. One of the most promising directions for preparation is systematic exposure to cognitive strategies; such strategies will prepare candidates directly for techniques needed in assessments. Examples of such strategies would be practice in categorization, sequencing, decision-making, deriving conclusions from given information, finding patterns and relationships, analyzing different linguistic constructions, comparison, applying logic, and using process of elimination. All of these cognitive strategies are generic in the sense that they assist the learner with many kinds of learning, but they also will prepare the learner,

whether hearing or deaf or hard of hearing, for a higher percentage of success on many kinds of assessments.

5. Equally important to the cognitive preparation for assessment situations is the affective (attitudinal and emotional) dimension; it is easy for a candidate who is deaf or hard of hearing to become discouraged when taking an assessment. Ways of dealing with discouragement and keeping an attitude of trying different strategies instead of giving up should be part of the professional preparation curriculum.

6. With the wide-scale inclusion of deaf and hard of hearing persons in the mainstream as students, it is more important than ever that university faculty who staff such preparation programs become far more knowledgeable about the language and learning needs of deaf and hard of hearing students; at this time, many well-meaning less-than-knowledgeable faculty members are unwittingly shortchanging deaf or hard of hearing students. Even at institutions that primarily serve deaf and hard of hearing students, some faculty may lack the language and communication skills needed to optimally meet student needs. Although students have rights under the Americans with Disabilities Act, and universities are responsible for implementing and promoting policies and practices that support these rights, some students may be wary of "rocking the boat," or may be unsure of how to approach faculty with whom they cannot readily communicate.

7. Additional experimentation must take place with various kinds of multiple measurements in order to demonstrate and analyze their reliability, validity, and utility as means of assessing candidates who are deaf or hard of hearing. With continued investigation, techniques can evolve that can ultimately ensure greater equity.

In sum, the agenda is long and serious; let all of us now move forward with this agenda promptly, so that the next generation of deaf or hard of hearing professionals will have an equitable opportunity to contribute their expertise to meeting the critical challenges posed by future students and clients.

Epilogue: Fort Monroe Revisited

Robert Clover Johnson

Many deaf and hard of hearing adults today are experiencing great difficulty passing professional certification and licensing examinations—what we call "high stakes" tests. This situation is most unfortunate considering their great strides in achieving professional status in recent decades in many fields. Today, there are deaf and hard of hearing K–12 teachers, university professors, social workers, clinical and school psychologists, certified public accountants, investment brokers, leisure services providers, linguists, lawyers, biologists, chemists, mathematicians, writers, historians, computer programmers, web designers, and even some physicians. This list would have astonished deaf and hard of hearing people as recently as the 1950s.

How did this happen? In his 1987 book, *Meeting the Challenge: Hearing-Impaired Professionals in the Workplace,* deaf scholar Alan B. Crammatte described the period of 1960 to 1982 as an era in which "a humanitarian revolution . . . brought many hearing-impaired citizens out of the closet of meek isolation into the active arena of competition for training, jobs, and recognition" (Crammatte, 1987, p. 1). Crammatte suggested that certain events led deaf and hard of hearing people to become increasingly assertive and seek changes that benefited all deaf and hard of hearing Americans. One such event, probably forgotten now by all but a few individuals, was a 1961 meeting in Hampton, Virginia, called "Fort Monroe Workshop #2." This meeting, Crammatte said,

. . . brought local and national deaf leaders and hearing professionals from across the nation to develop organizations and programs that would meet the needs of hearing-impaired people. The workshop was sponsored by the [U.S. Department of Health, Education, and Welfare's] Office of Vocational Rehabilitation (OVR) but was administered by deaf persons; it proved to be a watershed for hearing-impaired people. Many of the recommended actions became actualities in subsequent years. More importantly, a ferment grew among deaf leaders which led many a printer and craftsperson to aspire to more challenging roles as full-time professionals or administrators. (pp. 3–4)

In light of all that has happened since, it is fascinating to read this brief summary of an apparently seminal meeting that occurred in 1961, where deaf leaders were charting their vision of the kinds of organizations and programs needed to enable deaf and hard of hearing people to aspire to reach higher than previously had seemed possible. Equally interesting in a different way is the following glimpse of the preceding year's meeting, "Fort Monroe Workshop #1":

. . . an OVR-sponsored conference on research [that] involved mainly hearing school administrators (an ancient paternalistic pattern). However, the two deaf participants so impressed OVR officials that plans began soon after for a gathering of hearing-impaired leaders the next year. (p. 3)

My point in mentioning Fort Monroe Workshop #1, which consisted "mainly of hearing administrators," was not to compare them to a group so infamously paternalistic as, say, the hearing delegates at the 1880 Conference of Milan, but to contrast them to that group. Thinking, no doubt, of the Civil Rights movement, which focused national attention so unflinchingly on the plight of segregated black people, Crammatte said that the period beginning in the 1950s "constituted an era of humanitarian concern for minorities." Such concern had obviously affected the hearing delegates at the first workshop who paid attention to the two deaf attendees, recognized their mistake in not inviting a sufficient number of deaf people, and took action immediately to correct this error by arranging for a follow-up conference that would be led by deaf individuals. Crammatte describes the second Fort Monroe Workshop as a watershed, in other words, not only because many of the ideas presented led to genuine progress for deaf people, but also because deaf leadership was recognized and appreciated at the meeting.

In the conclusion of *Meeting the Challenge,* Crammatte commented on how promising it was that by that time, many deaf people had attained leadership roles at their own institutions, becoming superintendents of residential schools, coordinators of special programs in community colleges, college vice presidents, and deans. He added, "In time, we shall probably see a university provost or president." Crammatte did not have to wait long to witness such a development; but once again, deaf people had to assert themselves—in this case, through a dramatic rebellion—before the top job at Gallaudet University could be secured by a deaf person.

In March of 1988, Gallaudet University's Board of Trustees selected a hearing candidate to be president of the university even though there were qualified deaf applicants for the position (Christiansen & Barnartt, 1995). The selection of this candidate, who was not only hearing but who did not yet know sign language, offended Gallaudet students, many Gallaudet faculty and staff, and members of deaf organizations nationwide who had gone to great lengths to point out that deaf people were fully capable of running their own organizations and would benefit from having this readiness acknowledged by the selection of a deaf university president. They also effectively argued that it was vitally important that a president of Gallaudet University be able to communicate directly to deaf individuals, a skill that could not possibly be mastered overnight by a hearing person.

The conflict between the Deaf community and Gallaudet University's Board of Trustees became the focus of nationwide print and broadcast media attention, much if not most of it sympathetic with Gallaudet student and Deaf community demands. The bravery of the student leaders and the rightness of their cause became apparent and were lauded by people all over the world. Eventually, all student demands were accepted, and I. King Jordan, a deaf man who had previously been a psychology professor and the dean of the College of Arts and Sciences at Gallaudet, became Gallaudet University's seventh president.

Acceptance by the general public of this resolution to the "Deaf President Now!" movement confirmed Crammatte's thesis that beginning in the 1960s, there was a growing consensus among Americans that some of the barriers that prevent minority populations from realizing their aspirations are the result of prejudice and need to be reexamined and possibly discarded. The victory of I. King Jordan instantly sent a signal that deaf and hard of hearing people would no longer meekly accept the notion that some hearing person was surely more qualified than any deaf person for a particular professional or administrative position. Dr. Jordan's presidency, which continues to the time of this book's publication, is a lasting reminder that deaf and hard of hearing people, when well-matched to a particular job, can successfully manage their own affairs.

The assertiveness of deaf and hard of hearing people—which stunned the world in 1988—led to many promising changes for ambitious members of this population. Deaf people have boldly taken advantage of such legislation as the Americans with Disabilities Act of 1992, which enables qualified deaf and hard of hearing students to go to a broad range of colleges and universities with support services provided at the institution's expense. Deaf and hard of hearing students are indeed taking advantage of the openness of institutions of higher learning to consider, accept, and support deaf applicants. Today, deaf and hard of hearing individuals are obtaining degrees in more professional fields than ever before. These individuals, admittedly, constitute a small portion of the entire deaf and hard of hearing population, but their existence is a reminder that the events of the humanitarian era heralded by Crammatte have indeed opened doors of opportunity for those able to take advantage of them.

Although no one has declared that the humanitarian era is ending, the sensitivity to minority concerns Crammatte applauded in his book has been significantly affected by an equally ascendant accountability movement. Passing courses, getting a degree, and even performing effectively in a job are no longer a guarantee of lasting employment as a professional. As the chapters in this volume have made clear, the doors of opportunity can be abruptly slammed shut when deaf and hard of hearing people fail to pass licensing and certification tests ostensibly designed to measure capability objectively. Furthermore, the nationwide implementation of high-stakes testing in conjunction with the No Child Left Behind Act may prevent many dedicated deaf and hard of hearing students from obtaining high school diplomas and being able to attend Gallaudet University or other postsecondary education programs. It is even possible that this excessive emphasis and exclusive reliance on high-stakes testing may take deaf and hard of hearing people back to the 1950s.

The key question asked by this volume is: Are standardized tests developed for the general population reliable measures of the competence of deaf and hard of hearing individuals? If the answer were an unequivocal yes, then there would be little reason for this volume to have been assembled.

The trouble with licensing and certification examinations, as with most other tests, is that they generally are created on the unstated assumption that the test-taker has had unhampered access to spoken English throughout his or her life. Written English, a visual code that triggers associations with recorded speech patterns, is typically used as the medium through which the test designer tries to tease out the test-taker's knowledge of facts and concepts important within a particular domain of knowledge or professional discipline. Distinguishing between a correct or incorrect choice often depends on a full appreciation of every word or phrase presented in each multiple-choice item or reading passage. Deaf and hard of hearing individuals are at a disadvantage when taking such tests because the auditory base of much of the phonological coding that makes reading a relatively automatic process for hearing individuals is either partially or fully blocked. In spite of this, many deaf and hard of hearing people, through hard work and endless practice, have been able to develop sufficient awareness of English to be able to pass these tests.

Sometimes, as many chapters in this book have suggested, practice and preparation sessions addressing both general and specialized vocabulary, English language constructions typically used on tests, and other common testing conventions can sometimes help deaf and hard of hearing people significantly improve their scores. The point here is that although the content area of the subject being tested obviously needs to be mastered in deaf and hard of hearing students' course work or in on-the-job training, it is still quite likely that such a student or worker, though quite competent in his or her field, will fail a certification test simply because of the difficulty in understanding subtle distinctions in the written language of the test.

At a recent Gallaudet meeting of the National Task Force on Equity in Testing Deaf and Hard of Hearing Individuals, a deaf professional with a master's degree in social work and 20 years of experience working with deaf clients described her experience trying to pass an examination for social work licensure at the clinical (i.e., top) level. She had long held the intermediate-level license that can be obtained after completion of the master's of social work degree, but wanted to obtain the higher level license because her administrative position required it. Her state had since adopted a new series of licensure tests that are used nationwide and, to her dismay, when she took the clinical examination, she failed by a few points. She read books and study guides to prepare for a second test and failed that one as well by a narrow margin. Eventually, she went through the same ordeal five additional times. Each of these experiences involved months of test preparation and a not-insignificant expenditure of money. On one occasion, she took the test with two interpreters assisting who—though pleasant enough—made serious interpreting mistakes that she felt confused her more than the tests themselves would have. After seven tries, this individual still had not passed the test. She reported that the concepts on the tests were not at all alien to her. Her problem was that certain English terms and grammatical constructions puzzled her and made her choices somewhat uncertain, and in many instances, apparently wrong.

Yet her colleagues in the field of social work and her many clients and coworkers see this woman as a very intelligent, responsive, effective practitioner. Are these people mistaken? Or is the test somehow failing to measure what she knows? Many people believe that licensing and certification tests are inadequate for measuring the competence of deaf and hard of hearing professionals because test results so often reflect the difficulties these individuals experience with English rather than deficiencies in their professional knowledge. Much of the work performed by deaf and hard of hearing professionals, after all, is with deaf and hard of hearing students or clients. The interactions involved often, if not always, are conducted in sign language and rely on specialized skills not measured by the tests. Another way of putting this would be to point out that most of the hearing professionals currently passing certification tests with ease, but lacking those specialized skills, would quite likely be inept at practicing their profession with deaf and hard of hearing clients.

Having attended numerous meetings of the National Task Force on Equity in Testing Deaf and Hard of Hearing Individuals, I am struck by the contrast between the dispirited attitudes expressed in those meetings and the excitement felt in 1961 in the Fort Monroe Workshop #2. In some ways, looking back, it might seem that the deaf and hard of hearing individuals who assembled in Hampton, Virginia, were naïve in assuming that a society so overwhelmingly "hearing" in its notions of what is normal would ever allow or even encourage significant numbers of deaf and hard of hearing individuals to acquire the credentials and find the opportunities required to excel in a broad array of professions. So what was it about that time that gave rise to the conviction that such developments could actually be realized?

The key, I believe, was that beginning in the 1950s, the U.S. Supreme Court had begun to make decisions that brought to consciousness the injustices that had long been tolerated in America. These injustices did not square with the vision of the Bill of Rights in the U.S. Constitution or, for that matter, with the idealism of the Declaration of Independence. Americans at large, whether they wanted to think such thoughts or not, were reminded of the notion that "all men are created equal, that they are endowed by their Creator with certain inalienable rights, that among these are life, liberty, and the pursuit of happiness." The deep impact of these reminders on the American conscience and consciousness was largely responsible, I think, for the receptiveness of most Americans to the goals of the "Deaf President Now!" movement.

What is needed now, it seems, is for deaf and hard of hearing people and their advocates to find ways to explain to legislators, test designers, and organizations committed to ensuring competence in various professions the specific assessment needs of deaf and hard of hearing professionals. The goal, of course, would not be to water down professional standards but to make assessment instruments accessible to deaf and hard of hearing individuals through whatever means is determined to be most fair to this population.

The numbers of deaf and hard of hearing people in fields requiring licensure or certification testing are small enough that the damage that may be done to these individuals' professional identities could go almost unnoticed by society at large. The danger is that many students and clients who have been benefiting from their services may gradually experience a diminishing supply of deaf and hard of hearing professionals. In some ways, the situation is all too reminiscent of the period when oralism became the norm in deaf education programs more than a century ago, leading to a rapid thinning of the ranks of deaf teachers of deaf students in residential schools.

The voices of deaf and hard of hearing people need to be heard. For inspiration, think of Fort Monroe Workshop #2, which occurred after deaf and hard of hearing people made it clear to hearing individuals that deaf and hard of hearing representation was vital to the success of plans intended to benefit that population. Or think of "Deaf President Now!," which led to dramatic changes, once deaf and hard of hearing people made it clear that deaf professionals and deaf leaders must be respected and given a fair chance to succeed in realizing their professional goals. The time for action is now!

REFERENCES

Christiansen, J. B., and Barnartt, S. N. (1995). *Deaf president now! The 1988 revolution at Gallaudet University.* Washington, DC: Gallaudet University Press.

Crammatte, A. B. (1987). *Meeting the challenge: Hearing-impaired professionals in the workplace.* Washington, DC: Gallaudet University Press.

Contributors

Cara Cahalan-Laitusis is an Associate Research Scientist in the Center for Validity Research at Educational Testing Service (ETS) in Princeton, New Jersey. She received a Ph.D. in school psychology from Fordham University. Before coming to ETS, Dr. Cahalan was a school psychologist where she worked with a diverse student population, ranging from prekindergarten to high school students. Her applied specializations are in curriculum-based assessment and the diagnosis and treatment of students with learning disabilities. Since coming to ETS in 1998, Dr. Cahalan has been involved in research on validity and fairness, including examining the impact of testing accommodations on test score validity, differential item functioning for students with disabilities and English language learners, gender differences in mathematical problem-solving, and differential performance (by gender, race, and language groups) on paper-based and computer-based test formats.

Linda Cook is a Principal Research Scientist in the Research Division at Educational Testing Service (ETS) in Princeton, New Jersey. She received her Ed.D. in educational measurement and statistics from the University of Massachusetts in 1979; her M.E.D. in education of the deaf from Smith College in 1972; and her B.S. in chemistry from Ursinus College in 1960. Her primary research interests are evaluating the validity and fairness of assessments for individuals with disabilities and English language learners.

Cook has served in a number of roles since coming to ETS. She led the measurement work done on the Preliminary Scholastic Aptitude Test/National Merit Scholarship Qualifying Test (PSAT/NMSQT) and the SAT II subject tests. After spending five years as Executive Director of the admissions and guidance area, she became Vice President of the newly formed Assessment Division at ETS. Cook returned to the analysis area following the decentralization of the Assessment Division and later became the Research Director of the Center for Validity Research. Her professional activities outside of ETS consist of serving on a number of advisory groups and participating in professional organizations. Currently she is a member of the National Council on Measurement in Education's Board of Directors. Cook's interest in assessments for individuals with disabilities stems from her experiences with her son and grandson who are deaf.

Rosaline Hayes Crawford's interest in deaf and hard of hearing issues began in 1990 with the birth of her daughter who is deaf. Rosaline received a Jurist Doctor degree from the Columbus School of Law, Catholic University of America, and was admitted to the Maryland bar in 2002. Since then, she has been a staff attorney at the National Association of the Deaf, Law and Advocacy Center.

Contributors

Michael Ehringhaus is the Assistant Director of the MCAS (Massachusetts Comprehensive Assessment System) Client Division for Measured Progress. He is also responsible for the Massachusetts English Proficiency Assessment, developed to assess the English language proficiency of students whose native language is not English. Dr. Ehringhaus has been involved in the field of education for over 30 years and has extensive experience in large-scale assessment with respect to research, development, and administration of both criterion- and norm-reference tests. Prior to his work with Measured Progress, Dr. Ehringhaus worked with the Educational Testing Service and engaged in a wide range of research and test development activities related to large-scale assessment, to computer-based testing, and to deaf and hard of hearing students. Dr. Ehringhaus has taught math, English, history, and science in middle and high schools in North Carolina and New Zealand; trained teachers at the University of North Carolina; and developed and directed adult literacy services throughout Alaska's Interior Region. He has also published widely and made numerous presentations at international, national, state, and local conferences. He received his bachelor's and master's degrees from the University of North Carolina, and he earned both a Certificate of Advanced Study from Harvard University and a Ph.D. in adult education from Syracuse University.

Raylene Harris is currently a Research Fellow at the Department of Brain and Cognitive Sciences at the University of Rochester. She holds M.A. and Ph.D. degrees in clinical psychology from Gallaudet University. Dr. Harris was a research intern at Educational Testing Service (ETS) during the summer of 2003 while studying for her doctorate. During her time at ETS, she assisted with research on The Praxis Series: Professional Assessments for Beginning Teachers subject assessment in Education of Deaf and Hard of Hearing Students. Dr. Harris is a deaf native signer of American Sign Language (ASL), and her current research interest is the development of a better understanding of how ASL affects cognition.

Jason C. Immekus is an advanced doctoral student in the Educational Psychology program at Purdue University. His areas of specialization are applied measurement and research design. His research interests include test validity, structural equation modeling, and test development.

Robert Clover Johnson has been an editor for the Gallaudet Research Institute since 1983 and additionally for the Graduate School at Gallaudet University since 1995. He earned a B.A. from Duke University (1967) and an M.A. in English from the University of Virginia (1972). Prior to coming to Gallaudet University, he taught high school English in Charlottesville, Virginia, for a number of years. Mr. Johnson first became aware of issues related to deaf education and sign language while working as an editor for the National Rehabilitation Information Center (NARIC) in 1981–1982. He has written many articles about deaf education and related matters, particularly on research related to difficulties faced by deaf students, their parents, and their teachers. Clover is the author of a recent article on high-stakes testing, "Educational Reform Meets Deaf Education at a National Conference" in *Sign Language Studies,* vol. 4, issue 2, Winter 2004.

Neal Kingston is Vice President, General Manager at CTB/McGraw Hill. Dr. Kingston earned both his M.Ed. and Ph.D. in educational measurement and research design from Teachers College, Columbia University. He received his B.A. in biology and education from the State University of New York at Stony Brook. Dr. Kingston has published and presented more than 60 papers and chapters on technical aspects of psychometrics and on policy issues regarding the integration of assessment, instruction, and curriculum. He is particularly interested in the possibilities for applying principles of universal design to testing. Dr. Kingston has had the opportunity to work on testing issues with the Kentucky School for the Deaf, the Kentucky Commission on the Deaf and Hard of Hearing, and the Governor Baxter School for the Deaf in Maine.

Ruth Loew is the Assistant Director of the Office of Disability Policy at Educational Testing Service (ETS) in Princeton, New Jersey. She earned a B.A. in linguistics from Brown University, an M.A. in education of the hearing impaired from Northwestern University, and a Ph.D. in linguistics from the University of Minnesota, focusing on the structure and acquisition of American Sign Language. Before coming to ETS, Dr. Loew served on the faculty of the National Technical Institute for the Deaf in Rochester, New York, and held research positions with Rutgers University (Newark, NJ) and Children's Seashore House (Philadelphia). Her current responsibilities include consultation on adapting tests for individuals with disabilities; coordinating activities of ETS's Disability Policy Team; representing ETS on the National Task Force on Equity in Testing Deaf and Hard of Hearing Individuals; participating in test-accessibility research; and training staff involved in testing individuals with disabilities.

Susan J. Maller is Associate Professor of Educational Psychology and Research Methodology at Purdue University. She holds a doctorate from the University of Arizona, where she was named a Spencer Dissertation Fellow to conduct research on item bias in the WISC-III when administered to deaf people. She has served as Program Chair to the American Educational Research Association's Special Interest Group on Research on the Education of Deaf Persons. Dr. Maller currently serves as Associate Editor of Psychology in the Schools, and serves on the editorial review boards of *Educational and Psychological Measurement, Journal of School Psychology,* and *Journal of Psychoeducational Assessment.* She has published numerous journal articles on the psychometric properties of tests when administered to deaf people and recently published a chapter on intellectual assessment of deaf people in M. Marschark & P. Spencer's *Handbook of Deaf Studies, Language, and Education.* Dr. Maller has been acquainted with deaf people since childhood and initially pursued graduate studies at Gallaudet University.

David S. Martin is Professor/Dean Emeritus from Gallaudet University. He co-founded the National Task Force on Equity in Testing Deaf Persons in the late 1980s and has been involved as an expert consultant and advocate in a number of cases involving inequities experienced by test-takers who are deaf or hard of hearing. At Gallaudet, he was Professor of Education, established the undergraduate teacher education program to prepare deaf and hard of hearing candidates for licensure as teachers of hearing students, and served as Dean of the School of Education and Human Services. He has a B.A. from Yale, an Ed.M. and a C.A.S. from the Harvard School of Education, and a Ph.D. from Boston College in curriculum and instruction. He has published extensively in the areas of assessment, curriculum development, social studies education, and cognitive-strategy development of students who are deaf or hard of hearing.

Teresa V. Mason is an Associate Professor in the Department of Social Work at Gallaudet University and has worked in the Deaf community as a social worker since 1989. She received her Ph.D. from the University of Maryland at Baltimore in the School of Social Work and her master's degree in social work from Gallaudet University. Dr. Mason's research and scholarship interests include the creation of American Sign Language versions of standardized instruments and social work history regarding mental health and hospital social work.

Carolyn Emrick Massad is currently Director, Content Development, in the Testing Services Division of Harcourt Assessment, Inc., where she works on a variety of assessment programs. Prior to joining Harcourt in 2001, Dr. Massad was at Educational Testing Service (ETS) for thirty-one years, working on various assessment projects for all educational levels. A primary focus of her work at ETS was on licensure examinations for educators. She was involved in the research, planning, and coordination of the development of a new series of teacher licensure examinations, including one for certification of teachers of deaf and hard of hearing students. Dr. Massad received her B.S. in History and English, an M.Ed. in educational curriculum and instruction, and a Ph.D. in educational psychology and in Spanish from Kent State University. She also did postdoctoral work as a Spencer Foundation Fellow at the University of Stockholm (Sweden) where she began many years of research work in international assessment.

Judith L. Mounty directs the Center for American Sign Language Literacy at Gallaudet University and is Chair of the National Task Force on Equity in Testing Deaf and Hard of Hearing Individuals. She is also a social worker and educational consultant with the Center for Families in Transition in Bethesda, Maryland. Dr. Mounty holds a doctorate in applied psycholinguistics from Boston University and master's degrees in deaf education from Temple University in Philadelphia, PA, and in social work from Gallaudet University. She came to Gallaudet in 1996 as the first deaf woman to hold the Powrie Vaux Doctor Chair of Deaf Studies, during which time she also coordinated a job analysis study for the joint NAD-RID interpreter testing project. Dr. Mounty was a postdoctoral fellow at Educational Testing Service (ETS) in Princeton, New Jersey, and she worked there for six years as a research scientist addressing test equity issues affecting deaf and hard of hearing people. While at ETS, Dr. Mounty led the development of the Praxis Series: Professional Assessments for Beginning Teachers subject assessment in education of deaf and hard of hearing students. Prior to her time at ETS, she worked for many years as a teacher, teacher educator, and program administrator in the field of deaf education. Dr. Mounty's oldest daughter is deaf.

Marjorie Ragosta was a research scientist at Educational Testing Service (ETS) in Princeton, New Jersey, for 20 years, after receiving her Ph.D. in foundations of education from the University of Florida. Dr. Ragosta was instrumental in sensitizing the testing world to the unique issues regarding deaf and hard of hearing candidates. During her time at ETS, she led or collaborated on numerous studies related to equity in testing of deaf test-takers, established the ETS Committee on Testing People with Disabilities, and directed a federal study on progress in education and rehabilitation of deaf and hard of hearing individuals. Dr. Ragosta is now retired and living in Tallahassee, Florida.

Phyllis C. Rogers is a staff interpreter with Gallaudet Interpreting Service where she is responsible for a nationally recognized interpreter mentorship program. She holds a master's degree in deaf education from Gallaudet University and comprehensive skills certification from the Registry of the Deaf. In the past 25 years of professional interpreting experience, Ms. Rogers has worked in both staff and freelance positions, taught in interpreter training programs, conducted numerous interpreting workshops, and served as President of the Virginia Registry of Interpreters for the Deaf. Currently she also parents seven children by international adoption, five of whom are deaf. Her interest in interpreting tests has come from experiences with this content as an interpreter and interpreter trainer, as well as from her experiences with her children when they encountered testing in schools as well as medical and vocational/employment settings.

Anne Simonsen is a Professor and the former Coordinator of the Recreation and Leisure Studies Program in the Department of Physical Education and Recreation at Gallaudet University. Dr. Simonsen is a Certified Therapeutic Recreation Specialist (CTRS) and a Certified Park and Recreation Professional (CPRP). She holds a Ph.D. from the University of Maryland in recreation and master's degrees in education with a concentration in therapeutic recreation from the George Washington University and in legal and ethical studies from the University of Baltimore. Dr. Simonsen currently serves on the CPRP Exam Management Committee. She was a member of the Board of Directors of the National Council for Therapeutic Recreation in the early 1990s. She is a past President of the National Therapeutic Recreation Society and a member of the Board of Trustees of the National Recreation and Park Association.

Paul S. Singletary, is the Programming and Development Specialist/Certification Officer for the Office of the Dean, Graduate School and Professional Programs at Gallaudet University in Washington, DC, where he has been employed since 1984. Mr. Singletary holds a Certificate of Advanced Graduate Studies in Education Policy, Planning and Administration from the University of Maryland at College Park (specialization: higher education administration) as well as an M.A. in teaching English, an M.Ed. in reading, and an M.A. in teaching history from the University of South Carolina. He was a public high school teacher for 10 years. At Gallaudet, Mr. Singletary informs and advises students, faculty, and administrators about certification matters, including standardized teacher licensure test requirements. He also compiles data and writes annual reports for accreditation agencies and institutional educational surveys, and federally mandated Title II reports on student test performance. For over a decade, Mr. Singletary has represented Gallaudet University's professional education programs unit at meetings of the National Task Force on Equity in Testing Deaf and Hard of Hearing Individuals, and at the District of Columbia state education agency's unit heads meetings, where issues pertaining to the licensure and testing of teachers and other school-related professionals are routinely discussed.

Charlene Sorensen joined the chemistry faculty at Gallaudet University in 1996 and continues there as a Professor of Chemistry. Dr. Sorensen holds a bachelor's degree from St. Andrew's Presbyterian College with majors in chemistry and comparative religious studies. She received her Ph.D. in chemistry from the University of Tennessee in Knoxville, Tennessee. From 1993 until 1996, she was an Assistant Professor at Pikeville College, a small private college in the Appalachian Mountains. In working on a National Science Foundation grant project (starting in 1997) which focused on better preparing underrepresented groups for advanced studies in science, she recognized that the admission testing for graduate school posed a particularly significant obstacle for deaf and hard of hearing students. As a result, she continues to work with students to assess why this test is a significant barrier and to provide review and strategies to assist students in preparing for the exam.

Robert B. Weinstock is a trainer with Information Technology Services at Gallaudet University and also teaches in the Departments of English and Communication Studies. He holds B.A. and M.A. degrees from Gallaudet and has many years of experience in educational assessment and measurement. Mr. Weinstock previously worked at the Educational Testing Service as a senior editor in the SAT Program and as a test development specialist in the Praxis program. He currently serves as chief reader for the Praxis subject assessment in education of deaf and hard of hearing students. He is an active member of the National Task Force on Equity in Testing Deaf and Hard of Hearing Individuals, and he is widely known for his expertise in test and item review and for teaching deaf and hard of hearing individuals how to take and pass graduate and professional school and licensing examinations. Mr. Weinstock's oldest daughter is deaf.

Index

AACTE. *See* American Association of Colleges for Teacher Education accommodations, 34, 171.
   See also ended time; sign language interpretation
Bartlett v. New York State Board of Law Examiners, 100–1
  College Board list of eligibility, 102–3
  defined, 61
  difficulties in studying, 49–50
  Educational Testing Service, 140, 142
  history of, 38
  intelligence tests and, 78–79
  interpreter preparation and, 118
  research questions regarding, 64
  strategies when challenged, 104
  student age and, 97
  technology-based, 62–63
  types of, 39, 61–63, 103
ADA. *See* Americans With Disabilities Act adaptations. *See* modifications Advanced Placement courses/exams, 34, 40–41
AERA. *See* American Educational Research Association
AHSSPPE. *See* Association on Handicapped Student Service Programs in Postsecondary Education
Allen, Thomas, 19
alternate test versions, 7–9, 154
alternative-response questions, 67
American Association of Colleges for Teacher Education (AACTE), 157, 166
American Educational Research Association (AERA), 8–9, 66
American Psychological Association (APA), 66
American Sign Language (ASL)
  administration of tests and, 102
  differences with English, 114
  interpretation of exams and, 40–41
  linguistic variation and, 111
  as primary language, 141, 152, 162
  translation software and, 62
Americans With Disabilities Act (ADA), 3, 37, 173, 176
  accommodations and, 38
  definition of disability, 98–101
  goal of, 97
  overview of, 97–98
  practice tests and, 153
  requirements for testing, 101–4
  sign language interpreters and, 7

analytical test sections, 142, 145
Anderson, Glenn, 19
APA. *See* American Psychological Association
Army Alpha assessment, 56
assessments. *See also* certification exams; licensing exams; standardized tests; tests/exams
  alternative, 7–9, 154
  dilemmas in, 9–10
  need for equal standards, 4
  recommendations for future action, 172–73
  suggestions for improving, 171–72
Association of Graduate Schools, 138
Association of Social Work Boards (ASWB), 5, 32, 150–51, 153
Association on Handicapped Student Service Programs in Postsecondary Education (AHSSPPE), 18
ASWB. *See* Association of Social Work Boards
audio communications, 62
aural communications, 62

Babbidge, Homer, Jr., 18
Babbidge report, 18
back-translation, 62–63
Bahan, Ben, 5
Bartlett v. New York State Board of Law Examiners, 100–1
bias
  standardized tests and, 149–50, 161–63
  test-level, 81
Bill of Rights, 178
Binet, Alfred, 76
Binet and Simon scale, 76
blind persons/students, 11, 38

Canadian Teacher Federation, 160, 161
CDC. *See* Centers for Disease Control and Prevention
Center for ASL Literacy, 162
Centers for Disease Control and Prevention (CDC), 94
certification exams. *See also* Certified Therapeutic Recreation Specialist examination; licensing exams
  inadequacies of, 177–78
  negative impact of, 176
  suggestions for success in, 134–35
  test language and, 176–77

187

Index

Certified Park and Recreation Professional examination, 126
Certified Therapeutic Recreation Specialist (CTRS), 125–27, 136
Certified Therapeutic Recreation Specialist examination
  impact on deaf test-takers, 126–30
  percent who pass, 136
  problems with, 130–34
  suggestions for success in, 134–35
Children's Health Act, 94
Civil Rights movement, 175
Code of Fair Testing Practices in Education, 66
College Board, 11, 38, 40–41, 102–3
college-entrance examinations. *See* Scholastic Aptitude Test
colloquial English, 6
Committee for Handicapped People, 38
Committee on Assessment and Teacher Quality, 159–61
Comprehensive Test of Nonverbal Intelligence (CTONI), 77, 83
computer-based testing, 131
Conference of Milan (1880), 175
confirmatory factor analysis, 81–82
constructed-response questions, 71–73
construct-irrelevant variance, 80
constructs, 76
construct validity, 81–82
content area experts, 32
content validity, 58, 80
contexts, inadequate, 6
core profiles, 82
Council for Exceptional Children, 4
Council of Graduate Schools, 138
counseling license examinations, 29–30
CPRP examination. *See* Certified Park and Recreation Professional examination
Crammatte, Alan B., 174–75
criterion validity, 80–81
CTONI. *See* Comprehensive Test of Nonverbal Intelligence
CTRS. *See* Certified Therapeutic Recreation Specialist

deaf education, progress in, 19–20
"Deaf President Now!" movement, 175–76, 178–79
deaf teachers. *See also* state teacher licensing exams
  in nineteenth-century deaf schools, 44
  No Child Left Behind Act and, 157–58, 165–66
Declaration of Independence, 178
dependent clauses, 7
detractor items, 32
differential easiness, 15
differential item functioning, 44–50, 82–83
disability, legally defined, 98–101
Disability Policy Team (ETS), 38
disabled persons/students
  performance on state tests, 3–4
  problems in classifying, 50

discrimination, legal prohibitions, 97–98
distracters, 71
double negatives, 70
dyslexia, 100–1

Early Hearing Detection and Intervention (EHDI), 94
early identification, 94–97
early intervention, 94–97
easiness, differential, 15
EDHH. *See* Praxis II Education of Deaf and Hard of Hearing Students
Educational Testing Service (ETS), 4–5
  accommodations and, 39–42, 140, 142
  history of testing deaf or hard of hearing individuals, 38–39
  Office of Disability, 38
  Praxis II subject assessment, 29
  research pertaining to deaf and hard of hearing test-takers, 42–44
  SAT validity testing, 11–18
  test development process and, 30–33
  therapeutic recreation credentialing and, 126
Education for All Handicapped Children Act, 3
Education of the Deaf, 18
EEOC. *See* Equal Employment Opportunity Commission
EHDI. *See* Early Hearing Detection and Intervention
ELPT. *See* English Language Proficiency Test
Emmons, Jessica, 164
employment, 19
English. *See also* test language
  assessment exams, 21, 43, 119
  colloquial or figurative, 6
  differences with American Sign Language, 114
  idiomatic phrases, 61
  "sound" right issue, 27–29
English-as-a-second-language (ESL), 5
English assessment exams, 21, 43, 119
English Language Proficiency Test (ELPT), 21, 43
Equal Employment Opportunity Commission (EEOC), 99
ESL. *See* English-as-a-second-language
essay questions, 9, 41, 43, 67–68
ethics, intelligence tests and, 75–76
ethnic minorities, 13, 149–50, 161
ETS Committee on Testing People with Disabilities, 21
exploratory factor analysis, 81
extended-response questions, 72
extended time, 61, 104
  CTRS exam and, 134
  issues of fatigue, 118–19
  rationale for, 34, 39–40

factor analysis, 15, 81–82
FairTest, 160–61
Field of Dreams (movie), 35
figurative English, 6
first-year averages (FYAs), 16
First-Year Grade Point Average (FYGPA), 43, 55

flagging, of test scores, 11, 17, 142
Focus on Reaching Women in Academics, Research, and Development in Science, Engineering, and Mathematics, 138
foreign-language tests, 40
Forer, Douglas, 35
Fort Monroe Workshops, 174–75, 178
Fowler, R. Clarke, 159
Franklin, Edward, 19
French, 54–55
FYAs. *See* first-year averages
FYGPA. *See* First-Year Grade Point Average

Gallaudet College, 19
Gallaudet University, 4
   Center for ASL Literacy, 162
   "Deaf President Now!" movement, 175–76
   Department of Social Work, 151
   GRE preparation workshop, 138–48
   Recreation and Leisure Studies Program, 126–27
   Therapeutic Recreation Program, 126–30, 132, 136
   Title II pass rates, 163
Gallie, Beth, 164
George Washington University, 139
Governor's Office for Disabilities for the State of Maryland, 5
graduate admissions officers, 147
Graduate Record Examination Board, 11, 138
Graduate Record Examination (GRE), 13
   Deaf community and, 147–48
   student concerns over, 139–40
   test language and, 144–45
graduate schools, 147–48
grammatical constructions, 61
GRE. *See* Graduate Record Examination
GRE student preparation workshop
   beginnings of, 138–40
   lessons learned from, 147–48
   needs assessment, 141–42
   overview of, 140–41, 143
   post-test performance, 146
   pre-test performance, 143–44
   results, 144–45
Gustafson, Gerilee, 19

handicapped persons, definitions of, 95
Harcourt company, 5
hard of hearing persons, linguistic variation among, 112
Heller, Rachelle, 138
Higher Education Act, Title II
   future of, 167
   goals and requirements of, 156–57
   impact on teacher education programs, 166
   pass rates at Gallaudet University, 163
   validity of punitive sanctions questioned, 159–60
high school grade-point average (HSGPA), 13, 16
high-stakes testing, 3–4, 103. *See also specific test types*
Hiskey-Nebraska Test of Learning Aptitude, 80

history tests, 44
HSGPA. *See* high school grade-point average
Hurwitz, T. Alan, 19

IDEA. *See* Individuals With Disabilities Education Act
idiomatic English, 61
IEP. *See* individualized education program
Imig, David, 166
impact, 83
incidental learning, 115–16
inclusion, 93
Individualized Education Plan (IEP), 20, 95–96
Individualized Written Family Plan, 20
Individualized Written Rehabilitation Plan, 20
Individuals With Disabilities Education Act (IDEA), 3, 93–97
instant messaging, 63
intelligence, 76–77
intelligence tests
   accommodations and modifications, 78–79
   construct validity, 81–82
   content validity, 80
   criterion validity, 80–81
   deaf or hard of hearing individuals and, 76
   differential item functioning, 82–83
   ethical questions and, 75–76
   norms, 79
   performance scales and, 77
   professional guidelines, 77–78
   profile analysis, 82
   recommendations for using, 77, 83–84
   reliability, 79
   roots of, 76
interactive examinations, 153
interactive interviews, 9
Interpreters' Edge, The, 110
interpreting, 110–11
interviews, interactive, 9
invariant factor structure, 81–82
item bias, 6, 82–83
item-writing guides, 32–33

Joint Standards for Educational and Psychological Testing, 66–67
Jordan, I. King, 175–76

Kaufman Assessment Battery for Children, 80
keys, 32

language assessment exams. *See* English assessment exams
language deprivation, 96, 111
language skills
   difficulty in obtaining, 95
   variability in, 111–13
Laurent Clerc National Deaf Education Center, 5
learning disabilities, 96
learning problems, 96

Index

Legal Ramifications of an Incorrect Analysis of Tense in ASL, 114
Leiter-Revised, 77
licensing exams. *See also* state teacher licensing exams
   across-the-board challenges, 29–30
   deaf or hard of hearing students and, 55–56
   guidelines, 66
   inadequacies of, 177–78
   problems concerning, 57
   purpose and qualities of, 57, 65–66
   reliability and validity, 56–57, 66
   test language and, 66–68, 70, 176–77
   universal design, 60–63
   validation of, 57–58
licensing laws, 65
licensing requirements, 65
licensing test construction
   criteria for test-item structure, 69–73
   general guidelines, 67–68
   guiding principles, 68–69
listening test sections, 41
literacy skills. *See* language skills

Maine Center on Deafness survey, 163–65
Mann, Horace, 56
Massachusetts, 159
matching questions, 67
mathematics test sections, 55, 141–42, 145
Mavriplis, Catherine, 138
Measured Progress company, 5
Meeting the Challenge (Crammatte), 174–75
method bias, 80–81
minorities
   standardized tests and, 149–50
   state teacher licensing tests and, 161
Mississippi, 165
modifications
   intelligence tests and, 78–79
   strategies when challenged, 104
   student age and, 97
Montana, 165
Mounty, Judith, 19, 21–22, 151, 162
multimedia technology, 43–44
multiple-choice exams, 6–7, 56
multiple-choice questions, 67–71
multiple meanings, 6
multiple measures, 171

NACIQI. *See* National Advisory Committee on Institutional Quality and Integrity
National Academy of Sciences, 11
National Advisory Committee on Institutional Quality and Integrity (NACIQI), 157
National Assessment of Educational Progress, 22
National Board for Certification in Occupational Therapy, 4–5
National Center for Fair and Open Testing (FairTest), 160–61
National Certification Board (NCB), 126
National Commission for Health Certifying Agencies, 125
National Council for Accreditation of Teacher Education (NCATE), 157
National Council for Therapeutic Recreation Certification (NCTRC), 125–27, 136
National Council on Measurement in Education (NCME), 66
National Recreation and Park Association (NRPA), 126
National Research Council, 159
National Task Force on Equity in Testing Deaf and Hard of Hearing Individuals, 4, 151, 162, 177
National Task Force on Equity in Testing Deaf Persons, 18
National Task Force on Equity in Testing Deaf Professionals, 4, 127
National Task Force on Equity in Testing Deaf Teachers, 4
National Teacher Examinations, 44
National Technical Institute for the Deaf, 20
National Theatre of the Deaf, 20
National Therapeutic Recreation Association, 5
NCATE. *See* National Council for Accreditation of Teacher Education
NCB. *See* National Certification Board
NCLB. *See* No Child Left Behind Act
NCLB Teacher Toolkit, 158
NCME. *See* National Council on Measurement in Education
NCTRC. *See* National Council for Therapeutic Recreation Certification
NCTRC Candidate Bulletin, 128–30
Nebraska, 165
negative stems, 33
No Child Left Behind Act (NCLB)
   deaf teachers and, 157–58, 165–66
   future of, 167
   goals and requirements of, 157–58
   overview of, 96–97
   underlying premises, 156
   validity of punitive sanctions questioned, 159–60
norm-referenced tests, 79
norms, 79
NRPA. *See* National Recreation and Park Association
NTE Listening Comprehension Test, 21

observations, videotaped, 9
Office of Civil Rights, 11
Office of Vocational Rehabilitation (OVR), 174
"on-the-fly" translation, 41
open-ended questions, 9, 67–68
oral interpreters, 41
OVR. *See* Office of Vocational Rehabilitation

Panel on Testing of Handicapped People, 13
performance tests, 77
portfolios, 9, 153
PPST. *See* Praxis I Pre-Professional Skills Test

Index

practice tests, 35, 153
Praxis Core Battery, 41
Praxis I Basic Skill Assessment, 43
Praxis II Education of Deaf and Hard of Hearing Students (EDHH), 29, 32, 43–50
Praxis I Pre-Professional Skills Test (PPST), 164–65
Praxis teacher exams, 161, 163–64
primary language, 141
professional preparation programs, 153
   suggestions for improving, 135
   therapeutic recreational credentialing and, 128–30, 133–34
professionals with disabilities, 101
profile analysis, 82
psychometrics, 78
Public Law 99-457, 20

questionnaires, 13–14
Quigley, Stephen, 19

reading comprehension scores, 55
reading disorders, 100–1
reading test sections, 41
real-time translation, 41
recoding systems, 55
Recreation and Leisure Studies Program (Gallaudet University), 126–27
recreation generalist, 126
Reference and Reporting Guide for Preparing State and Institutional Reports, 156
rehabilitation, 19–20
Rehabilitation Act of 1973, Section 504, 3, 11, 17, 37–38, 93, 97–98, 104
reliability, 56–57, 66, 79
remediation. *See* accommodations
residuals, 16
restricted-response questions, 72
Riverside Community College, 19
Rochester Institute of Technology, 20

sample questions, 35
SAT. *See* Scholastic Aptitude Test
Scholastic Aptitude Test (SAT)
   accommodation eligibility and, 102–3
   blind students and, 38
   challenging of test items, 29
   performance of deaf or hard of hearing students, 13, 42–43, 55
   psychometric characteristics, 14–17
   research pertaining to deaf and hard of hearing test-takers, 42–43
   sign language translation and, 40–41
   student descriptive information, 13–14
   test validity studies, 11–18
science tests, 44
score comparability, 49
Section 504. *See* Rehabilitation Act of 1973, Section 504
short-answer questions, 67

sight translation, 110–11, 113
signed essays, 43
sign language. *See also* American Sign Language
   recognized as a "foreign" language, 19
   regional variations and, 114
   used with multimedia technology, 43–44
sign language interpretation
   challenges of, 109–11, 118–19
   content knowledge and, 109
   incidental learning and, 115–16
   interpreter error and, 116–17
   interpreter neutrality and, 117
   interpreter preparation and, 117–18
   nonstandard test administration and, 119–20
   problems with, 40–42
   sight translation and, 110–11
   suggestions for improving, 120–21
   test development and, 113–14
   test language and, 114–15
sign language interpreters, 7–8
   challenges facing, 118–19
   errors and, 116–17
   preparation, 117–18
   social work licensing exams and, 153–54
   training programs, 112–13
small community effect, 128
Snyder, H. David, 138
social sciences, 149
social workers, deaf, 28
social work licenses, 152
social work licensing, 150–54
Sorensen, Charlene, 138
speaking test sections, 42
special education, 95
specific learning disability, 96
SSI. *See* Supplementary Security Income
standardized tests
   access to test content and, 39
   accommodations (*see* accommodations)
   bias and, 149–50, 161–63
   challenges across-the-board, 29–30
   challenging test items, 28–29
   development process, 30–33
   extended time (*see* ended time)
   general use of, 149–50
   history of, 56
   importance of preparing for, 33–34
   performance of students with disabilities, 3–4
   problems in, 6–7
   sign language interpretation (*see* sign language interpretation)
   test language and, 5, 27–28, 37–38, 141, 152, 154, 162–63, 172
   using study guides and practice tests, 35
Standards for Educational and Psychological Testing, 77, 83
Stanford Achievement Test, 19, 38, 55, 80
Stanford Achievement Test for Hearing Impaired Students, 55

state teacher licensing exams, 29, 43. *See also* licensing exams
  bias against deaf and hard of hearing students, 161–63
  bias against minorities, 161
  criticisms of, 158–59, 166
  Maine Center on Deafness survey and, 163–65
  as neither valid nor adequate, 159–61
  No Child Left Behind Act and, 157–58, 165–66
  Title II and, 156–57
stems, 32–33, 69–70
Student Descriptive Questionnaire, 13
study guides, 35
subordinate clauses, 61
Supplementary Security Income (SSI), 19

Targeted Need Certificate, 164
TC. *See* Total Communication
teacher certification, 4
teacher education
  federal mandates effecting, 156
  No Child Left Behind Act and, 157–58
  programs, 160
  Title II and, 156–57
teachers. *See* deaf teachers
teaching licensing exams. *See* state teacher licensing exams
test completion rates, 14
test developers, 32
test development. *See also* licensing test construction
  goals of, 32
  process of, 30–33
  professional guidelines, 77–78
  sign language interpretation and, 113–14
  suggestions for improving, 135, 171
Testing Handicapped People (Willingham, Ragosta, Bennett, Braun, Rock, & Powers), 13
Testing Teacher Candidates, 159
test items, challenging, 28–29
test language. *See also* vocabulary
  access issues, 39–40
  difficulties for deaf or hard of hearing students, 5, 27–28, 37–38, 61, 103–4
  figurative or colloquial English, 6
  grammatical constructions and, 61
  GRE and, 144–45
  idiomatic English, 61
  licensing exams and, 66–68, 70, 176–77
  multiple embedded dependent clauses, 7
  on-demand simplification and contextualization, 63
  sign language interpretation and, 114–15
  standardized tests and, 5, 27–28, 37–38, 141, 152, 154, 162–63, 172
  as threat to test validity, 58–60
Test of English as a Foreign Language (TOEFL), 42
Test of Nonverbal Intelligence (TONI-2), 80
test preparation courses, 167
test reliability, 14–15
test research, 49–50
test scores
  of deaf or hard of hearing students, 13
  flagging, 11, 17, 142
tests/exams. *See also* assessments; licensing exams; standardized tests
  ADA requirements, 101–4
  alternative, 7–9, 154
  appropriate remediation, 7–8
  challenging, 28–30
  flagging scores, 11, 17, 142
  preparation for, 172–73
test-taking
  accommodations and, 34
  practice tests, 35
  preparing for, 33–34
  test language and, 27–28
  using study guides, 35
Texas Essential Knowledge and Skills battery, 30
therapeutic recreation, 125–26
Therapeutic Recreation Program (Gallaudet University), 126–30, 132, 136
Title II. *See* Higher Education Act, Title II
TOEFL. *See* Test of English as a Foreign Language
TONI-2. *See* Test of Nonverbal Intelligence
Total Communication (TC), 19
translations, 110–11. *See also* sign language interpretation
  intelligence tests and, 78–79
translation software, 62
Traxler, Carol, 162
true/false questions, 67

UNIT. *See* Universal Nonverbal Intelligence Test
U.S. Department of Defense Dependent Schools, 165
U.S. Department of Health, Education and Welfare, 18, 157, 159
U.S. Department of Justice, 5, 99
U.S. Office of Civil Rights, 5
U.S. Supreme Court, 99–100, 178
Universal Nonverbal Intelligence Test (UNIT), 77, 81–82

validity, 66
  defined, 57
  intelligence tests and, 79–80
  licensure testing and, 57–58
  reliability and, 56–57
  test language as threat to, 58–60
verbal test sections
  SAT, 55
  student concerns over, 141
  students' problems with, 144–45
Vermont, 165
video technology, 43–44, 62–63
Virginia, 165
visually-impaired persons, 11, 38

Index

vocabulary
   exam design and, 60, 162–63
   sign language interpretation and, 114–15
   word parts, 144–45
vocational rehabilitation, 20
Voluntary Registration Plan, 125

Wechsler Intelligence Scale for Children—Fourth Edition (WISC-IV), 83–84
Wechsler Intelligence Scale for Children—Revised (WISC-R), 77, 79–80
Wechsler Intelligence Scale for Children—Third Edition (WISC-III), 77, 80–84
Wechsler Performance Scales, 77, 80
Weschler Intelligence Scale—Revised, 81
Wide Range Achievement Test—Revised, 80
WISC-III. *See* Wechsler Intelligence Scale for Children—Third Edition
WISC-IV. *See* Wechsler Intelligence Scale for Children—Fourth Edition
WISC-R. *See* Wechsler Intelligence Scale for Children—Revised
word parts, 144–45
Wright, Gloria, 19